"How we understand the biblic
Unfortunately, the history of this
theology and dispensationalism. E
horizon, one that more accurately (......... A pioneer
book, *Progressive Covenantalism* guides us down a more faithful hermeneutical path, helping interpreters understand the nature of the new covenant in a way that does far more justice to the biblical and theological framework of the entire Bible."

Matthew Barrett, tutor in systematic theology and church history, Oak Hill Theological College

"It is thrilling to see so much fresh exegetical and theological work possible in so many areas as Christians are set free from the inaccurate biblical storylines offered by Covenant or Dispensational theology. I heartily recommend the contributions of this useful volume."

Peter J. Gentry, Donald L. Williams Professor of Old Testament Interpretation, The Southern Baptist Theological Seminary

"I am convinced that the bull's-eye sits somewhere between covenant theology and dispensationalism, and the contributors to this volume aim sure shots at it. We need more writing on progressive covenantalism, and this book continues the conversation in an admirable way."

James M. Hamilton Jr., professor of biblical theology, The Southern Baptist Theological Seminary

"Insightful and significant, *Progressive Covenantalism* freshly treats biblical eschatology with exegetical care and theological skill. And it treats other views with evenhandedness and an irenic spirit. Readers—no matter their preferred eschatological system—will find much to learn and some to rethink."

Christopher W. Morgan, dean and professor of theology, School of Christian Ministries, California Baptist University

"These ten essays exegetically and theologically support the argument that Steve Wellum and Peter Gentry present in *Kingdom Through Covenant* (2012). Unlike covenant theology, progressive covenantalism argues that the genealogical principle (a basis for infant baptism) significantly changes across redemptive history. Unlike dispensationalism, progressive covenantalism understands the land not ultimately as Canaan but as a type of the new creation. This book is now required reading for my biblical theology courses."

Andy Naselli, assistant professor of New Testament and biblical theology, Bethlehem College and Seminary

"With both careful exegesis and sensitivity to the unfolding plan of God across salvation history, *Progressive Covenantalism* will provide fresh stimulus to conversations among Bible-believing Christians that arise from broad how-to-put-your-Bible-together questions. Seemingly unconnected topics such as baptism, Sabbath observance, the role of Israel, and the role of the Mosaic law in the life of the Christian are all wisely examined here in the context of the relationship between God's covenants across Scripture. Whether or not you agree with all the points raised in these pages, this book will surely encourage greater attention to the richness, unity, and diversity of God's Word and gratitude to our Lord Jesus, the 'guarantee of a better covenant.' This significant contribution to biblical theology deserves to be widely read."

Alan J. Thompson, lecturer in New Testament, Sydney Missionary and Bible College

"*Progressive Covenantalism* fulfills its goal, and fulfills it well, as stated in the book's subtitle: *Charting a Course between Dispensational and Covenant Theologies*. The best way to understand the relationship between Israel and the church, and for that matter the progression from Old to New Testaments, is a constant challenge, and one that progressive covenantalists have taken seriously. Readers will encounter very thoughtful and biblically based interaction with dispensational and covenant conversation partners. While disagreements persist here with both of these broad traditions, including with progressive dispensationalism, one will find the chapters intensely interesting and of great value in assessing where the lines in the debates are drawn. I recommend this book strongly and am thankful for both its clarity and its charity."

Bruce A. Ware, T. Rupert and Lucille Coleman Professor of Christian Theology, The Southern Baptist Theological Seminary

"*Progressive Covenantalism* is an impressive work, characterized throughout by careful exegetical grounding, keen awareness of biblical-theological concerns, and close acquaintance with the developing Bible storyline and its recurring patterns. It is in many respects a model of how theology ought to be done. As biblical theology continues to come of age, traditional hermeneutical paradigms will inevitably require adjusting, and I have little doubt that this book will prove to be a focal point in that ongoing discussion. It is a pleasure to recommend it."

Fred G. Zaspel, pastor, Reformed Baptist Church, executive editor, Books at a Glance, and adjunct professor of Christian theology, The Southern Baptist Theological Seminary

Charting a Course between
Dispensational and Covenant Theologies

PROGRESSIVE
COVENANTALISM

EDITORS:

STEPHEN J. WELLUM
and BRENT E. PARKER

ACADEMIC

NASHVILLE, TENNESSEE

Progressive Covenantalism: Charting a Course between Dispensational and Covenant Theologies

© Copyright 2016 by Stephen J. Wellum and Brent E. Parker

B&H Academic
Nashville, Tennessee

ISBN: 978-1-4336-8402-9

Dewey Decimal Classification: 230
Subject Heading: COVENANTS / SALVATION / THEOLOGY

Printed in the United States of America
8 9 10 11 12 • 26 25 24 23 22
VP

To Kandace Parker
Whose constant support, encouragement, submissive spirit, and love
reflect the gospel of Christ and the blessings of the new covenant.
Proverbs 31:10–11

To Joel, Justin, Joshua, Janae, and Jessica Wellum
All of you are truly God's gracious gifts to me. May you know, love,
and serve our glorious, triune covenant Lord all the days of your life.
May he be your portion and delight, and may you stand firm without
compromise for the truth of the gospel in challenging times.
Ephesians 1:15–23

CONTENTS

ACKNOWLEDGMENTS

The current and prominent evangelical systems of theology broadly fall within the streams of covenant theology and dispensationalism. However, a growing number of biblical exegetes and theologians believe these two dominant systems, as helpful as they are, need careful revision in light of Scripture. "Always reforming" is necessary as we seek to bring all of our thoughts captive to God's Word, but we also realize that when treasured theological systems are questioned, resistance is often experienced. As a result, we appreciate and are grateful that B&H Academic has given us the opportunity to articulate an alternative theological viewpoint—Progressive Covenantalism—which seeks to tweak the reigning systems of theology at some key points. Specifically we are thankful for Andreas Köstenberger and Jim Baird, who listened to our proposal and were willing to publish this work. Their confidence and support of our work has been an encouragement to us and to each of the contributors. In addition, the support and help from the project team, especially Chris Cowan and Chris Thompson, have been indispensable. We are thankful for your support and hard work in making this project possible.

This book also would not be possible without the authors who have taken considerable time out of their busy schedules to contribute to this project. We are grateful for their efforts in producing excellent and thought-provoking essays.

I (Brent) would also like to express gratitude to my wife, Kandace, to whom this book is dedicated, for being an invaluable helpmate on this project. She thoughtfully read the manuscripts and offered helpful suggestions that have added clarity to make this work more lucid. Her unswerving love and support of me in the midst of working on this project reminded me how she is a truly one of God's greatest gifts to me.

I (Stephen) would like to express my gratitude to my family for their faithful support of me and encouragement to see this project to completion. My dear wife, Karen, has stood by my side now for thirty years as my loving, loyal, and faithful wife, and she has also helped me raise our five wonderful children, to whom this book is dedicated. It is an incredible privilege and sober responsibility to be gifted with children and to seek to raise them in the fear and the admonition of the Lord. It is my prayer for you that you will love, adore, and obey our great, gracious, and glorious triune God and, in so doing, make our Lord Jesus Christ the focus of your faith, confidence, affections, and joy. A new generation is necessary who will stand for the truth of God's Word without compromise and unashamedly serve and honor Christ Jesus, our glorious new covenant Lord and Redeemer. This is my prayer for you—glory in Christ and stand firm for the gospel!

Our prayer is that this book will be accepted in an irenic spirit and not be received as combative for our brothers and sisters in Christ who disagree. Questioning our theological systems is not easy, and we pray that our readers (and we ourselves!) will always be open to rethinking our views in light of Scripture. We look forward to ongoing discussion with those who disagree with us as we seek to bring our minds and hearts captive to the whole counsel of God. Even more, our earnest prayer is that this book will edify the church and bring much glory and honor to our Lord Jesus Christ.

Stephen J. Wellum
Brent E. Parker

ABBREVIATIONS

AB   Anchor Bible

BAR   *Biblical Archaeology Review*

BBR   *Bulletin for Biblical Research*

BDAG   Bauer, W., F. W. Danker, W. F. Arndt, and F. W. Gingrich. *Greek-English Lexicon of the New Testament and Other Early Christian Literature*. 3rd ed. Chicago: University of Chicago Press, 2001.

BECNT   Baker Exegetical Commentary on the New Testament

Bib   *Biblica*

BibSac   *Bibliotheca Sacra*

BJRL   *Bulletin of the John Rylands University Library of Manchester*

BNTC   Black's New Testament Commentary

BRev   *Bible Review*

BST   The Bible Speaks Today

BTNT   Biblical Theology of the New Testament

CTR   *Criswell Theological Review*

DOTP   *Dictionary of the Old Testament: Pentateuch*. Edited by T. Desmond Alexander and David W. Baker. Downers Grove, IL: InterVarsity, 2003.

DOTPR   *Dictionary of the Old Testament: Prophets*. Edited by Mark J. Boda and J. Gordon McConville. Downers Grove, IL: InterVarsity, 2012.

DPL   *Dictionary of Paul and His Letters*. Edited by G. F. Hawthorne, R. P. Martin, and D. G. Reid. Downers Grove, IL: InterVarsity, 1995.

EBS   Encountering Biblical Studies
EDNT   *Exegetical Dictionary of the New Testament*. Edited by H. Balz,
              G. Schneider. 3 vols. English translation. Grand Rapids:
              Eerdmans, 1990–1993.
ERE   *Encyclopædia of Religion and Ethics*. Edited by James Hastings.
              13 vols. New York: Charles Scribner's Sons, 1908–1926.
EV   English version
EvQ   *Evangelical Quarterly*
GKC   *Gesenius' Hebrew Grammar*. Edited by E. Kautzsch. Translated
              by A. E. Cowley. 2nd ed. Oxford: Clarendon Press, 1910.
GTJ   *Grace Theological Journal*
HAR   *Hebrew Annual Review*
HCSB   Holman Christian Standard Bible
ICC   International Critical Commentary
JAOS   *Journal of the American Oriental Society*
JBL   *Journal of Biblical Literature*
JETS   *Journal of the Evangelical Theological Society*
JSNT   *Journal for the Study of the New Testament*
JSNTSup   Journal for the Study of the New Testament Supplement
              Series
JSOT   *Journal for the Study of the Old Testament*
JSOTSup   Journal for the Study of the Old Testament Supplement Series
LXX   Septuagint
MJT   *Midwestern Journal of Theology*
NAC   New American Commentary
NDBT   *New Dictionary of Biblical Theology*. Edited by B. S. Rosner,
              T. D. Alexander, G. Goldsworthy, and D. A. Carson. Downers
              Grove, IL: InterVarsity, 2004.
NICNT   New International Commentary on the New Testament
NICOT   New International Commentary on the Old Testament
NIDOTTE   *New International Dictionary of Old Testament Theology and
              Exegesis*. Edited by Willem A. VanGemeren. 5 vols. Grand
              Rapids: Zondervan, 1997.
NIGTC   New International Greek Testament Commentary

NovT	*Novum Testamentum*
NSBT	New Studies in Biblical Theology
NT	New Testament
NTS	*New Testament Studies*
OT	Old Testament
PNTC	Pillar New Testament Commentaries
RB	*Revue biblique*
RBTR	*Reformed Baptist Theological Review*
RTR	*Reformed Theological Review*
SBJT	*Southern Baptist Journal of Theology*
SNTSMS	Society for New Testament Studies Monograph Series
STR	*Southeastern Theological Review*
TDNT	*Theological Dictionary of the New Testament*. Edited by G. Kittel and G. Friedrich. Translated by G. W. Bromiley. 10 vols. Grand Rapids: Eerdmans, 1964–1976.
TDOT	*Theological Dictionary of the Old Testament*. Edited by G. Johannes Botterweck, Helmer Ringgren, and Heinz-Josef Fabry. Translated by John T. Willis, David E. Green, and Douglas W. Stott. 15 vols. Grand Rapids: Eerdmans, 1974–2006.
TMSJ	*The Masters Seminary Journal*
TNTC	Tyndale New Testament Commentaries
TOTC	Tyndale Old Testament Commentaries
TrinJ	*Trinity Journal*
TynBul	*Tyndale Bulletin*
UBCS	Understanding the Bible Commentary Series
VT	*Vetus Testamentum*
WBC	World Biblical Commentary
WCF	Westminster Confession of Faith
WTJ	*Westminster Theological Journal*
WUNT	Wissenschaftliche Untersuchungen zum Neuen Testament
ZECNT	Zondervan Exegetical Commentary on the New Testament
ZTK	*Zeitschrift für Theologie und Kirche*

Introduction

STEPHEN J. WELLUM WITH BRENT E. PARKER

From the beginning the church has wrestled with how to put together the biblical covenants and understand the nature of fulfillment in Christ Jesus our Lord. In fact, it is impossible to understand many of the early church's struggles apart from covenantal debates. For example, think about the debate regarding the Jew-Gentile relationship in the church (Matt 22:1–14; Acts 10–11; Romans 9–11; Eph 2:11–22; 3:1–13), the Judaizers' false covenant theology (Galatians 2–4), the need for the Jerusalem Council (Acts 15), the strong and weak debate (Romans 14–15), and the question of how Christians ought to relate to the Mosaic law (Matt 5–7; 15:1–20; Acts 7; Romans 4; Hebrews 7–10). All of these debates are simply the wrestling with the larger debate regarding the relationship between the covenants, specifically the old and new covenants.

Today, especially within evangelical theology, this debate continues unabated as represented by the two dominant biblical-theological systems of dispensational and covenant theology (and their varieties). Although these two views agree on many areas central to the gospel, they differ on their respective understanding of the nature and interrelationship of the biblical covenants. On these points of disagreement, there is still much division, especially on questions of how the Mosaic law applies to Christians today, the Israel-church relationship, and the various entailments of these discussions for ecclesiology and eschatology. In this ongoing discussion a consensus seems difficult to reach, especially if one remains within the confines of the two views.

In recent years a number of people have sensed the need for a mediating position on these debates, especially arising from the discipline of biblical theology.[1] This is why Peter Gentry and I wrote *Kingdom Through Covenant (KTC)*,[2] in which we proposed a slightly different way of thinking through the narrative plot structure of the Bible in contrast to the current views. Although we have benefited much from dispensational and covenant theology, we were also convinced an alternative view was needed to resolve some of these disputes.

We labeled our view *progressive covenantalism* (PC) to distinguish it from various alternatives. *Progressive* seeks to underscore the unfolding nature of God's revelation over time, while *covenantalism* emphasizes that God's plan unfolds *through* the covenants and that *all* of the covenants find their fulfillment, *telos*, and terminus in Christ. We strongly argue for the *unity* of God's plan-promise culminating in the new covenant. Our focus on the new covenant is *not* to exclude the other covenants since in God's plan each covenant is significant. In order to discern that significance, each covenant must be placed in its own covenantal location and then placed in terms of what covenant(s) preceded it and follow it before we can rightly discern how God's entire plan is fulfilled in Christ. By doing this, we interpret Scripture on its own terms *and* discover God's glorious plan unveiled before our eyes. We learn how in Christ all of God's promises are yes and amen (2 Cor 1:20).

In *KTC* we said that our view was a subset of *new covenant theology* (NCT), but we did not prefer that label, hence the reason for the title of this

---

[1] See especially the multivolume works in the New Studies of Biblical Theology, ed. D. A. Carson (Downers Grove, IL: InterVarsity).

[2] Peter J. Gentry and Stephen J. Wellum, *Kingdom Through Covenant: A Biblical-Theological Understanding of the Covenants* (Wheaton, IL: Crossway, 2012); and see the abridged version, *God's Kingdom through God's Covenants: A Concise Biblical Theology* (Wheaton, IL: Crossway, 2015).

present work. Even though we respect many who are identified with NCT, our hesitation to use the label was because we were not in full agreement with the diverse views fitting under its banner.[3] For example, some in NCT deny a creation covenant and Christ's active obedience and imputation of righteousness and hold little instructive place for the Mosaic law in the church's life—all points we reject.[4] In addition, some distinguish the old and new covenants merely in terms of the categories of external and internal, or that the old covenant was not gracious, or follow the "unconditional-conditional" covenantal distinction—all ideas we cannot endorse.[5] Yet some who embrace NCT also resonate with our proposal, although we prefer to use the "progressive covenantal" label.[6]

When *KTC* was written, we only scratched the surface of the debate. In one volume it was impossible to say everything—which many of our critics were quick to point out, although few critical reviews actually engaged the argument of the book.[7] In fact, in a number of reviews it was hard to

---

[3] For some examples of helpful NCT, see Tom Wells and Fred Zaspel, *New Covenant Theology* (Frederick, MD: New Covenant Media, 2002); John G. Reisinger, *Abraham's Four Seeds* (Frederick, MD: New Covenant Media, 1998); A. Blake White, *The Newness of the New Covenant* (Frederick, MD: New Covenant Media, 2007).

[4] See, e.g., Steve Lehrer, *New Covenant Theology: Questions Answered* (n.p.: Steve Lehrer, 2006).

[5] For the "unconditional-conditional" distinction as a way of distinguishing the covenants, see Fred Zaspel's evaluation of progressive covenantalism at http://books ataglance.com/book-reviews/gods-kingdom-through-gods-covenants-a-concise-biblical-theology-by-peter-j-gentry-and-stephen-j-wellum.

[6] See Gary D. Long, *New Covenant Theology: Time for a More Accurate Way* (n.p.: Gary D. Long, 2013); A. Blake White, *What Is New Covenant Theology? An Introduction* (Frederick, MD: New Covenant Media, 2012), and in many areas, Fred Zaspel.

[7] For a helpful review from a sympathetic critic, see Douglas Moo at http://thegospelcoalition.org/article/kingdom-through-covenant-a-review-by-douglas-moo. For two dispensationalist critiques of *KTC*, see Darrell Bock at http://www.thegospelco-alition.org/article/kingdom-through-covenant-a-review-by-darrell-bock, and Michael J. Vlach, "Have They Found a Better Way? An Analysis of Gentry and Wellum's, *Kingdom Through Covenant*," *TMSJ* 24 (2013): 5–24. For two critiques of *KTC* from the standpoint of covenant theology, see Michael Horton at http://www.thegospelcoalition. org/article/kingdom-through-covenant-a-review-by-michael-horton, and Jonathan M. Brack and Jared S. Oliphint, "Questioning the Progress in Progressive Covenantalism: A Review of Gentry and Wellum's *Kingdom Through Covenant*," *WTJ* 76 (2014):

recognize the actual book we had written; nevertheless we knew a follow-up book was necessary to unpack some of the points left underdeveloped or not discussed.

This present work is a continuation of *KTC*. Its purpose is to develop the overall view in more detail and depth. It is not the final word, but it is an attempt to continue the conversation on these important matters. All of the authors work from within the basic view of PC although not everyone agrees on every point. On certain doctrinal matters we do not take a position. For example, on the millennium, PC advocates can accept historic premillennialism or amillennialism, yet all the authors are united in their rejection of a dispensational understanding of the land promise to national Israel "apart" from Gentile Christians. Or, with regard to a text such as Romans 9–11, people within our view may differ, yet all agree that this text does not demand a dispensational interpretation.

In the ten chapters that follow, chapters 1–4 are general essays that discuss various topics crucial to putting together the biblical covenants. They continue to develop progressive covenantalism in relation to dispensationalism and covenant theology and show key similarities and differences.

In chapter 1, Jason DeRouchie presents an engaging discussion concerning the meaning of the "seed of Abraham" and how this theme is developed from the Abrahamic covenant across the OT and brought to fulfillment in the NT. By doing so, he provides further exegetical warrant *in the OT* to new covenant ecclesiology in contrast to dispensational and covenant theology.

In chapter 2, Brent Parker turns to the much-debated relationship of Israel-Christ-church. Dispensational theology tends to separate Israel and

---

189–217. Not surprisingly, in the dispensational and covenant critiques, each view retreated to their theological system without directly engaging the arguments of *KTC*. In a similar way, from the 1689 Reformed Baptist side, Samuel Renihan, "Kingdom Through Covenant: A Biblical-Theological Understanding of the Covenants: A Review Article," *Journal of the Institute of Reformed Baptist Studies* 1 (2014): 153–76, also does not engage the argument of the book, wrongly assumes we deny the covenant of grace (because we do not define it the way he does), employs the tripartite division of the Mosaic law without grappling with the problems with this understanding, and thus argues for the ongoing application of the Sabbath.

the church, while covenant theology tends to flatten the one into the other. Parker demonstrates that through the covenants the proper relationship is Israel to Christ and then to the church, so that in Christ not only is Adam's role fulfilled but so is Israel's role. In Christ the identity, vocation, and prophesied roles of corporate Israel are fulfilled; and thus nothing is left outstanding for national Israel apart from Christ.

In chapters 3–4, Jason Meyer contrasts progressive covenantalism with dispensational and covenant theology's understanding of the Mosaic law and its relationship to the new covenant, while Ardel Caneday rounds out our initial essays by showing the unconditional-conditional distinction of the covenants is incorrect and unnecessary.

In the next four chapters (chaps. 5–8), specific issues related to covenant theology are discussed and developed. In chapter 5, John Meade discusses the issue of circumcision with specific focus on its meaning in its covenantal location and its typological development through the covenants. He argues that circumcision of the flesh marked one out for service to God, but in the OT this sign did not truly equal the thing signified in the life of the old covenant people of God. This sign of circumcision was also a type, foreshadowing a heart circumcision, which would bring about the devotion to God signified by the sign. As such, heart circumcision has become the sign for all members of the new covenant who are true Jews in God's kingdom. Baptism, therefore, is not a fulfillment or replacement of circumcision in the flesh; but rather it is an external sign or testimony to the heart circumcision of the member of the new covenant. As a result, it should not be applied to anyone who has not undergone the circumcision of the heart and who has not repented of sin and believed and confessed that Jesus Christ is Lord.

In chapter 6, Tom Schreiner investigates the contentious issue of the Sabbath. He rejects covenant theology's tripartite distinction of the law and lays out how progressive covenantalism views the Sabbath in light of Christ and contends that the Sabbath command is not required for new covenant believers.

In chapter 7, Chris Cowan critiques one of covenant theology's main arguments for its mixed view of the church, that is, the warning passages of

Scripture. By these warning texts, covenant theology insists that there are nonelect members of the new covenant who will commit apostasy. Cowan rejects this interpretation by providing a critique of their arguments and an alternative view that better accounts for the biblical data.

In chapter 8, I wrestle with how new covenant believers apply the whole Bible as our ethical standard. I also reject covenant theology's tripartite division of the law and demonstrate how a progressive covenantal view seeks to determine what the moral law is and thus establish the biblical norm for doing ethics.

In the last two chapters (chaps. 9–10), specific issues related to dispensational theology are discussed and developed. In chapter 9, Richard Lucas analyzes the dispensational appeal to Romans 11 to warrant their view of national Israel in the millennium. Lucas argues that their view is not justified from this text, especially when it comes to reading in a future *restoration* of Israel since none of these "restoration" features of Israel are explicitly mentioned in Romans 11. Arguments for their view will have to be found elsewhere, for they are not in Romans 11.

In chapter 10, Oren Martin critiques the dispensational argument that the OT land promise must be fulfilled by national Israel in the millennial age. He argues that this view does not do justice to the biblical story line. Instead, the land promised to Abraham begins the process of recapturing and advancing what was lost in Eden and will not be fulfilled until a "new Eden" is regained in the new creation.

It is our sincere desire that this book will contribute to our understanding of Scripture and continue the conversation between differing theological viewpoints, with the goal of resolving those differences that separate us. It is not enough to affirm the authority of Scripture; we must also seek rightly to handle the Word of truth and bring our entire thought captive to it and to Christ. Ultimately our desire is to give glory to our great triune God for his glorious plan of redemption, of which we are the beneficiaries by his sovereign grace in Christ Jesus our Lord.

CHAPTER 1

Father of a Multitude of Nations: New Covenant Ecclesiology in OT Perspective[1]

Jason S. DeRouchie

Jews and Gentiles as "the Seed of Abraham"

Paul refers to *both* Jews and Gentiles in Christ as Abraham's "seed" [σπέρμα].[2] This is clear in Galatians 3:28–29 where he asserts: "There is neither Jew nor Greek, there is neither slave nor free, there is no male and female, for you are all one in Christ Jesus. And if you are Christ's, then you are Abraham's offspring, heirs according to promise" (ESV). This echoes his

---

[1] *Author's Note*: This essay is condensed from a longer study published in *JETS* 58 (2015) titled "Counting Stars with Abraham and the Prophets: New Covenant Ecclesiology in OT Perspective." Sections 1–5 in the present paper correspond generally to sections 1, 4, 5.2, 7, 8 in the more extended study. I am grateful to each of the editorial teams for granting the opportunity to publish both the shorter and longer versions.

[2] The noun σπέρμα occurs 43 times in the NT, and all but seven refer to "descendants, children, posterity" (BDAG, s.v. "σπέρμα"). Of these, the most predominant occurrence is to the "seed" of Abraham (22x), which refers either to Christ himself or to the whole family of God including both Jews and Gentiles in Christ (Luke 1:55; John 8:33, 37; Acts 3:25; 7:5, 6; Rom 4:13, 16, 18; 9:7[2x], 8; 11:1; 2 Cor 11:22; Gal 3:16[3x], 19, 29; Heb 2:16; 11:11, 18).

stress in 3:8–9 that all "those who are of faith [whether Jews or Gentiles] are blessed along with Abraham, the man of faith" (ESV).

Similarly, citing Genesis 17:5, Paul affirms in Romans 4:16–17 that the promised inheritance "depends on faith, in order that the promise may rest on grace and be guaranteed to all his offspring—not only to the adherent of the law but also to the one who shares the faith of Abraham, who is the father of us all, as it is written, 'I have made you the father of many nations'" (ESV). In the next verse Paul links Abraham's fatherhood of the nations with the promise in Genesis 15:5 that the patriarch's "seed" (KJV) would be as numerous as the stars (Rom 4:18). The apostle views the Gentile Christian participation in the new covenant community as fulfilling OT promises regarding the "seed" of Abraham.

Within the original OT context of the Abrahamic and Mosaic covenants, "seed" [זֶרַע/σπέρμα] most directly designates a category of biology or ethnicity often distinguished from the "nations/Gentiles" [גּוֹיִם/ἔθνη]. Indeed, through the "seed" the "nations" would be blessed—God's overcoming Adam's curse and reconciling to himself some from all the families of the earth (Gen 22:18; 26:4; 28:14).[3]

How then can Paul in Romans 4:18 link Abraham's fatherhood of many nations (Gen 17:5) with the promise that his "offspring" (ESV) would be as numerous as the stars (15:5)? Genesis 15:5 appears to address most immediately only *natural* "seed": "Please look to the heavens and count the stars if you are able to count them. . . . So shall your offspring be."[4] Within Genesis 15, the "seed" promise specifically answers the dilemma raised by Abram's assertion that Eliezer of Damascus is his heir but not his "seed." God stresses that the "offspring" that would "come from your loins" (15:4)[5] would inherit the land (15:13, 18). Also, Abram's struggle here is directly associated with the earlier parallel promise that his "seed" would become like "the dust of the earth" and claim the land (13:16; cf. 22:17; Heb 11:12).

---

[3] Cf. Gen 12:3; 18:18; Jer 4:2; Ps 72:17; Acts 3:25; Gal 3:16.

[4] So too G. K. Beale, *The Book of Revelation*, NIGTC (Grand Rapids: Eerdmans, 1999), 430.

[5] Unless otherwise indicated, Scripture translations are mine.

Genesis associates the "seed" promise most immediately with the patri-arch's *natural* descendants, a select group of whom would inherit the prom-ised land (e.g., Gen 28:13–14). Elsewhere, references to the "stars" and "dust" focus on the promise of land and on the old covenant nation of Israel (Exod 32:13; Deut 1:10; 10:22; Neh 9:23)—the land that would be lost and the nation that would dwindle to a small remnant through the curse of exile (Deut 28:62; cf. Isa 48:18–19). Furthermore, later OT texts, especially from Esther and Ezra-Nehemiah, explicitly restrict "seed" language to bio-logical lineage when associated with the old covenant age.

Nevertheless, Genesis itself and several OT prophetic texts antici-pate the expansion of "the seed of Abraham" to include those redeemed from both ethnic Israel and the nations during the eschatological age of the Messiah. As Paul recognizes, including "nations/Gentiles" among the "seed" (Rom 4:16–18 KJV) fulfills a new covenant eschatological hope that is associated directly with the representative saving work of the promised royal deliverer, Messiah Jesus (Gal 3:8, 14, 16, 29).[6]

This chapter considers some OT roots to new covenant ecclesiology, specifically from the perspective of the language of "seed."[7] Space con-straints have required focusing principally on two texts: Genesis 17 and portions of Isaiah. Following a synthesis of the argument and an assess-ment of Paul's use of the OT, the final segment of this paper will unpack the implications of the study for new covenant ecclesiology, arguing for the legitimacy of a progressive covenantal framework in contrast to the systems of dispensational and covenant theologies.

---

[6] For more on this, see Jason S. DeRouchie and Jason C. Meyer, "Christ or Family as the 'Seed' of Promise? An Evaluation of N. T. Wright on Galatians 3:16," *SBJT* 14 (2010): 36–48, esp. 40–43.

[7] G. K. Beale provides a broader, helpful overview of the OT data concerning the latter-day true Israel including a remnant from the nations (*A New Testament Biblical Theology: The Unfolding of the Old Testament in the New* [Grand Rapids: Baker, 2011], 656–65). For other overviews of the "seed" data that support the schema of progressive covenantalism, see John G. Reisinger, *Abraham's Four Seeds: A Biblical Examination of the Presuppositions of Covenant Theology and Dispensationalism* (Frederick, MD: New Covenant Media, 1998); Peter J. Gentry and Stephen J. Wellum, *Kingdom Through Covenant: A Biblical-Theological Understanding of the Covenants* (Wheaton, IL: Crossway, 2012), 632–33, 696.

Abraham, Father of a Multitude of Nations

I have already noted how Paul applies Genesis 17:5 to Jews *and* Gentiles in Christ (Rom 4:17). With this, Paul most likely cites Genesis 17:8 when he states in Galatians 3:16, "Now the promises were made to Abraham and to his seed. It does not say, 'And to seeds,' referring to many, but referring to one, 'And to your seed,' who is Christ."[8] These references demand a closer look at Genesis 17.

Abraham's Fatherhood—by Nature or Adoption?

In Genesis 17:5, Yahweh changes the patriarch's name from *Abram* "exalted father" to *Abraham* "father of a multitude" (ESV), highlighting his revealed destiny (cf. Gen 4:1, 25; 5:29; 16:15).[9] Specifically, God would make Abraham "the *father* of a multitude of *nations*" (17:4–5 ESV), the fulfillment which Paul identifies, "In you [Abraham] shall all the nations be blessed" (Gal 3:8 ESV).[10] Yahweh further promised, "I will give you for nations, and kings will come from you" (Gen 17:6), and then he reiterated the same proclamation with respect to Sarah (17:16). Similar promises were reiterated to Jacob: "A nation and a company of nations will come from you, and kings will come from your loins" (35:11; cf. 48:4).

Two observations suggest that the paternal language used in Abraham's, Isaac's, and Jacob's relationship to the nations connotes a family tie that is *not* restricted to or perhaps even associated with biological descent. First,

---

[8] DeRouchie and Meyer write ("Christ or Family as the 'Seed' of Promise?," 38): "The reference in Gal 3:16 to plural 'promises . . . made to Abraham and to his offspring' immediately sends us back to Genesis suggesting the likelihood of multiple promise texts in Paul's mind. The inclusion of the conjunction in the phrase 'καὶ τῷ σπέρματί σου' implies that Paul is indeed *quoting* Gen 13:15; 17:8; and/or 24:7—the only texts in the LXX of Genesis that include the entire phrase and addresses Abraham. In our view, the most likely candidate of these three is 17:8, for the mention of Abra(ha)m becoming 'the father of a multitude of nations' in the immediate literary context anticipates the inclusion of Gentiles in the people of God—one of the key issues at stake in Galatians 3."

[9] So Gordon J. Wenham, *Genesis 16–50*, WBC 2 (Dallas: Word, 1994), 21.

[10] See also Gen 18:18; 22:18; 26:4; cf. 12:3; 28:14.

throughout the OT, the plural form "nations" [גּוֹיִם] most commonly refers to political entities larger than tribes and usually not including Israel.[11] As such, because the promise to Sarah that "she shall become nations" (17:16 ESV) most likely reiterates the parental promise made to Abraham (17:6) and because two nations (Israel through Jacob and Edom through Esau) seem far from the "multitude" promised, the parenthood to which Genesis 17:4–6, 16 refer most likely points to a nonbiological relationship of authority.[12] Second, while the Ishmaelites, Edomites, Midianites, and several other peoples mentioned in the genealogy lists of Genesis 25 and 36 biologically derived from Abraham, only the one nation of Israel is known to have descended from Jacob.[13] Consequently, the fact that Jacob is to bring forth a "company of nations" suggests his "family" is larger than Israel and will include some

---

[11] On my count, of the 504 instances of גּוֹי in the Hebrew OT, only 53 refer to what would become known as Israel (= 10.52%; see Gen 12:2; 18:18; 35:11; 46:3; Exod 19:6; 33:13; Deut 26:5; 32:28; Josh 3:17; 5:6, 8; 10:13; Judg 2:20; 2 Sam 7:23; 1 Chr 17:21; 2 Chr 15:6; Pss 33:12; 43:1; 83:4; 106:5; Isa 1:4; 9:3; 10:6; 26:2, 15; 49:7; 58:2; Jer 2:11; 5:9, 29; 7:28; 9:8[9]; 31:36; 33:24; Ezek 2:3; 36:13–14; 37:22; Mic 4:7; Zeph 2:1, 9; Hag 2:14; Mal 3:9). If one only treats the 108 singular instances, 52 point to Israel (48.15%). Ezekiel 2:3 is the only occurrence of plural גּוֹיִם referring to Israel's "tribes" and not "nations," unless the plural references in the Abrahamic promises also point only to Israel and not the Gentiles (see Gen 17:4–6, 16; 35:11; 48:19), which seems unlikely in light of the contrast of Israel with the "nations" in these contexts (see 18:18; 22:18; 26:4) (cf. Victor P. Hamilton, *The Book of Genesis: Chapters 18–50*, NICOT [Grand Rapids: Eerdmans, 1995], 381; Moshe Greenberg, *Ezekiel 1–20*, AB 22 [New Haven, CT: Yale University Press, 1983], 63). For a discussion of these texts that shows how unlikely it is that גּוֹיִם refers to Israel's "tribes," see Chee-Chiew Lee, "גים [sic] in Genesis 35:11 and the Abrahamic Promise of Blessing for the Nations," *JETS* 52 (2009): 468–70.

[12] Cf. W. J. Dumbrell, *Covenant and Creation: A Theology of the Old Testament Covenants* (Carlisle, UK: Paternoster, 1984), 73; T. Desmond Alexander, "Abraham Re-Assessed Theologically: The Abraham Narrative and the New Testament Understanding of Justification by Faith," in *He Swore an Oath: Biblical Themes from Genesis 12–50*, ed. R. Hess et al. (Grand Rapids: Baker, 1994), 17–18; idem, "Royal Expectations in Genesis to Kings: Their Importance for Biblical Theology," *TynBul* 49 (1998): 200–201; Francis Watson, *Paul and the Hermeneutics of Faith* (London: T&T Clark, 2004), 210.

[13] Along with the nation of Israel, the nations that biologically derive through Abraham come from the descendants of Ishmael (Gen 25:12–18), the descendants of Abraham's concubine Keturah (25:1–5), and the descendants of Esau (36:1–19, 31–43).

adopted from other nations. T. Desmond Alexander' explains the fact that Genesis 35:11 distinguishes between a "nation" and a "company of nations" seems to imply that "whereas many nations will be closely associated with [Jacob], only one nation will be directly descended from him."[14]

Abraham's paternal relationship over the nations is principally an elected rather than a formal/biological association.[15] This more figurative use of "father" language parallels the ancient world's use of the term for various authoritative or shepherding social roles, whether advisor (Gen 45:18), priest (Judg 18:19), king (1 Sam 24:11), master (2 Kgs 2:12; 5:13), prophet (2 Kgs 6:21), governor (Isa 22:20–21), or legal protector (Job 29:12–16).[16] Perhaps most significant is the designation of kings as "fathers" of their vassal peoples (cf. 1 Sam 24:11, 16).[17] While Abraham himself is never called a king in the Hebrew text, numerous textual pointers both in and outside Genesis suggest we are to view him like one.[18] It seems plausible then to understand Abraham's fatherhood over the nations primarily as a royal

---

[14] Alexander, "Royal Expectations in Genesis to Kings," 201n22.

[15] Paul R. Williamson has further observed that in every other place where the construction found in Gen 17:4 occurs (i.e., the inseparable preposition לְ + the noun אָב in a resultative sense), a nonphysical concept of fatherhood is always in view (*Abraham, Israel, and the Nations: The Patriarchal Promise and Its Covenantal Development in Genesis*, JSOTSup 315 [Sheffield, UK: Sheffield Academic Press, 2000], 158–60; idem, *Sealed with an Oath: Covenant in God's Unfolding Promise*, NSBT 23 [Downers Grove, IL: InterVarsity, 2007], 88).

[16] Christopher J. H. Wright, "אָב," in *NIDOTTE*, 1:221; cf. Helmer Ringgren, "אָב *'abh*," in *TDOT*, 1:1–19. See also Alexander, "Abraham Re-Assessed Theologically," 17–18; idem, "Royal Expectations in Genesis to Kings," 201; Williamson, *Abraham, Israel, and the Nations*, 158–60; Lee, "גים in Genesis 35:11," 473–74.

[17] For an example in Mesopotamian literature, see Ringgren, "אָב *'abh*," *TDOT*, 1:3; on the use of adoption language in covenant relationships, see Moshe Weinfeld, "The Covenant of Grant in the Old Testament and in the Ancient Near East," *JAOS* 90 (1970): 190–94.

[18] For royal ideology in the Abrahamic narrative, see Ronald E. Clements, *Abraham and David* (London: SCM, 1967); E. Ruprecht, "Der traditionsgeschichtliche Hintergrund der einzelnen Elemente von Gen. 12:2–3," *VT* 29 (1979): 444–64; Gordon J. Wenham, *Genesis 1–15*, WBC 1 (Dallas: Word, 1987), 275; Victor P. Hamilton, *The Book of Genesis: Chapters 1–17*, NICOT (Grand Rapids: Eerdmans, 1990), 465n15; Alexander, "Royal Expectations in Genesis to Kings," 205; James Hamilton, "The Seed of the Woman and the Blessing of Abraham," *TynBul* 58 (2007): 266–72.

designation by which he and his wife Sarah, the "princess" (Gen 17:15), are regarded as the founders of a new dynasty that will climax in a specific, royal descendant who will rule Israelites (both native-born and alien residents) and those from vassal nations.

The Implications of Abraham's Fatherhood

With the blood tie not determinative in Abraham's "fatherhood," his status and role, at least with all nations other than Israel, must be established on the basis of covenantal adoption. Nevertheless, while this adoption will *result from* the "covenant of circumcision" (Genesis 17), the adoption is *not into* this specific covenant in its original form, for all circumcised members of the community (whether the alien resident or the father, son, or household servant among the native born) were considered part of *one nation* later named Israel (Gen 17:12; Josh 8:33)—a nation that is here only one part of "the multitude of nations" parented or overseen by Abraham (likely through his royal representative, Gen 17:6).[19]

These observations give rise to at least three significant implications. First, Genesis 17 highlights the progression of two distinct covenant eras anticipated in the framework of Genesis 12:1–3, where Abra(ha)m must first "go" to the land in order to become a nation (realized in the Mosaic covenant) and then once there "be a blessing" in order for all the families of the earth to be blessed (realized through Christ in the new covenant).[20] The initial period is shaped by Abraham's biological descendants living in the promised land as a nation that would become known as Israel under the Mosaic covenant. They would claim the promised land, bearing the charge to heed God's voice in order to serve as mediators and displayers of God's

---

[19] Cf. Beale, *The Book of Revelation*, 429.

[20] When two imperatives are linked via the conjunction *waw* (as in Gen 12:1–2 and 17:1), the second imperative is in some way contingent on the first (captured in *GKC* by the term "consequence," §110f and i), while still maintaining its imperatival force (so esp. Gentry and Wellum, *Kingdom Through Covenant*, 230–34; cf. Williamson, *Sealed with an Oath*, 78–79, 82–84). With this, when imperatives are followed by volitional *yiqtols*, the latter often expresses purpose (*GKC* §108d; Thomas O. Lambdin, *Introduction to Biblical Hebrew* [New York: Scribner's, 1971], §107c).

holiness to the world (Exod 19:4–6; Deut 4:5–8). That is the initial era. Next comes the final period, the age of fulfillment, which is enjoyed only after Abraham's "seed" (realized in Jesus Messiah) serve(s) as agent(s) of curse-overcoming blessing. During this new covenant period, God would reconcile mankind, and Abraham would stand as the father of many nations—a fatherhood manifest through an earthly royal descendant who would rule over all (Gen 17:4–6; cf. 22:17b–18; 49:8, 10; Isa 9:6).

Second, at one level both the old covenant and the land promise should be treated as "eternal," for God would fulfill his purposes for the Abrahamic covenant progeny and property (Gen 17:7–8; cf. Deut 4:31). Nevertheless, at another level, the eternality is qualified by the period of fulfillment. That is, while the Abrahamic covenant is eternal, the participation and property aspects get transformed in the age of the Messiah. Genesis 17 envisions a day when Abraham's "fatherhood" will expand beyond ethnic Israelites to include the nations. The fact that God chose to use Israel as the agent of the world's deliverance will ever establish a temporal, positional distinction within the one family of Abraham (see Rom 1:16; 2:9; cf. Acts 13:46). Yet, as Paul would note, there are *natural* and *wild* branches in the tree of new covenant life (Rom 9:11–27; cf. 3:1–2; 9:4–5; Eph 2:11–22), for the promise of a global inheritance is for both Jews and Gentiles, who share "the faith of Abraham, who is the father of us all" (Rom 4:16; cf. Gal 3:18). With this, there is an implication that God's kingdom will no longer be limited to the promised land but will, like the original vision for the garden of Eden, expand to include the whole world (Gen 1:28; Matt 5:5; Rom 4:13),[21] God's blessed glory filling the earth as the waters cover the sea (Num 14:21; Ps 72:19; Hab 2:14).[22] This kind of expansion is suggested in Genesis 22:17b–18 where the unique, male deliverer will not only bless "all the nations of the earth," but will also possess "the gate of his enemies," claiming once-enemy territory, his kingdom expanding to fill the earth (cf. 24:60). The same expansion appears evident in 26:3–4 where, in the context of the

---

[21] Cf. Eph 6:2–3; Heb 11:13–16.

[22] See Beale, *The Temple and the Church's Mission,* 81–167. Cf. Gentry and Wellum, *Kingdom Through Covenant,* 468–70; cf. 703–16.

global blessing promise, God pledges to give Isaac and his "seed" not only "the land" but also "these lands" (plural).

Third, because Abraham will oversee Israel and many nations as covenant father and because the particular male, royal descendent of Abraham alone will inaugurate the age of blessing (Gen 22:17b–18; Acts 3:25–26; Gal 3:14, 16, 29), *Genesis 17 works with 15:5 to set the stage for Paul, in a context of eschatological fulfillment in Christ, to identify Jews and Gentiles as having a place in the one family of Abraham apart from circumcision and the law that would later be associated with it.* That is, the progression from the Abrahamic and Mosaic administrations to the new covenant in Jesus answers how Paul can apply "seed" language to Christian Gentiles who never became Jewish proselytes. They are counted as "seed" only because they are identified by faith with *the* "seed, who is Christ."[23] The makeup of the new covenant community is shaped around the connection with Christ through a faith like Abraham's (Gen 15:6; Rom 4:3–5). Whether Jew or Gentile, covenant membership requires adoption into Christ by faith (Rom 8:15; Gal 3:26; 4:4–5; Eph 1:5). This new covenant community stands distinct from that of the previous era because: (1) the members include elect from both ethnic Israel and many other nations of the world (Gen 17:4–5); (2) all of whom are heirs of the life-giving, barrenness-overcoming, miraculous power of God (17:21; 18:14; cf. Rom 4:19); (3) who have witnessed a pattern of faithfulness (Gen 12:2; 17:1); and (4) through this have become recipients of divine blessing (12:2–3; 22:18); and (5) who are now serving together under a king in the line of Abraham who bears global influence and rule (17:6; 49:8, 10). All of these are features of progressive covenantalism that highlight the centrality of Christ in God's redemptive purposes.

The Servant and His "Seed" in Isaiah

While tagging Abraham as the future "father of a multitude of nations" sets the stage for non-Israelites in the age of fulfillment to be considered part

---

[23] See DeRouchie and Meyer, "Christ or Family as the 'Seed' of Promise?" 36–48, esp. 40–43. Cf. Beale, *The Book of Revelation*, 430.

of the Abrahamic "family," we have thus far not focused on any OT texts that overtly apply the term "seed" to nonbiological descendants of Abraham (though Gen 15:5 and similar promises do so through their long-range fulfillment). The Pentateuch teaches that nonnative aliens and household slaves could become Israelites and their children would be considered the patriarch's "seed" (e.g., Rahab, Ruth, Uriah the Hittite), but this required full incorporation into the Abrahamic and (later) Mosaic covenant communities, including male circumcision and other law keeping (see Exod 12:48–49; Lev 19:34; Num 9:14).[24] A number of OT eschatological texts, especially in Isaiah, explicitly anticipate a broadening in how "seed" language is applied in the new covenant age of the Messiah.

More than any other OT prophet, Isaiah detailed the nature of the messianic age that would fulfill the Abrahamic promises of worldwide curse-destruction. Like other OT prophets (e.g., Hos 3:1–5; Zech 3:9; 12:10; 13:1; Dan 9:2, 24–27), he envisioned Israel's restoration coming in two stages, the second of which parallels the second stage of the Abrahamic covenant highlighted in Genesis 12:2–3 and 17:4–5: (1) initial physical restoration to the promised land (Isa 42:18–43:21) and then (2) spiritual reconciliation with God (43:22–44:23).[25] Stage one (liberation), later associated with Jeremiah's "seventy years" (Jer 25:11–12; 29:10), would be wrought by one named Cyrus (Isa 44:24–48:22; cf. 2 Chr 36:20–22). Stage two (atonement) would be secured by the royal Davidic servant (Isa 49:1–53:12) and would include blessing reaching the nations, the fulfillment of the Abrahamic covenant (stage 2). The book ends with the proclamation of such glories to Zion and the world (54:1–55:13) and the climactic vision of the new creation (56:1–66:24). Wrapped into the midst of these eschatological texts are a number of

---

[24] Cf. Lev 24:22; Num 15:29; Ezek 47:22. See R. J. D. Knauth, "Alien, Foreign Resident," in *DOTP*, 26–33; cf. also G. H. Haas, "Slave, Slavery," in *DOTP*, 778–83; K. Kuhn, "προσήλυτος," *TDNT*, 6:728–29.

[25] For the following breakdown of Isaiah, see Gentry and Wellum, *Kingdom Through Covenant*, 437–38; and Peter J. Gentry, "The Atonement in Isaiah's Fourth Servant Song (Isaiah 52:13–53:12)," *SBJT* 12 (2007): 21–24.

references to "seed" that help clarify Paul's application of "offspring" language in the NT.

The "Survivors of the Nations" as the "Seed" of Israel

It is intriguing that the assertion in Isaiah 45:25 that "in Yahweh all the offspring of Israel shall be justified and will glory" directly follows the identification of Cyrus as the agent of exilic release (45:1, 13), a comment regarding the salvation of the nations (45:14), and an extended call for "the survivors of the nations" [פְּלִיטֵי הַגּוֹיִם] to repent (45:20–24). Who are the "survivors" (45:20), and what is their relationship to the "offspring" (45:25)?

"Survivors" in 45:20 is the plural form of the masculine noun פָּלִיט and could refer to the remnant of Israelites who experienced exile. Nevertheless, elsewhere in the book the restored Jews are called "the survivors of Israel" (4:2 ESV) and "the survivors of the house of Jacob" (10:20; 37:31; cf. 37:32), all with the plural form of the feminine noun פְּלֵיטָה. Furthermore, the fact that God calls "all the ends of the earth" to turn to him and be saved (45:22) suggests that the "survivors" are actually members of the nations amid which Israel was exiled. In Isaiah's words elsewhere, "Yahweh has bared the arm of his holiness before the eyes of all the nations, and all *the ends of the earth* shall see the salvation of our God" (52:10; cf. 5:26; 24:15–16; 41:5). Similarly, though using a singular instead of a plural, Isaiah wrote of the representative messianic servant's mission: "It is too light a thing that you [Israel] should be my servant to raise up the tribes of Jacob and to bring back the preserved of Israel; I will make you as a light for the nations, that my salvation may reach to *the end of the earth*" (Isa 49:6 ESV; cf. Acts 1:8; 26:23).[26] Though plagued by idolatry (Isa 45:20), the nations were being called to recognize the superiority and authority of Israel's God (45:15–17).

These observations are significant because, after the climaxing declaration that "to me [i.e., Yahweh] every knee will bow and every tongue will swear [allegiance]" (45:23 ESV; cf. Rom 14:11; Phil 2:10) and noting

---

[26] Here the Davidic servant is named "Israel" (Isa 49:3), whom God in turn commissions to redeem a remnant from both "Israel" and the "nations" (49:5–6; cf. 42:6; 52:13–53:12). See Beale, *A New Testament Biblical Theology*, 656.

the shame that God will place on all nations that remain angry with him (Isa 45:24), verse 25 then speaks of the righteousness and praise of "the offspring of Israel." While the point may simply be that the saving of the nations does not nullify the promises to Israel,[27] the prophet is more likely suggesting that in the new age of fulfillment Yahweh will consider *all* who turn to him, both from Israel and the nations, full "offspring" of the patriarchs, as if all were biological descendants of Abraham.[28] This latter possibility is grounded by two facts: (1) The phrase "offspring of Jacob/Israel" in 45:19 and 25 shapes an inclusio around the call for Gentile repentance, and (2) the remark about "the seed of Israel" in verse 25 (KJV) would be extremely abrupt if indeed it bore no reference to the nations just addressed.

The "Many" Becoming "Seed" through the Servant King's Atoning Work

Does Isaiah clarify what generates the broader application of "seed" language in the age of fulfillment? He elucidates this in the last servant song, which highlights the Davidic servant's substitutionary atoning work (Isa 52:13–53:12). The prophet earlier highlighted that following the fires of judgment against Israel, Yahweh would cause a "holy seed" in the line of David to sprout (6:13)—a royal "seed" whose kingdom would be eternal, whose life would bear fruits mirroring the likeness of God and in a new and consummate garden of Eden, and whose reign would include a remnant from every nation (6:13; 9:6–7[5–6]; 11:1–5, 10–11).[29] Building off this botanical imagery (6:13; 11:1), the prophet later says of Yahweh's servant, "He grew up as a tender plant before him [i.e., Yahweh], and like a root from dry ground, neither form nor majesty was to him" (53:2). Thus the servant

---

[27] So John N. Oswalt, *The Book of Isaiah: Chapters 40–66*, NICOT (Grand Rapids: Eerdmans, 1997), 225n83.

[28] So F. Delitzsch, *The Prophecies of Isaiah* (Grand Rapids: Eerdmans, 1991), 2:231; Edward J. Young, *The Book of Isaiah* (Grand Rapids: Eerdmans, 1972), 3:218; Claus Westermann, *Isaiah 40–66*, Old Testament Library (Philadelphia: Westminster, 1969), 176; Brevard S. Childs, *Isaiah*, Old Testament Library (Louisville: Westminster John Knox, 2001), 356; Robert L. Hubbard Jr., "פלט," in *NIDOTTE*, 3:624.

[29] Cf. Jer 23:5–6; 33:14–26.

of Isaiah 53 is none other than the promised royal Son of David anticipated throughout the book. While he would indeed be exalted overall and enable spiritual sight and understanding to nations and their kings (52:13–15; cf. Rom 15:21), such would be accomplished only by his bearing the sins of "many" in his death so that the "many" could in turn be counted righteous (Isa 53:11–12; cf. Rom 5:18–19; 2 Cor 5:21; Phil 3:9). This righteous servant would suffer as a substitutionary guilt offering under Yahweh's just wrath, but having fulfilled his purpose unto death, he would rise and be completely satisfied at the sight of "*his* offspring" now redeemed (Isa 53:10–11). What is the identity of the "many," the servant's "seed"?

Recognizably, when Isaiah speaks of redemption accomplished and applied in this unit, he regularly uses the first common plural: "And he was being pierced on account of *our* wrongdoings, being crushed on account of *our* iniquities. The chastisement that secured *our* peace was on him, and with his stripes he has secured healing for *us*" (Isa 53:5). While Isaiah was an old covenant enforcer, the "us" referred to did not include most of his Israelite peers, who were never granted ears to hear (6:9–13) and from whom the prophet's visions were "sealed" (29:9–12; cf. 8:16). Indeed, anticipating that the rebel majority would remain unmoved at the messianic servant king's coming, Isaiah declared, "Who has believed unto our report?" (53:1)—a passage both Jesus and Paul cite in relation to Jewish hard-heartedness (John 12:37–38; Rom 10:16). Certainly the "us" included a remnant of ethnic Israelites, but at least five reasons suggest that a saved, adopted remnant from the nations is also included and is part of the "many" and the "offspring" in Isaiah 53:11–12, fulfilling the Abrahamic promises (cf. Rev 7:9). (1) The book has highlighted the international nature of the royal servant's saving work (Isa 42:1–4, 6; 49:6; 51:4–5). (2) Leading into the servant song, we are told that the age of fulfillment would include testament that "God reigns" in Zion (52:7) and a vision of "the salvation of our God" by all the nations at the ends of the earth (52:10).[30] (3) This servant song explicitly opens with a message of *global* salvation (52:13–15), with

---

[30] Directly following this statement in Isa 52:10 is a call to purity that Paul applies in 2 Cor 6:17 to the new covenant church. The same group of OT quotations in 2 Cor 6:18 includes the "sons and daughters" reference in Isa 43:5–6.

the mention of "kings" perhaps echoing the Abrahamic promise of Genesis 17:6, the "many" nations of Isaiah 52:14–15 paralleling the redemption of the "many" in 53:11–12, and the "sprinkling" of the nations in 52:15 highlighting direct benefit from the servant's sacrifice.[31] (4) Isaiah explicitly shifts from the first common plural referents ("our," "we") to the generic "many." (5) The NT authors readily draw on these texts with application to all the redeemed in Christ, both Jews and Gentiles (e.g., Rom 4:24; 1 Pet 2:24). Significantly, Messiah Jesus neither married nor fathered physical children. His "offspring" in whom he delights (Isa 53:10), therefore, must be identified through spiritual adoption. This means the "offspring" of the new covenant community will only include the "many to be accounted righteous" in Christ (53:11 ESV). This bears significant implication for new covenant ecclesiology.

New Covenant "Seed" as the Fulfillment of the Abrahamic Covenant

The next chapter of Isaiah supports this view of "offspring" and develops a portrait of this messianic age. The text opens: "Sing, O barren one—she did not bear! Break forth a song and cry aloud—she did not experience labor pain, but many more are the children of the desolate one than the children of the married one!" (Isa 54:1). Here the "barren one" recalls Sarah's barrenness (Gen 11:30), whereas "the married one" appears to point to Hagar, maidservant whom Sarah gave to Abram as wife in order to answer the "offspring" problem (16:3–4). Like Paul years later (Gal 4:21–31), what Isaiah sees in this historical account is a layer of prophetic allegory that anticipates the certain fulfillment of the Abrahamic covenant in the new and that also

---

[31] Cf. J. Alec Motyer, "'Stricken for the Transgressions of My People': The Atoning Work of Isaiah's Suffering Servant," in *From Heaven He Came and Sought Her: Definite Atonement in Historical, Biblical, Pastoral Perspective*, ed. David Gibson and Jonathan Gibson (Wheaton, IL: Crossway, 2013), 252; cf. 264–66.

foresees the new covenant's superseding of the Mosaic covenant through the death and resurrection of the servant king.[32]

Earlier, while unpacking his message of eschatological *global* salvation (Isa 51:4–5; cf. 45:14–25), Isaiah urged any who pursued righteousness and sought Yahweh to return to their roots, looking "to the Rock [צוּר] from which you were hewn" and "to Abraham your father and to Sarah who bore you through birth pain [חִיל], for as one I called him so that I might bless him and multiply him" (Isa 51:1–2). The "Rock" is probably an allusion to Deuteronomy 32:18, which designates Yahweh as the "Rock" [צוּר] who bore Israel through birth pain [חִיל]—likely an enigmatic reference to the symbolic representative judgment Yahweh underwent in redeeming Israel from Egypt, specifically during their sixth act of rebellion (Exod 17:1–7).[33] The initial call, then, is for the audience to consider the implications of divine mercy.

With this Isaiah grounds his discussion of the eschatological hope for salvation in the original patriarchal promises that Abraham's headship over a blessed multitude would be assisted by his "princess," matriarch Sarah (Gen 17:4–6, 16). Furthermore, the mention of Sarah in Isaiah 51:2 enables the prophet to use her life in chapter 54 to explain the greatest covenantal progression of the ages. For like Sarah, whose barrenness continued until there appeared to be no hope of promise fulfillment (Gen 18:13–14; cf. Rom 4:18–21; Heb 11:11–12), so too the Abrahamic covenant had extended through centuries without fulfillment (Gen 12:3; 17:4–5). Nevertheless, in calling his audience to "look to Abraham . . . and Sarah," Isaiah reminded them of the Genesis promises and pushed them to anticipate salvation

---

[32] Cf. Charles H. Cosgrove, "The Law Has Given Sarah No Children (Gal. 4:21–30)," *NovT* 29 (1987): 231. For an argument that the allegory is original to Genesis itself and not simply part of prophetic interpretation, see A. B. Caneday, "Covenant Lineage Allegorically Prefigured: 'Which Things Are Written Allegorically' (Galatians 4:21–31)," *SBJT* 14 (2010): 50–77; cf. Karen H. Jobes, "Jerusalem, Our Mother: Metalepsis and Intertextuality in Galatians 4:21–31," *WTJ* 55 (1993): 317–18.

[33] Jesse R. Scheumann, "A Biblical Theology of Birth Pain and the Hope of the Messiah" (ThM Thesis, Bethlehem College and Seminary, 2014), 54 with 26–29; cf. Edmund P. Clowney, *The Unfolding Mystery: Discovering Christ in the Old Testament* (Phillipsburg, NJ: P&R, 1988), 120–28. We will see that the veiled reference to Deut 32:18 in Isa 51:2 (first exodus) works with the reference in 42:14 (new exodus) to set the stage for the fulfillment of the Abrahamic covenant promises in the new covenant age.

rising out of the exilic judgment. Just as Sarah in her old age did give birth to Isaac and ultimately the Israelite nation, so too the Abrahamic covenant would reach its goal: the children of the desolate one would become even more numerous than those of the rival old covenant, represented by Hagar (Isa 54:1; cf. 49:21).

In that future day the covenant community's dwelling place ("tent") would need to be expanded because of the family's abounding growth— "your offspring will inherit the nations" (54:3; cf. 49:20). In light of the Abrahamic context, this phrase suggests not only the expansion of the promised land to include the world (see Gen 1:28; 22:17b; 26:3–4; Matt 5:5; Rom 4:13)[34] but also the fulfillment of the blessing reaching all the families of the earth (Gen 12:3; 22:18; cf. Isa 49:22–23).[35] Abraham will have become the father of a multitude of nations. And because the redeemed nations operate as an "inheritance," they appear to be fully identified with and incorporated into the "offspring" of Abraham, their head (cf. Jer 3:17–18 with 4:2; 12:16; 30:8–11).

Importantly, Isaiah 54:1 notes that the generating of "offspring" in the new covenant occurs *without* labor and *without* birth pain for the covenant people: "Sing, O barren one—*she did not bear!* Break forth a song and cry aloud—*she did not experience labor pain*, but more are the children of the desolate one than the children of the married one!" (cf. 49:21). We can draw two significant implications from this, one ecclesiological and the other soteriological.

First, in contrast to previous covenants, the "seed" of the new covenant are *not* physically born into covenant membership. Even Sarah ultimately experienced labor and pain at Isaac's birth (Isa 51:2), but the "barren one's" lack of labor and childbearing in 54:1 suggests that *spiritual adoption, not physical birth, would characterize the identity of the new children.*[36] The physical genealogical principle so evident in the Abrahamic and Mosaic covenants does *not* continue once the Abrahamic covenant reaches its fulfillment in the new, for membership is now solely conditioned on *spiritual*

---

[34] Cf. Eph 6:2–3; Heb 11:13–16.

[35] See Gentry and Wellum, *Kingdom Through Covenant*, 442.

[36] Scheumann, *A Biblical Theology of Birth Pain and the Hope of the Messiah*, 57.

rebirth, generated through the sacrificial death of the servant king (53:10). While nothing in the text suggests that ethnic distinction will be eradicated in the new covenant, the wording does mean that membership will not be assumed simply because of ethnicity. Furthermore, because Abraham's "offspring" have now been reidentified as only the servant king's spiritual "offspring" who have thus been accounted righteous (53:10–11), Isaiah would not affirm the view of covenant theologians that an infant's birth into a family with at least one believing parent grants the child full membership in the new covenant.

Second, because throughout Scripture labor pain is directly associated with judgment (Gen 3:16) and only rarely accompanied by hope,[37] the absence of birth pain in Isaiah 54:1 most likely means that the judgment through which new covenant salvation is birthed was borne by another—namely, the servant king of the previous chapter (Isa 52:13–53:12), whose sacrificial death would satisfy God's wrath against the people and display the curse-bearing mercy of God himself.

That the royal servant's substitutionary atonement described in Isaiah 52:13–53:12 is indeed the "birth pain" punishment that brings forth the new covenant family in chapter 54 is suggested by four parallels.[38] (1) The "many" in 52:14–15 and 53:11–12 are the "many" in the "miracle family" of 54:1. (2) The servant's "offspring" in 53:11 are Sarah's "offspring" in 54:3 who have been expanded by inheriting nations. (3) In 53:11 the "righteous" servant king makes many "righteous," and in 54:14 the redeemed city is established in "righteousness" (cf. Jer 23:6; 33:16). (4) The "servant" singular in Isaiah 52:13 and 53:11 gives rise to "servants" plural in 54:17 and beyond (cf. 65:8–9, 13–15; 66:14)—servants that explicitly include a remnant from the tribes of Israel (63:17) *and* the nations (56:6).

Furthermore, it is important to see that two times already in Isaiah, Judah has declared herself unable to "give birth"—that is, to generate her own deliverance (26:16–18; 37:3). Instead, the people continued godless and desolate under the Lord's judgment (49:19; 64:10). Because no one was "being a blessing," divine favor was not reaching all the families of the

---

[37] See Scheumann's summary of the evidence with implications in ibid., 112–19.

[38] Adapted from Gentry and Wellum, *Kingdom Through Covenant*, 441.

earth (Gen 12:2–3). Thus the Abrahamic covenant remained unfulfilled, while the Mosaic covenant flourished in carrying out its judgment curses on the unfaithful people (Leviticus 26; Deuteronomy 28). Yet Yahweh, in alignment with his character and in fulfillment of his past promise (Exod 34:6; Deut 4:30–31), announces that he would act in mercy on his people's behalf. Though they were unable to rescue themselves from divine wrath, Yahweh promises concretely and completely to bear Israel's judgment of "labor pain" in their place and complete a new, antitypical exodus: "I have been quiet; I have restrained myself. Like a woman in labor, I will groan, gasp, and pant altogether. . . . And I will lead blind ones in a way they do not know; in paths they do not know I will guide them. I will change darkness before them into light and rough places into a plain" (Isa 42:14, 16).[39]

Isaiah 51:1 charges the audience to consider the first exodus labor pain that Yahweh symbolically endured on behalf of Israel (Deut 32:18 with Exod 17:7). In contrast, in Isaiah 42:14 the prophet emphasizes that the new covenant and second exodus would be marked by an actual penal substitution for sin, accomplished by Yahweh, ultimately through his royal servant (52:13–53:12).[40] Yahweh's actions in 42:10–17 closely parallel those of the servant king in the first servant song (42:1–9), thus identifying how closely the two work together. Both bear influence among the coastlands (42:4, 10, 12), redeem the blind (42:7, 16), serve as guides (42:4, 16), overcome darkness with light (42:6–7, 16), and put to shame carved idols (42:8, 17). The servant would be the "the arm of Yahweh" (53:1; cf. 51:9), the Spirit-endowed agent of God (Isa 42:1; cf. 11:2; 61:1; Luke 4:18) who would be given "as a covenant for people, a light for nations" (Isa 42:6; cf. Luke

---

[39] For the second exodus theme in Isaiah, see G. P. Hugenberger, "The Servant of the Lord in the 'Servant Songs' of Isaiah: A Second Moses," in *The Lord's Anointed: Interpretation of Old Testament Messianic Texts*, ed. P. E. Satterthwaite, R. S. Hess, and G. J. Wenham (Grand Rapids: Baker, 1995), 105–40, esp. 126–28; Bernard W. Anderson, "Exodus Typology in Second Isaiah," in *Israel's Prophetic Heritage: Essays in Honor of James Muilenberg*, ed. Bernard W. Anderson and Walter J. Harrelson (New York: Harper, 1962), 177–95.

[40] "What was symbolic substitution at the rock (Exod 17:1–7; Deut 32:18) becomes actual substitution for sin in this Fourth servant song" (Scheumann, *A Biblical Theology of Birth Pain and the Hope of the Messiah*, 55).

2:32). Yahweh would be pleased to crush him in order to secure far-reaching atonement (Isa 53:6, 10, 12), but this servant king would also die the substitutionary death willingly for the joy set before him (42:4; John 10:17–18; Heb 12:2).[41] This royal figure would embody the presence of God and bear the character of God (Isa 7:6; 9:6),[42] and through him God would establish his reign on the earth (9:7; 52:7; 53:10). As the representative royal "offspring" of Abraham and David (Gen 22:17b–18; 2 Sam 7:12; Jer 33:26), the royal servant's faithful covenant obedience would secure new life for all who submit to his kingship (Isa 55:3–5),[43] and these redeemed would then be counted "his offspring" (53:10)—a children no longer desolate but now flourishing and expanded, having inherited the nations (54:1, 3; cf. Gen 28:14). What hope is found in Isaiah's "good news" (Isa 40:9; 52:7; 61:6)!

Summary

Other texts address becoming "sons and daughters" of God by identifying with the royal Son (Isa 43:5–7; 44:4; 45:25; cf. 2 Cor 6:18) or the multiethnic "seed" as servants of Yahweh in the new creation (Isa 59:20–21; 61:9; 65:9, 23; 66:18–23). Nevertheless, the noted texts show that Isaiah envisioned the new covenant age to be fulfilled by the Servant King, who would have Jewish and Gentile "offspring" identified with him solely by spiritual adoption. As Israel's representative, he would become the agent of universal blessing, the instrument by which Abraham's royal fatherhood would be realized on a global scale.

Synthesis and Fulfillment in Christ

Abraham's Fatherhood Realized through Christ

As noted earlier, Paul's application of the "seed" designation to both Jews and Gentiles in Christ (Rom 4:16–18; Gal 3:28–29) marks a

---

[41] Cf. Isa 50:6–7; 53:3, 5, 7–8, 10, 12; Heb 10:4–7.
[42] Cf. Isa 28:29; 10:21; 63:16; 66:12; Matt 1:23.
[43] On this text, see Gentry and Wellum, *Kingdom Through Covenant*, 406–21.

redemptive-historical shift from an age of promise to an age of fulfillment. Both the Abrahamic and Mosaic covenants incorporate "seed" language in three primary ways: (1) all those who by physical birth were part
of Abraham's family, (2) a subset of Abraham's biological descendants who
would take on national status as Israel within the promised land, and (3) a
unique individual biological son who would play a significant typological
role in redemptive history (types leading to Christ, the antitype). While the
Abrahamic and Mosaic covenants did not regard first-generation proselytes
as "seed," their children were considered to be such, almost completely
overlapping covenant membership and "offspring" status.

While the Abrahamic and Mosaic covenants initially restricted "seed"
language to physical descent, they also pointed ahead to a day when covenantal, spiritual adoption would replace ethnicity as the foundational mark
of the patriarch's "fatherhood." The promise that Abraham would become
an adoptive "father" of many nations anticipated this shift (Gen 17:4–6; cf.
22:17b–18), and then prophets like Isaiah (esp. Isa 53:10; 54:3; 66:22) predicted it through their eschatological new covenant promises (see above).
Together these prophets envisioned an international people gathering in an
eschatological Zion under a single Davidic king whose own penal substitutionary death would exalt him over all. At the cross Christ experiences
the divine labor-pain judgment (Isa 42:14; 52:13–53:12) that births salvation for the many (49:20–21; 52:15; 53:11–12; 54:1), securing for him
the inheritance of the nations (49:22–23; 54:3; cf. Ps 2:8). Since Christ's
atoning work, the *true* "offspring" of Abraham are those who have become
the "seed" of the messianic servant king (Isa 53:10; cf. 59:21; Gal 3:29)
through spiritual rebirth (Isa 54:1–3; cf. 49:20–21). They have experienced
the great exchange that their representative head supplies: he bears their
sins and counts his righteousness as their own (53:11; Rom 5:18–19; 2 Cor
5:21; Phil 3:9; 1 Pet 2:24).

The Narrowing of the "Seed" and the Hope of the Promised "Offspring"

The Abrahamic and Mosaic covenant texts often identify a continuum of various types of "offspring" in the covenantal community. Not all the "offspring" are the same. For instance, Asaph writes that the "Israel" to which God is good is only "those who are pure in heart" (Ps 73:1 ESV). Such narrowing resulted in a "mixed" community, made up of those "offspring" associated with Abraham only by biology or ethnicity and those *true* "offspring" linked to him by faith in God. Both types of members received the covenant sign of circumcision and were ultimately called upon to keep the Mosaic law, but only the latter group typologically pointed to those in the new covenant: "Those from faith are blessed with the believing Abraham" (Gal 3:9).

Within the new covenant Paul speaks of his fellow ethnic Israelites, saying, "Not all who are descended from Israel belong to Israel" (Rom 9:6 ESV). Similarly, Paul earlier affirms, "No one is a Jew who is merely one outwardly, . . . but a Jew is one inwardly" (2:28–29 ESV). Elsewhere we learn that God regards both Jews and Gentiles as part of the *true* "Israel of God" (Gal 6:16; cf. 3:28–29) if they are joined by faith to Christ Jesus, the *true* Israel (Isa 49:3, 5) and Abraham's *true* "seed" (Gal 3:16).[44]

From the beginning the revealed goal of the national aspects of the Abrahamic covenant (Gen 12:1–2; 17:7–9) was that the progeny and property associated with the patriarch would expand into a global kingdom with Abraham serving as the father of a multitude of nations through his representative king (12:2–3; 17:4–6; 22:17b–18; 26:3–4). Faith in God to fulfill the "offspring" promise fueled Abraham's life of obedience (15:4–6; Heb

---

[44] For "the Israel of God" in Gal 6:16 referring to the whole church (Jews and Gentiles in Christ), see Christopher W. Cowan, "Context Is Everything: 'The Israel of God' in Galatians 6:16," *SBJT* 14 (2010): 78–85; G. K. Beale, "Peace and Mercy upon the Israel of God: The Old Testament Background of Gal. 6,16b," *Bib* 80 (1999): 204–23; cf. idem, *A New Testament Biblical Theology*, 722–23.

11:17–19),[45] and it testifies to the patriarch's inability to bless the world (Gen 12:2–3); only the true "offspring" could fulfill it.[46] That is, from the beginning the believing remnant viewed the promised royal deliverer as representative of the many, and only through his representative obedience and substitutionary sacrifice would blessing ultimately reach worldwide. This one, Messiah Jesus, is the *true* "offspring" of Abraham (Gal 3:16) in that he, in fulfillment of the Genesis promises (Gen 17:4–5; 22:17b–18), bears the role of father, enemy destroyer, and blessing mediator on Abraham's behalf. But he is also the patriarch's superior, for the hopes of both Abraham and the world rested upon him (John 8:56, 58; cf. Heb 6:20 with 7:8). Those who surrender to Jesus' representative authority will participate in the single family of God and be counted as Abraham's "seed" (Gal 3:29).

The Centrality of Christ in OT Interpretation

In Romans 4:16–18 and elsewhere, when Paul applies the "seed" promise of Genesis 15:6 ("So shall your offspring be" ESV) to spiritually reborn Jews and Gentiles in Christ, he identifies the ultimate fulfillment of Genesis's original predictions. Following closely Moses's argument, Paul recognizes that Abraham's fatherhood of a multitude of nations is the intended ultimate realization of his "offspring" being as numerous as the stars. Employing a redemptive-historical and canonical hermeneutic that

---

[45] See Walter C. Kaiser Jr., "Is It the Case That Christ Is the Same Object of Faith in the Old Testament? (Genesis 15:1–6)," *JETS* 55 (2012): 291–98.

[46] Yahweh charged Abra(ha)m, "And you shall be a blessing *so that* . . . in you may be blessed all the families of the land" (Gen 12:2–3). Ultimately, the "in you" [בְּךָ] (12:2) becomes "in your offspring" [בְּזַרְעֲךָ] (22:18)—that is, "in Christ" [ἐν (τῷ) Χριστῷ]. For the grammatical uses and theological import of this phrase in Paul, see Murray J. Harris, *Prepositions and Theology in the Greek New Testament: An Essential Reference for Exegesis* (Grand Rapids: Zondervan, 2012), 122–28; and Constantine R. Campbell, *Paul and Union with Christ: An Exegetical and Theological Study* (Grand Rapids: Zondervan, 2012), 67–199.

finds its basis in the OT itself, Paul reads all Scripture in light of the fulfillment secured in Christ.[47]

Following this pattern, those "on whom the end of the ages has come"
(1 Cor 10:11 ESV) must see Jesus as the center of history, to whom all
promises point, and from whom all fulfillment comes (Matt 5:17–18; Luke
24:44; 2 Cor 1:20). He is the last Adam (1 Cor 15:45; cf. Rom 5:18–19),
the hoped-for "Offspring"-Deliverer who discloses true humanity by imag-
ing God as a royal Priest-Son (Gen 1:26–28; 5:1–3) and by serving as
the ideal provider and protector (2:15). He also fulfills Israel's mission
(Exod 19:4–6; Deut 4:5–8), representing the nation as the true royal
"seed" of Abraham (Gen 22:17b–18) and son of God (Exod 4:22; 2 Sam
7:12, 14; Ps 2:7), through whom blessing (i.e., reconciliation with God)
reaches the nations (Gen 12:3; Ps 72:17; Isa 42:1–6; 49:5–6; 51:4–5),
ultimately through his perfect obedience unto substitutionary death (Isa
52:13–53:12; 55:3–5). The NT uniformly asserts that Christ's teaching
through the apostles provides the essence of Christian instruction (Matt
17:5; 28:19–20; John 16:12–14; 2 Thess 2:15). As such, Christian doctrine and preaching of the whole counsel of God must work through the
lens that the apostles provide, which is colored by the fulfillment realized
in Christ (Acts 2:42; Heb 1:1–2). As Stephen J. Wellum asserts, the NT
places the revelation that comes through Jesus in a "qualitatively different
category" to previous revelation, highlighting how everything that preceded
him was "incomplete and by its very nature was intended by God to point
beyond itself to God's full self-disclosure in his Son" (Gal 3:24–26; Heb
1:1–2).[48] Christ's new covenant work fulfills the hope of OT saints; therefore, the NT provides confirmation that our OT interpretations are correct.[49]

---

[47] For more on the NT authors' redemptive-historical, canonical hermeneutic, see
Gentry and Wellum, *Kingdom Through Covenant*, 82–108; cf. G. K. Beale, "Did Jesus
and His Followers Preach the Right Doctrine from the Wrong Texts?," in *The Right
Doctrine from the Wrong Texts? Essays on the Use of the Old Testament in the New*, ed.
G. K. Beale (Grand Rapids: Baker, 1994), 393–95, 401.

[48] Gentry and Wellum, *Kingdom Through Covenant*, 90. Cf. Matt 11:13–14; Acts
13:22–26; 19:4.

[49] E.g., *hope*: Matt 13:17; John 8:56; Acts 13:32–33; Rom 1:1–6; Heb 11:13, 39–40;
1 Pet 1:10–12; *fulfillment*: Matt 5:17–18; 11:13–14; John 5:39, 45–47; 2 Cor 2:20.

In Christ alone does proper understanding of the OT come (2 Cor 3:14; cf. Isa 30:8; Jer 30:24; Dan 12:4).

Implications for Theological Systems

In conclusion, let us consider how the biblical portrayal of the "seed" of Abraham supports a progressive covenantal framework. To do so, I will distinguish my interpretation from that of dispensational and covenant theologies. I write this section with deepest affections for my brothers and sisters who see these other frameworks evidenced in Scripture, and I pray that my words will nurture greater pursuit of the truth rather than discord.

Progressive Covenantalism and Dispensational Theology

Highlighting discontinuity between the testaments, *dispensational theology* has traditionally viewed the new covenant church not as a continuation or replacement of Israel but as a unique people of God in redemptive history. In this framework ethnic Jews in Christ still maintain a distinct privilege to the promised land that they will enjoy in a future millennium separate from believing Gentiles.

This study affirms the newness of the new covenant community without distinguishing the privileges of any members within it. In Christ, Jews and Gentiles alike are "co-inheritors, fellow body members, and co-partakers of the promise in Christ Jesus through the gospel" (Eph 3:6; cf. 2:12). The inheritance is "out of faith, in order that, according to grace, the promise may be certain to all the offspring—not only to those out of law but to those out of the faith of Abraham, who is the father of us all, just as it is written, 'A father of many nations I have made you'" (Rom 4:16–17). Furthermore, Christ fulfills *in the church* God's long-range purposes given to Abraham. Because all the world's hopes for reconciliation with God rested on God's work through Abraham (Gen 12:3), national Israel's disloyalty and punishment heightened the world's condemnation, greatly distancing all from hope (Rom 3:19–20). Nevertheless, when King Jesus, Abraham's ultimate "seed" and Israel's representative (Isa 49:3, 5–6; Gal 3:16), performs all required obedience, he secures life and blessing for redeemed Jews and Gentiles alike (Gen 22:17b–18; Jer 4:2; Ps 72:17; Gal 3:8, 14), who together make up one regenerate people of God, the "seed" of Abraham (Gal 3:29). Rather than being an unexpected formation, the new covenant church in Christ is the natural, anticipated end in the progress of the biblical covenants.

Many progressive dispensationalists today affirm Scripture's teaching that "Christ is the true and ultimate Israel, temple, seed of Abraham, and so on."[50] Most of these, however, would agree with Michael Riccardi that the application of "seed" language to Gentiles in Galatians 3:28–29 ("There is neither Jew nor Greek. . . . And if you are Christ's, then you are Abraham's offspring" ESV) requires only that Gentiles enjoy the "blessing" promise; the patriarchal nation-land promises continue only for ethnic Jews who are in Christ: "In Galatians 3 Paul presents justification by faith in Messiah as the fulfillment of the promise of universal blessing to the nations through Abraham's true Seed. It does not cancel or reinterpret the promise of land for that 'great nation.'"[51] Further, Robert Saucy states, "The promises concerning the physical seed constituting the nation of Israel remain alongside the universal promise even as they did in the original statement in the Old Testament."[52]

I believe this line of reasoning falters on a number of fronts. First, this view fails to appreciate the two-stage *progression* evident within the Abrahamic covenant itself (see above). Stage one was realized in the temporary Mosaic covenant, wherein Israel became a nation enjoying the land. Stage two was inaugurated when this nation, through its representative head, fulfilled the charge to "be a blessing" (Gen 12:2) and thus served as the instrument of blessing to the world (12:3; cf. 22:18; Jer 4:2; Ps 72:17; Acts 3:25–26; Gal 3:8, 14). In fulfillment of the OT hopes, stage two—realized in the eschatological, everlasting new covenant in Christ—sees the

---

[50] Michael Riccardi, "The Seed of Abraham: A Theological Analysis of Galatians 3 and Its Implications for Israel," *TMSJ* 25 (2014): 59.

[51] Ibid., 60–63, quote from 63. See also Robert L. Saucy, *The Case for Progressive Dispensationalism: The Interface Between Dispensational and Non-Dispensational Theology* (Grand Rapids: Zondervan, 1993), 200.

[52] Saucy, *The Case for Progressive Dispensationalism*, 50.

"seed" and land promises fulfilled in a way that includes the nations, yet
without geopolitical barriers (Eph 2:13–17). This is accomplished as the
true "seed" of Abraham narrows first to Christ, the ultimate "seed," and
then to those identified with him by faith (Gal 3:16, 29). Christ, the royal
"offspring" deliverer, claims once enemy strongholds (Gen 22:17b; 24:60;
cf. plural "lands" in 26:3–4) through his ever-expanding new royal family,
who now globally bears witness to him (Acts 1:8) and offensively confronts
the gates of hell (Matt 16:18) with the testimony of Christ's victory over
evil and with the certainty of the new heavens and earth. Within this family
Jews and Gentiles are "one in Christ Jesus" (Gal 3:28), "one new man" (Eph
2:15), together enjoying "adoption as sons" (1:5) with equal partnership in
the "inheritance of the saints" (Col 1:12; cf. Gal 3:18; Eph 3:6).

Second, the view that Gentiles in Christ participate only in the blessing promise but not also in the ultimate fulfillment of the "seed" and land
promises fails to recognize the reference to plural "promises . . . made to
Abraham and to his offspring" (Gal 3:16 ESV). Paul in Galatians 3 had in
mind *multiple* promises in Genesis, not just the one focused on blessing.[53]
I agree with Saucy that, "because the concept of 'nation' [promised in Gen
12:2] carries a territorial aspect, the land must be viewed as the necessary
corollary to the promised seed that would constitute the 'great nation.'"[54]
Nevertheless, if the blessing promises include a reconstituting of the "seed"
with a global identity in Christ, then one should be cautious to separate the
land promise from this same transformation. Indeed, within the argument
of Galatians 3, the eschatological fulfillment of the land promise appears
to stand behind Paul's argument.[55] We see this in at least two ways: (1) The
inclusion of the conjunction in the phrase "*and* to your seed" [καὶ τῷ σπέρματί σου] in Galatians 3:16 implies that Paul is indeed quoting Scripture,
most likely Genesis 13:15; 17:8; and/or 24:7, for they are the only instances
of the phrase addressed to Abraham in the LXX of Genesis. Of these,

---

[53] DeRouchie and Meyer, "Christ or Family as the 'Seed' of Promise?" 38.

[54] Saucy, *The Case for Progressive Dispensationalism*, 44.

[55] Contra F. F. Bruce, who says, "The reference to the land . . . plays no part in the
argument of Galatians" (*The Epistle to the Galatians: A Commentary on the Greek Text*,
NIGTC [Grand Rapids: Eerdmans, 1982], 171).

the most likely candidate is Genesis 17:8, "for the mention of Abra(ha)m becoming 'the father of a multitude of nations' in the immediate literary context anticipates the inclusion of Gentiles in the people of God—one of the key issues at stake in Galatians 3."[56] Regardless, all three texts in Genesis address the *land* promise, which means Paul in Galatians 3 is stressing that the blessing, "seed," *and* land promises find their culmination in Christ, that each can be understood rightly only in light of him, and that the eschatological fulfillment of the land promise is part of the "inheritance" enjoyed by the reconstituted "seed" of Abraham (Gal 3:29). (2) Paul's language of "inheritance" in Galatians 3:18 likely is rooted in the OT land promise (e.g., Num 26:53–56; Josh 11:23),[57] which marked the context wherein God's global kingdom purposes first highlighted to Adam and Eve (Gen 1:27–28) would be realized. That is, the inheritance of Canaan always anticipated the expansion of the kingdom to include the world.[58] And because the male, royal deliverer's global work of blessing was to reverse the serpent's kingdom-thwarting purposes (Gen 3:15) and to result in possessing enemy gates (22:17b–18; 24:60), Paul likely saw Messiah Jesus as inaugurating the fulfillment of the original Edenic vision to see God's earthly sanctuary expanding to fill the earth through his royal-priestly imagers.[59] In Christ,

---

[56] DeRouchie and Meyer, "Christ or Family as the 'Seed' of Promise?" 38. For more on this theme, see Oren Martin's essay on the land promise in the present volume and Gentry and Wellum, *Kingdom Through Covenant*, 703–16.

[57] So too Thomas R. Schreiner, *Galatians*, ZECNT (Grand Rapids: Zondervan, 2010), 230; cf. Ronald Y. K. Fung, *The Epistle to the Galatians*, NICNT (Grand Rapids: Eerdmans, 1988), 155. Cf. Num 18:20; 32:18–19; 33:54; 34:2; Deut 4:21, 38; 12:9; 15:4; 19:14; 20:16; 24:4; 25:19; 26:1; Josh 13:6–8; 24:28.

[58] E.g., Gen 22:17b; 24:60; 26:3–4; Pss 22:27–28; 47:7–9; 72:8–11; Zeph 3:9–10; Rom 4:13; Heb 11:10, 13–16; 13:14; 2 Pet 3:13; Rev 21:1–22:5.

[59] For arguments that Gen 3:15 and 22:17b–18 indeed point to a single, male deliverer, see Jack Collins, "A Syntactical Note (Genesis 3:15): Is the Woman's Seed Singular or Plural?" *TynBul* 48 (1997): 139–48; T. Desmond Alexander, "Further Observations on the Term 'Seed' in Genesis," *TynBul* (1997): 363–67; cf. C. John Collins, "Galatians 3:16: What Kind of Exegete Was Paul?" *TynBul* 54 (2003): 75–86; DeRouchie and Meyer, "Christ or Family as the 'Seed' of Promise?" 36–48, esp. 38–40; Jason S. DeRouchie, "The Blessing-Commission, the Promised Offspring, and the *Toledot* Structure of Genesis," *JETS* 56 (2013): 228–29.

God's blessings of "seed" and land are becoming universalized, just as the OT itself anticipated would happen in the age of the fulfillment.

Progressive Covenantalism and Covenant Theology

As for *covenant theology*, this system has traditionally viewed the church as a continuation or renewal of Israel, though some view it more as a replacement.[60] In both views, however, the makeup of the new covenant community remains substantially the same as those of past eras, for all the biblical covenants are simply various expressions of one covenant of grace. Because membership in the covenants associated with Abraham and Moses was always guided by physical birth into the family of the mediator or by a reorientation in spiritual loyalty (e.g., Ruth 1:16), covenant theologians have seen no reason both features would not remain operative in the new covenant. Thus, they baptize babies born into homes with at least one Christian parent, convinced that covenant membership and election, ecclesiology and soteriology, may be overlapping in this age but are never aligned preconsummation. While more regenerate members are present this side of the cross, the new covenant community continues to be "mixed" with remnant and rebel, saved and unsaved.

In my view covenant theology's construal does not fully account for Scripture's teaching of the newness of the new covenant and the distinctiveness of Jesus and his work in redemptive history. First, by treating the Abrahamic covenant as a monolithic reality substantially equated with the new covenant, many covenant theologians miss that Genesis 17 distinguishes *two* progressive eras for the everlasting Abrahamic covenant—the first national (Gen 17:7–8) with a genealogical principle as its guide and circumcision as its sign (17:9–13); and the second international with the

---

[60] For the continuation model, see e.g., Beale, *A New Testament Biblical Theology*, 656; Michael S. Horton, *Introducing Covenant Theology* (Grand Rapids: Baker, 2006), 130–31; idem, *The Christian Faith: A Systematic Theology for Pilgrims on the Way* (Grand Rapids: Zondervan, 2011), 730. For renewal, see Jeffrey D. Niell, "The Newness of the New Covenant," in *The Case for Covenantal Infant Baptism*, ed. Gregg Strawbridge (Phillipsburg, NJ: P&R, 2003), 127–55.

patriarch's fatherhood being established by spiritual adoption and no longer bound by biology, ethnicity, or the distinguishing mark of circumcision
(17:4–6) (see above; cf. Gen 12:1–3). Elsewhere, Genesis clarifies that the
initial stage would find fulfillment only in the second when an obedient
king, *the* "seed" of the woman and of Abraham from the line of Judah, would
rise, overcoming all enemy hostility and blessing all the nations of the earth
(3:15; 22:17b–18 with 26:3–4 and 49:8–10). Christ's arrival inaugurates
the age of fulfillment, thus shifting the covenant community's makeup away
from the genealogical principle to one of corporate identity, established
through spiritual adoption by faith. "But when the fullness of time had
come, God sent forth his Son, born of woman, born under the law, in order
that he might redeem those under the law, so that we might receive adoption" (Gal 4:4–5). "In love he predestined us for adoption as sons through
Jesus Christ" (Eph 1:4–5 ESV).

G. K. Beale rightly articulates the OT hopes in this way: "When the
Messiah came, the theocracy of Israel would be so completely reconstituted that it would continue only as the new organism of the Messiah
(Jesus), the true Israel. In him Jews and Gentiles would be fused together
on a footing of complete equality through corporate identification."[61] We

---

[61] Beale, *A New Testament Biblical Theology*, 654. Beale, himself a paedo-baptist,
seems inconsistent in the working out of his own model with respect to baptism. On the
one hand, in alignment with the quote above, he affirms in a comment on Col 2:11–13
that "OT physical circumcision as a type *has been fulfilled* in eschatological spiritual
circumcision and is no longer relevant for entrance into the new covenant community.
Instead, spiritual 'circumcision made without hands' and 'baptism' are ongoing realities designating entrance into the covenant community. . . . Physical circumcision can
be seen to have its *typological fulfillment* also in the physical rite of baptism" (*A New
Testament Biblical Theology*, 808–9, emphasis added). In these quotations (both in the
footnote and the one cited in the body), Beale appears to be affirming a high view of fulfillment that marks substantial discontinuities between old and new. Indeed, to speak
of a type's "fulfillment" is to speak of escalation, of reaching a goal, and of antitype,
which identifies physical baptism as something distinct from and superseding physical
circumcision. In contrast, when later arguing that baptism should be applied to infants,
Beale is forced to change his wording: "[Water] baptism is the redemptive-historical
and typological *equivalent* to circumcision" (816). In moving from fulfillment language
to equivalence language, he minimizes the significance and centrality of the work of

must see covenantal progression in the move from promise to fulfillment. In Christ, spiritual adoption, not physical descent, becomes the mark of the new covenant community. While ethnic distinctions are not eradicated (e.g., Rom 1:16; 2:9; 9:25–27; cf. Acts 13:46), new covenant membership is grounded solely in "corporate identification" with the Messiah and is no longer assumed simply because of biological connection. In this and many other senses, Christ's new covenant work marks an escalation beyond all previous eras.

Second, covenant theologians must consider further the significance of Jesus' being the *last* Adam (1 Cor 15:45; cf. Rom 5:18–19), the head of a *new* creation (2 Cor 5:17; Gal 6:15), *the* "offspring" of Abraham and David who mediates a *new* covenant (Heb 9:15; 12:24) that creates the church as one *new* man (Eph 2:15). All members in the new covenant are identified with Christ in the heavenly realms (Eph 2:5–6; Col 2:12–13; 3:3); they are children of "the Jerusalem above" (Gal 4:26, 31; cf. Heb 12:22–24), meaning that, regardless of one's original heritage, all have new birth certificates declaring, "This one was born there"—in Zion (Psalm 87). Indeed, as Isaiah asserts, every member of this community is spiritually reborn and thus regenerate (Isa 54:1, 3), having become "offspring" of the servant king by his bearing their iniquities and counting them righteous (53:10–11). Similarly, Jeremiah stresses that, in distinction from the mixed nature of the old covenant, *all* in the new covenant know Yahweh for *all* are forgiven (31:34). The fact that the new covenant "has been enacted" in Christ (Heb 8:6, using the perfect passive νομοθετέομαι and thus stressing the completed action with continuing results) means that *already* the new covenant community is made up of only the regenerate, even if some aspects of salvation are *not yet* complete. Jesus' atoning sacrifice both effects and is effectual; and within the new covenant, soteriology gives birth to ecclesiology in a way that the two are completely overlapping *already*.[62]

Christ and the distinctiveness of the new covenant community that he had earlier so beautifully articulated.

[62] As Wellum rightly states, "Unlike Israel of old, by definition, the locus of the covenant community and the locus of the redeemed are one" (Gentry and Wellum, *Kingdom Through Covenant*, 689). In contrast, in an attempt to maintain a "mixed"

Because Messiah Jesus had no physical children and yet enjoys "offspring" (Isa 53:10), and because new covenant membership comes without birth-pain judgment for all but the covenant head (54:1; cf. 42:14), the genealogical principle is no longer operative. Abraham's "fatherhood" of a multitude of nations becomes fully enacted through the spiritual adoption effected by his "offspring," Christ (Gal 3:14, 16). Just as Yahweh stressed

---

nature to the new covenant while affirming the clear teaching of Jer 31:34, covenant theologian Richard L. Pratt Jr. is forced to substantially deny the "already" nature of Christ's work, claiming that the full establishment of a regenerate community is yet future: "Many evangelicals object to infant baptism because the new covenant distributes salvation to all of its participants. As with the previous objections, this point of view is correct insofar as it relates to the complete fulfillment of the new covenant in the consummation" ("Infant Baptism in the New Covenant," in *The Case for Covenant Infant Baptism*, ed. Gregg Strawbridge [Phillipsburg, NJ: P&R, 2003], 172). But such a view cannot stand for several reasons. (1) Every promise is *already* yes in Christ (2 Cor 1:20). (2) As James R. White correctly notes of Heb 8:6: "There is nothing in the text that would lead us to believe that the full establishment of this covenant is yet future, for such would destroy the present apologetic concern of the author; likewise, he will complete his citation of Jer. 31 by asserting the obsolete nature of the first covenant, which leaves one to have to theorize, without textual basis, about some kind of intermediate covenantal state if one does not accept the full establishment of the new covenant as seen in the term νομοθέτηται" ("The Newness of the New Covenant [Part I]," *RBTR* 1 (2004): 157; cf. idem, "The Newness of the New Covenant [Part II]," *RBTR* 2 [2005]: 83–104). (3) Other paedo-baptists like G. K. Beale correctly recognize that when the writer of Hebrews declares, "By a single offering he [Christ] *has perfected* [perfect active indicative of τελειόω] for all time those who are being sanctified" (Heb 10:14), and then supports it by citing Jer 31:33–34 (Heb 10:15–18), he is asserting the *inaugurated* nature of forgiveness (i.e., positionally, through our identification with Christ our representative) and the *already* completed certainty of final, complete cleansing from sin (*A New Testament Biblical Theology*, 735; cf. Heb 12:2, 23). (4) Samuel E. Waldron observes that, in alignment with its inaugurated nature, the new covenant's ordinances have *already* been established (Luke 22:20; 1 Cor 11:25), its officers have *already* been installed (2 Cor 3:6; Eph 2:20; 4:11; Heb 8:1–6), and the knowledge of God predicted in Isa 54:13 and Jer 31:34 is *already* being enjoyed whenever a believer is redeemed (John 6:45; Heb 10:26) ("A Brief Response to Richard L. Pratt's 'Infant Baptist in the New Covenant,'" *RBTR* 2 [2005]: 106–7). (5) Pratt's delayed-fulfillment view of the new covenant removes the clear pastoral hope for perseverance in *this age* found in passages like Jer 32:40: "And I will cut for them an eternal covenant that I will not turn away from after them from doing good to them, and my fear I will place in their heart to not turn from unto me."

to Abraham that the nations of the earth would be blessed "in your off-spring" [בְּזַרְעֲךָ/ἐν τῷ σπέρματί σου] (Gen 22:18 ESV; cf. Ps 72:17; Jer 4:2; Gal 3:14, 16), so now "God . . . has blessed us *in Christ* [ἐν Χριστῷ] with every spiritual blessing in the heavenly places," even as we await the full inheritance (Eph 1:3, 14 ESV; cf. 1 Pet 1:3–5).[63] Christ is the "seed" of Abraham and of David (Gen 17:4–5; 2 Sam 7:12, 16; Jer 33:26; Acts 3:25–26; Gal 3:16) and the one through whom both Abraham's fatherly head-ship over a multitude and David's eternal throne find fulfillment (Luke 1:32–33; 2:68–75; John 8:53–59; Rom 1:3; 2 Tim 2:8). Today—whether Jews or Gentiles, slaves or free, males or females—all become "offspring" of Christ and then of Abraham (Isa 53:10; Gal 3:28–29) only through union with Jesus by faith.[64] The NT knows no new covenant community apart from this relationship; and, therefore, the church should apply the new covenant sign of baptism only to those who are reborn through faith in Christ. It is those who are *in Christ* who are "sons of God," those *who have put on Christ* who are baptized, and those *who are Christ's* who are counted "Abraham's offspring, heirs according to promise" (Gal 3:26–27, 29 ESV; cf. Rom 6:1–4; 1 Pet 3:21).[65]

---

[63] On reading "seed" here as a single, male descendant of Abraham, see the resources in footnote 59.

[64] Troy W. Martin argues that the three antitheses mentioned in Gal 3:28 are con-text specific to the argument in Galatians, each pair pointing to spheres in which the old covenant made distinctions by circumcision but where the new covenant does not ("The Covenant of Circumcision [Genesis 17:9–14] and the Situational Antithesis in Galatians 3:28," *JBL* 122 [2003]: 111–25, esp. 117–19). If correct, Paul is stressing high discontinuity between the old and new covenants in a way that discourages a mere equating of the covenant signs of physical circumcision and water baptism, the latter being linked solely with faith in Christ.

[65] G. R. Beasley-Murray, "Baptism," in *DPL*, 62; cf. Richard N. Longenecker, *Galatians*, WBC 41 (Dallas: Word, 1990), 154–56; Douglas J. Moo, *Galatians*, BECNT (Grand Rapids: Baker, 2013), 249–52.

CHAPTER 2

The Israel-Christ-Church Relationship

BRENT E. PARKER

The relationship between Israel and the church is of paramount importance for all theological systems. Covenant and dispensational theology, while both undergoing some modification in the late twentieth century,
still have sharp differences on this hotly debated and contentious subject.
For covenant theologians their understanding of the unity of the covenant
of grace and God's plan of redemption leads them to a position of strong
continuity. The nature of the church is essentially one with Israel, the relationship being one of substitution or fulfillment,[1] thus viewing the church

---

[1] Louis Berkhof, *Systematic Theology*, new ed. (Grand Rapids: Eerdmans, 1996),
570–72; Herman Bavinck, *Holy Spirit, Church, and the New Creation*, vol. 4 of *Reformed
Dogmatics*, ed. John Bolt, trans. John Vriend (Grand Rapids: Baker, 2008), 277–79,
665–67; Michael S. Horton, *The Christian Faith: A Systematic Theology for Pilgrims
on the Way* (Grand Rapids: Zondervan, 2011), 729–33; Herman Ridderbos, *Paul:
An Outline of His Theology*, trans. John Richard DeWitt (Grand Rapids: Eerdmans,
1975), 333–41, 360–61; O. Palmer Robertson, *The Israel of God: Yesterday, Today, and
Tomorrow* (Phillipsburg, NJ: P&R, 2000), 33–51; Marten H. Woudstra, "Israel and the
Church: A Case for Continuity," in *Continuity and Discontinuity: Perspectives on the
Relationship Between the Old and New Testaments*, ed. John S. Feinberg (Wheaton,
IL: Crossway, 1988), 221–38; Anthony A. Hoekema, *The Bible and the Future* (Grand
Rapids: Eerdmans, 1979), 194–201, 215–16.

as the "new Israel."[2] In other words, even if Romans 9–11 teaches a mass conversion of Jews in the future, all the prerogatives, promises, and prophecies to OT Israel are translated to the church.[3] On the other hand, the *sine qua non* of dispensationalism is the Israel-church distinction such that OT promises and prophecies to Israel must be fulfilled during the millennium (Rev 20:4–6).[4] Distinguishing Israel and the church consistently with the

---

[2] Some covenant theologians and other theologians who hold to the continuity between Israel and the church will use the terminology of "replacement" in delineating the Israel-church relationship. For example, Bruce K. Waltke, "Kingdom Promises as Spiritual," in *Continuity and Discontinuity*, 274 says that "national Israel and its law have been permanently replaced by the church and the New Covenant." Bavinck, *Reformed Dogmatics*, 4:667 states, "The community of believers has in all respects replaced carnal, national Israel. The Old Testament is fulfilled in the New." Mark Karlberg, "The Significance of Israel in Biblical Typology," *JETS* 31 (1998): 257–69 advances a similar line of thinking (263, 269). Others, such as Hans K. LaRondelle (*The Israel of God in Prophecy: Principles of Prophetic Interpretation* [Berrien Springs, MI: Andrews University, 1983], 101) and R. T. France (*Jesus and the Old Testament: His Application of Old Testament Passages to Himself and His Mission* [Vancouver: Regent College Publishing, 1998], 67) also advocate the replacement thesis.

[3] This is not indicative of the entire tradition of covenant theology, as a case has been made for a "remarkable 'fluidity'" on the future and restoration of Israel in Reformed theology. See Willem A. VanGemeren, "Israel as the Hermeneutical Crux in Interpretation and Prophecy," *WTJ* 45 (1983): 122–32 and idem, "Israel as the Hermeneutical Crux in Interpretation and Prophecy (II)," *WTJ* 46 (1984): 254–97.

[4] The distinctive features of dispensationalism are explored in Charles C. Ryrie, *Dispensationalism*, rev ed. (Chicago: Moody, 2007), 46–48. He also mentions a literal historical-grammatical hermeneutic and the glory of God as other defining marks of dispensationalism, but clearly the essence of dispensationalism is the Israel-church distinction (39, 41, 90); cf. Robert Saucy, "The Crucial Issue Between Dispensational and Non-Dispensational Systems," *CTR* 1 (1986): 155–56. For progressive dispensational works, see Craig A. Blaising and Darrell L. Bock, *Progressive Dispensationalism* (Grand Rapids: Baker, 1993), 267–70; Craig A. Blaising and Darrell L. Bock, eds., *Dispensationalism, Israel, and the Church: The Search for Definition* (Grand Rapids: Zondervan, 1992); Robert L. Saucy, *The Case for Progressive Dispensationalism: The Interface Between Dispensational and Non-Dispensational Theology* (Grand Rapids: Zondervan, 1993), 28–29, 187–218; idem, "Israel and the Church: A Case for Discontinuity," in *Continuity and Discontinuity*, 239–59. For more traditional dispensationalists on the subject of the future of Israel, see H. Wayne House, "The Future

future existence of national, political, and ethnic Israel "is probably the most basic theological test of whether or not a person is a dispensationalist."[5] Israel will be restored as a national entity in the future under the reign of Christ as the Davidic king and thereby exercise her mediatorial[6] role to the nations in the promised land. The Israel-church emphasis is clearly one of discontinuity, for even in the affirmation of one people of God, the church and Israel still have distinct purposes and roles in the outworking of God's kingdom for all forms of dispensationalism even if there are variances within the viewpoint.

The battle lines could not be more clearly drawn on this difficult subject that pulls together one's understanding of how the biblical story line unfolds and how the covenants relate to one another with direct impact on areas of Christology, ecclesiology, and eschatology. For dispensationalists, covenant theologians are deemed guilty of "supersessionism," and so covenant theology is often labeled with the popular, pejorative moniker of "replacement theology."[7] On the other side, nondispensational theo-

---

of National Israel," *BibSac* 166 (2009): 463–81; Arnold G. Fruchtenbaum, *Israelology: The Missing Link in Systematic Theology*, rev ed. (Tustin, CA: Ariel Ministries, 1993), 766–819; Michael Vlach, "What About Israel?," in *Christ's Prophetic Plans: A Futuristic Premillennial Primer*, ed. John MacArthur and Richard Mayhue (Chicago: Moody, 2012), 103–22.

    [5] Ryrie, *Dispensationalism*, 46. Blaising and Bock, *Progressive Dispensationalism*, 50, write: "The same redeemed Jews and Gentiles will be directed and governed by Jesus Christ according to their different nationalities. The national identities and political promises of Israel and the Gentiles in the last dispensation testifies in turn to this aspect of redemption."

    [6] For Israel's mediation to the nations in the future see Saucy, *The Case for Progressive Dispensationalism*, 259, 306–23; idem, "The Progressive Dispensational View," in *Perspectives on Israel and the Church: 4 Views*, ed. Chad O. Brand (Nashville, TN: B&H, 2015), 170–74, 198. Not all dispensationalists would agree with the description of Israel having a *mediatorial* role to the nations in the millennium and beyond. Some prefer to describe Israel's future restoration and role in terms of prominence or being a channel of blessing or having a functional role of service to the nations.

    [7] See Michael J. Vlach, *Has the Church Replaced Israel? A Theological Evaluation* (Nashville, TN: B&H Academic, 2010) and idem, "Various Forms of Replacement Theology," *TMSJ* 20 (2009): 57–69. For Vlach, anyone who does not believe in both a future salvation and restoration for Israel is a supersessionist, thus basically anyone who

logians have sought to highlight the dangers of dispensationalism, given their rejection of dispensationalism's understanding of the Israel-church relationship, particularly warning of "Christian Zionism" and its political impact associated with the modern state of Israel.[8] Given the back-and-forth on these issues, there is significant doubt that evangelicalism will ever come to a consensus.

does not adhere to some form of dispensationalism would be considered a supersessionist. For other dispensational writings on the topic of replacement theology, see Barry E. Horner, *Future Israel: Why Christian Anti-Judaism Must Be Challenged* (Nashville, TN: B&H Academic, 2007); Craig A. Blaising, "The Future of Israel as a Theological Question," *JETS* 44 (2001): 435–50. Cf. Walter C. Kaiser Jr., "An Assessment of 'Replacement Theology': The Relationship Between the Israel of the Abrahamic-Davidic Covenant and the Christian Church," *Mishkan* 21 (1994): 9–20. Not all covenant theologians apply the terminology of "replacement," and many repudiate such a description. For example, Horton, *The Christian Faith*, writes that "the church does not replace Israel; it fulfills the promise God made to Abraham that in him and his seed all the nations would be blessed" (730) and further, "Israel is not replaced by the church, but is the church *in nuce,* just as the church is the anticipation of the kingdom of God" (731). Likewise, Michael D. Williams, *Far as the Curse is Found: The Covenant Story of Redemption* (Phillipsburg, NJ: P&R, 2005), 251–52 concludes that "the church does not replace Israel, nor is it simply identical to Israel. Some new historical and redemptive development has forever transformed and redefined the people of God. That development is the incarnation and work of Christ the Messiah." For other responses to the charge of "replacement theology," see Colin Chapman, "God's Covenant—God's Land?" in *The God of Covenant: Biblical, Theological and Contemporary Perspectives*, ed. Jamie A. Grant and Alistair I. Wilson (Leicester, UK: InterVarsity, 2005), 221–56 and Sam Storms, *Kingdom Come: The Amillennial Alternative* (Fearn, Ross-shire, Scotland: Mentor, 2013), 177–227, esp. 195–96.

[8] Philip A. F. Church, "Dispensational Christian Zionism: A Strange but Acceptable Aberration or a Deviant Heresy?" *WTJ* 71 (2009): 375–98; Stephen Sizer, *Zion's Christian Soldiers? The Bible, Israel and the Church* (Nottingham, UK: InterVarsity, 2007); Colin Chapman, *Whose Promised Land? The Continuing Crisis over Israel and Palestine* (Grand Rapids: Baker, 2002), 241–66; Gary M. Burge, *Jesus and the Land: The New Testament Challenge to "Holy Land" Theology* (Grand Rapids: Baker, 2010), 110–31; Tom Wright, "Jerusalem in the New Testament," in *Jerusalem Past and Present in the Purposes of God*, 2nd ed., ed. P. W. L. Walker (Grand Rapids: Baker, 1994), 53–77, esp. 73–75.

A Summary of the Progressive Covenantal Position: Israel to Christ, Christ to Church

A mediating position—*progressive covenantalism*—offers a corrective to both theological systems on the topic of the Israel-church relationship.[9] Most of the writings by covenant and dispensational theologians have sought *directly* to address the Israel-church relationship, but progressive covenantalism seeks first to analyze the relationship between Israel and Israel's Messiah—Jesus Christ—and then to address the relationship between Christ and the church before making theological conclusions on this matter. The above claim is not to suggest that covenant and dispensational theologians have ignored the Israel-Christ relationship; quite the contrary, covenant theologians have often claimed that Jesus is the "true Israel,"[10] and to a much lesser extent, dispensationalists have also examined the Israel-Christ relationship.[11] Nevertheless, significant theological

---

[9] See Peter J. Gentry and Stephen J. Wellum, *Kingdom Through Covenant: A Biblical-Theological Understanding of the Covenants* (Wheaton, IL: Crossway, 2012), 24–25; hereafter *KTC*.

[10] G. K. Beale, "Did Jesus and His Followers Preach the Right Doctrine from the Wrong Texts? An Examination of the Presuppositions of Jesus' and the Apostles' Exegetical Method," in *The Right Doctrine from the Wrong Texts?*, ed. G. K. Beale (Grand Rapids: Baker, 1994), 392, 395; idem, *Handbook on the New Testament Use of the Old Testament: Exegesis and Interpretation* (Grand Rapids: Baker, 2012), 53, 95–102; idem, *A New Testament Biblical Theology: The Unfolding of the Old Testament in the New* (Grand Rapids: Baker Academic, 2011), 406–12, 651–56, 920–21; Robert B. Strimple, "Amillennialism," in *Three Views on the Millennium and Beyond*, ed. Darrell L. Bock (Grand Rapids: Zondervan, 1999), 87–90; Kim Riddlebarger, *A Case for Amillennialism: Understanding the End Times* (Grand Rapids: Baker, 2003), 37, 69–70; David E. Holwerda, *Jesus and Israel: One Covenant or Two?* (Grand Rapids: Eerdmans, 1995), 27–58; Alistair W. Donaldson, *The Last Days of Dispensationalism: A Scholarly Critique of Popular Misconceptions* (Eugene, OR: Wipf & Stock, 2011), 53–59.

[11] This is most noticeable in Michael J. Vlach, "What Does Christ as 'True Israel' Mean for the Nation Israel?: A Critique of the Non-Dispensational Understanding," *TMSJ* 21 (2012): 43–54, as he accepts Jesus' identity as Israel but views the restoration and future role of Israel as continuing on the basis of Jesus as the true Israelite. See also Robert Saucy, "Is Christ the Fulfillment of National Israel's Prophesies? Yes and No!," (paper presented at the national meetings of the Evangelical Theological Society,

differences remain in terms of how Israel is understood to relate to Christ and the church via the unfolding of the covenants and in conjunction with the vital subject of typology, a crucial area in resolving the Israel-Christ-church debate in systems of theology.[12]

Progressive covenantalism argues that the biblical covenants and typological structures converge and climax in Christ with entailments for the eschatological people of God—the church. First, if OT Israel's identity and promises, along with their prophesied national and mediatorial roles, find their fulfillment in Jesus and by extension, the church, then fundamental principles of dispensationalism are called into question. Progressive covenantalism argues this precisely: the NT presents Jesus as the fulfillment of Israel and all the OT covenant mediators, for he ushers in the promises to Israel (restoration and return from exile, the land, etc.), embodies their identity, and completes Israel's role, calling, and vocation. All the institutions (the sacrificial system, tabernacle, temple, Sabbath, feasts, the law), identity markers (e.g., circumcision),[13] offices (prophet, priest, king), and

---

Atlanta, GA, 18 November 2010) and Craig A. Blaising, "A Premillennial Response," in *Three Views on the Millennium and Beyond*, 145–46.

[12] For the importance of typology to bridging the divide between dispensationalism and covenant theology, see W. Edward Glenny, "Typology: A Summary of the Present Evangelical Discussion," *JETS* 40 (1997): 627–38. Others have affirmed that further agreement on the nature and function of typology would help resolve the covenant and dispensational theological divide: John S. Feinberg, "Systems of Discontinuity," in *Continuity and Discontinuity*, 74–75; Mark W. Karlberg, "Legitimate Discontinuities Between the Testaments," *JETS* 28 (1985): 19. Vern S. Poythress, *Understanding Dispensationalists*, 2nd ed. (Phillipsburg, NJ: P&R, 1994), 117, suggests that further "reflection on problems with typology may therefore help to bring us together." Likewise, Darrell L. Bock, "Summary Essay," in *Three Views on the Millennium and Beyond*, 290–97 highlights the relationship of the OT to the NT, typology, and the role of Israel as key areas in the millennial debate. For a survey of how typology is understood in covenant and dispensational theology, see Friedbert Ninow, *Indicators of Typology Within the Old Testament: The Exodus Motif*, Friedensauer Schriftenreihe: Reihe I, Theologie, Band 4 (Berlin: Peter Lang, 2001), 65–75.

[13] N. T. Wright, *The New Testament and the People of God*, vol. 1 of *Christian Origins and the Question of God* (Minneapolis: Fortress, 1992), 237, identifies boundary markers or badges as circumcision, Sabbath, and kosher laws that particularly distinguished Jews from Gentiles in the first century. For Jesus as the only identity marker for the NT people of God, see Beale, *A New Testament Biblical Theology*, 873–78.

key events (e.g., the exodus) of Israel find their culmination in the life, death, resurrection, and ascension of Christ.[14] As Patrick Fairbairn correctly surmises, the Israelite nation "with their land and their religious institutions, were, in what distinctively belonged to them under the old covenant, of a typical nature; the whole together, in that particular aspect, has passed away—it has become merged in Christ and the Gospel dispensation."[15] Jesus is the "true Israel" in that he typologically fulfills all that the nation of Israel anticipated and hoped for; Jesus is the one who brings to completion the covenants, inaugurates the kingdom, and establishes the prophesied new covenant with his blood.

Second, if Jesus is the antitypical fulfillment of Israel and all the OT covenant mediators, what implications are there for the community—the church—in faith union with this Messiah? The coming of Christ introduces a significant epochal shift entailing structural changes to the covenant community. Our comprehension of the redemptive-historical progression centered in Christ and the bestowal of the Spirit at Pentecost impacts how we understand the nature of the church's relationship to Israel. The church, made up of Jew and Gentile believers in union with Christ through faith, does not have the same essential nature as OT Israel in contrast to how paedo-baptist covenant theologians construe the nature of the church and the continuity of "signs and seals" (the Passover and circumcision having direct continuity to the Lord's Supper and baptism, respectively). The church is a new redemptive-historical reality—the heavenly, eschatological, Spirit-empowered, new covenant community, which is the new creation

---

[14] Graeme Goldsworthy has correctly summarized how the OT stages, epochs, and structures move along redemptive history to their fulfillment in Christ as all things are summed up in him (Eph 1:10). See his *Gospel-Centered Hermeneutics: Foundations and Principles of Evangelical Biblical Interpretation* (Downers Grove, IL: InterVarsity, 2006), 253–56. Cf. F. F. Bruce, *This Is That: The New Testament Development of Some Old Testament Themes* (Exeter, UK: Paternoster, 1968), 21.

[15] Patrick Fairbairn, *The Interpretation of Prophecy* (Carlisle, PA: Banner of Truth Trust, 1964), 255. Thomas R. Schreiner, *New Testament Theology: Magnifying God in Christ* (Grand Rapids: Baker Academic, 2008), 173, in a similar vein states that "Jesus is the true Israel who fulfills what God always intended when he chose Israel to be his people."

(2 Cor 5:17; Gal 6:15) and new humanity in Christ (Eph 2:15).[16] Therefore, the church is linked to Israel only indirectly through its relationship with Jesus. "[T]he relationship between the church and Israel . . . is neither one of direct succession nor radical disjunction, but one of mediated continuity. One may describe the church as the 'true Israel,' but its continuity with the rejected Israel is found in the representative figure of Jesus, who bridges salvation-history even while fulfilling it."[17] Covenant theologians will argue for the Israel-church typological relationship, but the greater nature of the new covenant community is distorted resulting in the nullification of the intrinsic escalation of this typological relationship.[18] If the church continues to be a mixed community comprised of covenant breakers and keepers like Israel of old, then there is little typological development between Israel and the church.

---

[16] As Christ followers, Jewish and Gentile believers alike are those upon "whom the end of the ages has come" (1 Cor 10:11). The eschatological and heavenly nature of the church is also indicated by such passages as Eph 2:5–6; Col 1:12–14; 3:3; Heb 12:22–24; 13:14. For other points on the definition of the church offered above, see D. A. Carson, "Evangelicals, Ecumenism, and the Church," in *Evangelicals, Ecumenism and the Church*, ed. Kenneth S. Kantzer and Carl F. H. Henry (Grand Rapids: Zondervan, 1990), 358–67; P. T. O'Brien, "Church," in *DPL*, 123–31; Stephen J. Wellum, "Beyond Mere Ecclesiology: The Church as God's New Covenant Community," in *The Community of Jesus: A Theology of the Church*, ed. Kendell H. Easley and Christopher W. Morgan (Nashville, TN: B&H, 2013), 183–212; Schreiner, *New Testament Theology*, 675–754; and Ronald Y. K. Fung, "Some Pauline Pictures of the Church," *EvQ* 43 (1981): 89–107, esp. 105–7.

[17] William L. Kynes, *A Christology of Solidarity: Jesus as the Representative of His People in Matthew* (Lanham, MD: University Press of America, 1991), 202. Stephen Motyer agrees as he also understands that the Israel-church relationship must be understood Christologically. He suggests that the label "renewed Israel" would be a more fitting designation for the church ("Israel, New," in *Evangelical Dictionary of Theology*, 2nd ed., ed. Walter A. Elwell [Grand Rapids: Baker Academic, 2001], 618–19 and idem, "Israel (Nation)," in *NDBT*, 581–87).

[18] One reviewer of *KTC* rightly recognizes that "while dispensationalism has an insufficient view of typology, paedobaptist covenant theology has an under-realized view of typological fulfillment, for in the new covenant there is no gap between the sign (baptism) and the thing signified (circumcision of heart)" (Christopher R. Bruno, *Themelios* 37 [2012]: 504–5).

This chapter focuses on how Jesus typologically fulfills OT Israel and how the church, through Christ, inherits the promises of Israel. The goal is to provide further ground for the progressive covenantal view on the Israel-Christ-church relationship, particularly in light of recent dispensational criticisms of progressive covenantalism. The church does not displace Israel but is the restored, new covenant community that Israel looked forward to. Before addressing these crucial issues, it is important to first briefly define and lay out the nature of biblical typology.

The Nature and Importance of Typology

Putting the whole Bible together, tracing themes across the canon, and understanding the NT authors' citations and allusions to OT texts all interface in one degree or another with the complex subject of typology. While difficult to define, Davidson's evaluation of the hermeneutically significant usages of the τύπος word group in the NT (Rom 5:12–21; 1 Cor 10:1–13; Heb 8:5; 9:24; 1 Pet 3:18–22) along with attention to clearer and more explicit typological patterns such as Adam, Melchizedek, David, the exodus, and the Passover means that a general evangelical consensus of the nature of typology has emerged.[19] Typology is the study of how OT historical persons, events, institutions, and settings function to foreshadow,

---

[19] Richard M. Davidson, *Typology in Scripture: A Study of Hermeneutical ΤΥΠΟΣ Structures*, Andrews University Seminary Doctoral Dissertation Series 2 (Berrien Springs, MI: Andrews University Press, 1981). Note the classic works of Leonhard Goppelt, *Typos: The Typological Interpretation of the Old Testament in the New*, trans. Donald H. Madvig (Grand Rapids: Eerdmans, 1982), and Patrick Fairbairn, *Typology of Scripture* (New York: Funk & Wagnalls, 1900; repr., Grand Rapids: Kregel, 1989). For other helpful works see D. A. Carson, "Mystery and Fulfillment: Toward a More Comprehensive Paradigm of Paul's Understanding of the Old and the New," in *The Paradoxes of Paul*, vol. 2 of *Justification and Variegated Nomism*, ed. D. A. Carson, Peter T. O'Brien, and Mark A. Seifrid (Grand Rapids: Baker, 2004), 404–7; Ninow, *Indicators of Typology*; Beale, *Handbook on the New Testament Use of the Old*; Paul M. Hoskins, *Jesus as the Fulfillment of the Temple in the Gospel of John*, Paternoster Biblical Monographs (Eugene, OR: Wipf and Stock, 2006), 21–31; idem, *That Scripture Might Be Fulfilled: Typology and the Death of Christ* (LaVergne, TN: Xulon, 2009); Gentry and Wellum, *KTC*, 102–8; Charles T. Fritsch, "Biblical Typology," *BibSac* 104 (1947): 214–22.

anticipate, prefigure, and predict the greater realities in the new covenant age. The correlation between the OT type and the NT antitype is not just one of analogy or basic correspondence. Analogies are drawn between OT persons and events to NT persons and events, but typological patterns are more. Typological patterns are prospective in that God has designed and intended certain OT figures, institutions, settings, and events to serve as advance presentations, which are then transcended and surpassed by the arrival of the NT antitype.[20] Typology really belongs in the category of indirect prophecy because the fulfillment wrought by Christ brings to completion what the OT type prefigured.

Three Fundamental Aspects of Typology

Three further points are critical to the subject of typology. First, the typological patterns develop along the textual, epochal, and canonical horizons or, more specifically, along the backbone of the biblical covenants.[21] Careful consideration is required to recognize the typological indicators in the text,

---

[20] Types are prospective in that the patterns are within the providential scope and plan of God. Characterizing typological patterns as retrospective confuses the matter. We may come to *knowledge* of the type by looking back and seeing how God's plan unfolded as previously hidden mysteries come to light, and thus some typological patterns may be discerned retrospectively from an interpretative standpoint. But the nature of typological patterns themselves is prospective in that they point ahead and are prophetic in their design. Beale, for example, recognizes rightly that types foreshadow and are indirectly prophetic, but he still confusingly lists retrospection as an essential characteristic of typology in his *Handbook on the New Testament Use of the Old*, 14–15; cf. 17–19, 23–24, 98. Types are prospective by nature even if interpreters discover them retrospectively. In other words, identifying and recognizing scriptural types is an epistemological problem that may be retrospective, but since types are divinely designed, they are ontologically prospective. See Carson, "Mystery and Fulfillment," 405–6, and Douglas J. Moo, "The Problem of Sensus Plenior," in *Hermeneutics, Authority, and Canon*, ed. D. A. Carson and John D. Woodbridge (Grand Rapids: Zondervan, 1986), 197. For a helpful case on the prospective nature of types, see Todd A. Scacewater, "The Predictive Nature of Typology in John 12:37–43," *WTJ* 75 (2013): 129–43.

[21] Richard Lints, *The Fabric of Theology: A Prolegomenon to Evangelical Theology* (Grand Rapids: Eerdmans, 1993), 293–311; Gentry and Wellum, *KTC*, 92–100; Edmund P. Clowney, *Preaching and Biblical Theology* (Phillipsburg, NJ: P&R, 1979), 15–16.

for "some indication of the existence and predictive quality of the various OT types should occur already in the OT *before* their NT antitypical fulfillment—otherwise there would be no predictive element. Thus some inherent textual indicators identifying the OT types should be apparent already in the OT."[22] The goal is to read the Bible on its own terms and allow the typological patterns to emerge from the text, based on the Bible's own interpretative matrix. In this way the interpreter avoids forging arbitrary typological links and, in the other direction, missing the typological patterns that are legitimately there. There cannot be selective acceptance of certain typologies, such as an event like the exodus or a person like Adam, while dismissing or reinterpreting the typological function of other patterns. For example, dispensationalism recasts the typological aspects of the nation of Israel and the land in terms of mere analogy, but that is not how they treat other typological patterns. On the other hand, the typological aspects of the Abrahamic covenant (i.e., the seed theme) and circumcision are neglected in covenant theology.[23]

---

[22] Richard M. Davidson, "The Nature [and Identity] of Biblical Typology—Crucial Issues" (paper presented at the meeting of the Midwest Evangelical Theological Society, St. Paul, MN, 14 March 2003), 15; see also Ninow, *Indicators of Typology*, and Beale, *Handbook on the New Testament Use of the Old*, 15–16.

[23] For discussion of the error covenant theologians make with respect to circumcision and the seed theme, see John Meade's and Jason DeRouchie's chapters in this volume. In regard to dispensationalism, Michael J. Vlach, "Have They Found a Better Way? An Analysis of Gentry and Wellum's *Kingdom Through Covenant*," *TMSJ* 24 (2013): 5–24, critiques Gentry and Wellum's approach to typology (12–17) with respect to the Israel-Christ typological relationship. But none of the passages he cites (Matt 19:28; Luke 21:24; Acts 1:6; 3:19–21; Romans 9–11) actually proves a future role for Israel as a national political ethnic entity (13–16). For discussion of Romans 11, see Richard Lucas's chapter in this volume; and for the key passages in Acts, see Eckhard J. Schnabel, *Acts*, ZECNT (Grand Rapids: Zondervan, 2012). Further, if the "'antitype negates type' approach" is evident in other typological patterns, why would this not also be the case of Israel (in terms of its role, vocation, identity) as a typological pattern of Jesus (16)? Vlach needs to offer his own proposal for the nature of typology, for typology is about the move from shadow to substance (Col 2:16–17; Heb 10:1) as the antitype fulfills the type; yet Vlach wants it both ways in admitting a typological connection between Israel and Jesus but then nullifying the fulfillment aspect of the typology in arguing that national Israel still has a central role in God's future plan.

Second, typology always has an eschatological aspect that is usually described as an escalation or heightening with the arrival of the antitype along the lines of inaugurated eschatology.[24] The text must dictate whether the type is completely annulled or fulfilled in Christ's first advent, or if there may be additional fulfillment or appropriation in the church and in the eschaton (the new creation).

For example, the whole OT sacrificial system has been rendered obsolete and fulfilled in the sacrifice of Christ (John 1:29, 36; Rom 8:3; 1 Cor 5:6–8; 1 Pet 1:18–19; Hebrews 9–10; Rev 5:6–10; 13:8). The only possible appropriation of this typological pattern for the church is that Christians can now offer acceptable spiritual sacrifices (Heb 13:15; 1 Pet 2:5; cf. Rom 15:16). Every indication from the NT is that Christ's one-time perfect sacrifice means that the ceremonial sacrificial practices of OT Israel under the Mosaic covenant are done away with now and forever. Some more traditional dispensationalists argue that memorial or actual ceremonial nonatoning sacrifices will be offered in the future millennium.[25] But such a position misses how the sacrificial system as a whole, tied to the old covenant, being typological and prophetic (e.g., Isaiah 53), terminates in Christ's sacrificial death on the cross. Positing the shadows of the OT cult practices into the future is a failure to read the Bible in a redemptive-historical manner, missing how such themes are developed within the Bible's own categories and progressively unfold along the covenantal epochs.[26]

---

[24] See footnote 19 and additionally, see the helpful examples of the characterization of escalation in typological patterns by Thomas R. Schreiner, *Commentary on Hebrews*, Biblical Theology for Christian Proclamation (Nashville, TN: B&H, 2015), 36–45.

[25] Jerry M. Hullinger, "The Compatibility of the New Covenant and Future Animal Sacrifice," *Journal of Dispensational Theology* 17 (2013): 47–64; idem, "The Function of the Millennial Sacrifices in Ezekiel's Temple, Part 1," *BibSac* 167 (2010): 40–57; idem, "The Function of the Millennial Sacrifices in Ezekiel's Temple, Part 2," *BibSac* 167 (2010): 166–79; John C. Whitcomb, "Christ's Atonement and Animal Sacrifices in Israel," *GTJ* 6 (1985): 201–17; Fruchtenbaum, *Israelology*, 810–13.

[26] Benjamin L. Merkle, "Old Testament Restoration Prophecies Regarding the Nation of Israel: Literal or Symbolic?" *SBJT* 14 (2010): 23, rightly observes the problem with dispensationalists who read Ezekiel 40–48 literalistically in finding the reinstitution of animal sacrifices in the millennium: "[A]ffirming that the restored people of Israel will rebuild the temple, reinstate the priesthood, and restore animal sacrifices,

A second illustration of how a type culminates in Christ but with further realization in the church and beyond may be helpful. Tracing out the temple typology through the canon reveals that Christ is the antitypical fulfillment and replacement of the temple (Matt 12:6; John 1:14, 51; 2:18–22; 4:20–24).[27] With the eclipse of the temple through Jesus, however, the temple pattern is appropriated to the church, since believers are united to the true Temple through faith and are indwelt with God's Spirit. Formerly, the presence of God was housed in the tabernacle and the temple. Temple imagery is applied to believers both corporately (2 Cor 6:16; Eph 2:19–22; 1 Pet 2:4–8) and individually (1 Cor 3:16–17; 6:19) as God's presence is now among them through the Spirit. The pattern takes further shape and additional realization in the new creation with God as the perfect temple dwelling with his people for eternity (Revelation 21–22). In this way typological patterns are always either completely fulfilled with the coming of the Christ, the primary antitype, or they are

---

minimizes the complete and perfect work of Christ. His death and resurrection is the focal point of God's great work in redemptive history. To go back to the shadows and images of the Old Testament is to neglect the centrality of Christ's finished work on the cross." Merkle also points out that God has already given his people a memorial of Christ's sacrifice—the Lord's Supper (25n26). Why this covenant meal, which is the continuing rite of the new covenant, would be replaced by animal sacrifices in the millennium is an argument with no warrant from the NT. The Lord's Supper will cease upon Christ's return (1 Cor 11:26), but it gives way to the messianic banquet, the marriage supper of the Lamb (Luke 22:15–18; Rev 19:7–9) and not to the OT cultic practices of sacrificing animals. Furthermore, arguing for animal sacrifices in the future millennium but not the reinstitution of the Mosaic covenant rips the sacrifices out of their covenantal setting. To deposit any sacrificial system after Christ's return misses the fact that the climax of the kingdom is still within the new covenant age (God's final covenant is the new covenant). The new covenant sacrifice of Christ has been offered once for all as taught in Heb 8:8–13, cf. Hebrews 9–10.

[27] See G. K. Beale, *The Temple and the Church's Mission: A Biblical Theology of the Dwelling Place of God*, NSBT 17 (Downers Grove, IL: InterVarsity, 2004). Cf. Hoskins, *Jesus as the Fulfillment of the Temple*; Holwerda, *Jesus and Israel*, 59–83; T. Desmond Alexander and Simon Gathercole, eds., *Heaven on Earth: The Temple in Biblical Theology* (Carlisle, UK: Paternoster, 2004); Edmund Clowney, "The Final Temple," *WTJ* 35 (1972): 156–89; P. W. L. Walker, *Jesus and the Holy City: New Testament Perspectives on Jerusalem* (Grand Rapids: Eerdmans, 1996); Rob Dalrymple, *Understanding Eschatology: Why It Matters* (Eugene, OR: Wipf & Stock, 2013), 56–99.

initially inaugurated by Christ with appropriation directed to the church, living in the "already-not yet" tension of the new covenant era. Finally, the typological pattern may have, as the temple example showed, additional realization with the second coming of Christ and the consummation of God's kingdom.[28] Even when the type has ongoing or continuing fulfillment, it is important to observe that there is always a transformation from the type to the antitype, hence the escalation embedded within typological relationships because of the shifts that have occurred with the dawning of the new age through Christ.

Third, it is important to recognize that when a person or entity is identified as typological, this does not include every aspect of the person or entity. David is a type of Christ in terms of his roles, king and servant of Yahweh, and as God's son (2 Sam 7:12–16; Psalms 2; 89). But not everything in David's life, such as his sinful actions with Bathsheba, are typological of Christ. Similarly, Israel as an ethnic people group is not a type, but our claim is that national Israel in terms of its role, vocation, calling, and identity is typological of Christ and thus rules out the notion of a future national role of Israel in the plan of God. Ethnic Jews and Gentiles in Christ are co-heirs and fellow partakers of promise.

In summary, typological patterns involve certain OT persons, events, institutions, and settings that God has orchestrated to prefigure greater realities centered in Christ and the new age he brings. Some types are completely fulfilled in Christ's first coming while others are initially fulfilled while also having antitypical fulfillment and realization in the church and finally the new creation. Even so, with the arrival of the antitype, namely Jesus Christ, the type is surpassed since the "antitype fills the role of the type in a way that makes the type unnecessary and effectively obsolete."[29] This is precisely the case because Jesus inaugurates the kingdom and ratifies the new covenant, which is the goal of the OT prophecies, promises, and covenants.

---

[28] On these points, see Davidson, "The Nature [and Identity] of Biblical Typology," 7–8.

[29] Hoskins, *Jesus as the Fulfillment of the Temple*, 23.

Christ as the "True Israel"

Before examining the biblical evidence, it is necessary to define what is meant when Jesus is described as the "true Israel." The case will be made that Jesus is the "true Israel" in the sense that eschatological fulfillment has come in Christ as he embodies the identity, vocation, and prophesied roles of corporate Israel. Jesus is the last Adam, the true Servant, the true Son, the ultimate Prophet, the final Priest, and the reigning, exalted King (David's greater Son). He is the true Israel, the faithful Israelite, in that he fulfills all that God had promised and intended for the nation of Israel. Identifying Jesus as the "true Israel" is a shorthand way, while recognizing that the term *Israel* is not applied to Jesus in the NT, of concisely describing who Jesus is in realizing and completing the destiny and function of national Israel in the plan of God.

Such terminology is frequently attacked in dispensational circles. Vlach argues that the language of "true Israel" is a "combination of terms [that] is not found in the Bible. Jesus does not call himself 'true Israel' and neither do the other NT writers."[30] Many bank on word studies of the use of *Israel* in the NT, asserting that the term always refers to the national, ethnic, covenant people of the OT and thus drawing the theological conclusion that OT Israel is not typological since Israel never loses its status as a national entity in the future of God's eschatological plan.[31] Even if dispensationalists are correct about the ethnic limitations to the term *Israel* in the NT (though good cases can be made for the term *Israel*

---

[30] Vlach, "What Does Christ as 'True Israel' Mean?," 47. He further complains that calling Jesus "true Israel" gives the impression that the nation of Israel is not truly Israel anymore. But the issue is how we define our terms and how we understand the redemptive historical trajectory of the Bible. Jesus can be referred to as the "true David" because he fulfills the Davidic covenant as the Messiah even though the NT never uses this label for him.

[31] See for example, Saucy, *The Case for Progressive Dispensationalism*, 194–207; Blaising, "A Premillennial Response," 146–48; Ryrie, *Dispensationalism*, 148–50; see also Peter Richardson, *Israel in the Apostolic Church*, SNTSMS 10 (Cambridge: Cambridge University Press, 1969), 7, 71, 83n2.

extending beyond a nationalistic, ethnic sense in Gal 6:16; Rev 7:4; and 21:12[32]), Israel's identity is not exclusively bound to the term *Israel*. Many other titles, designations, and imagery characterize and identify Israel and its vocation.[33] For instance, Israel is referred to as God's treasured possession (Deut 7:6), called to serve and worship him alone (Exod 7:16; Deut 4:39; see the Psalms) and to be a kingdom of priests and a holy nation (Exod 19:6). Having received its name from Jacob (Genesis 32; and often called *Jacob* later in the OT), Israel is known as the seed or offspring of Abraham (Genesis 12; 15; 17; Ps 105:6; Isa 41:8; 51:2; Jer 33:26), and becomes God's elect, covenant nation through his sovereign choice (Deut 4:37; 7:7; 10:15; Jer 33:24) and covenant faithfulness to Abraham (Exod 19:4; Deut 7:8). The defining and catalyzing event for Israel as a nation is their miraculous redemption from slavery in Egypt, which in turn becomes the archetype of Israel's future (Isa 11:10–16; 51:1–52:15; Zech 10:6–12).[34] Furthermore, the exodus is also the context where Israel is summoned as the son of God (Exod 4:22; Deut 14:1; Jer 31:20; cf. Israel as the children of God in Isa 1:2, 4; Hos 1:10; 11:1). As the firstborn son, Israel is to serve the Lord (e.g., Exod 4:23) and is denoted with the title *Servant* or referred to as "my servant" in the second half of Isaiah and elsewhere (cf. Jer 30:10; 46:27–28).[35] Other covenantal imagery describes who Israel is in relationship to Yahweh: Israel is the wife (Isa 54:5; and as an adulterous wife in

---

[32] See Graham Harvey, *The True Israel: Uses of the Names Jew, Hebrew and Israel in Ancient Jewish and Early Christian Literature* (Leiden: Brill, 1996), 225–56. On the difficulty of answering who a Jew is from political and religious perspectives, see Holwerda, *Jesus and Israel*, 27–30.

[33] For helpful discussions, note Iain M. Duguid, "Israel," in *DOTPR*, 391–97; R. J. D. Knauth, "Israelites," in *DOTP*, 452–58; Charles H. H. Scobie, *The Ways of Our God: An Approach to Biblical Theology* (Grand Rapids: Eerdmans, 2003), 469–80; LaRondelle, *The Israel of God*, 81–98.

[34] See also Isa 40:3–11; 49:8–12; Jer 23:5–8; Ezek 11:15–20; Mic 7:15–20; Hos 2:14–15.

[35] See Stephen G. Dempster, "The Servant of the Lord," in *Central Themes in Biblical Theology: Mapping Unity in Diversity*, ed. Scott J. Hafemann and Paul R. House (Grand Rapids: Baker, 2007), 128–78 and John Goldingay, "Servant of Yahweh," in *DOTPR*, 700–707.

Ezekiel 16; Hosea 1–3) or bride (Jer 2:2; cf. Jer 31:32) of the Lord. Agrarian imagery is applied to Israel as well, as God is the shepherd to his sheep (Isa 40:11; Ps 100:3) or flock (Ezekiel 34; Ps 77:20), and Israel is described as a *vine* planted and typically judged by the Lord for its fruitlessness (Ps 80:8, 14; Isa 5:1–7; Ezek 19:10–14; Hos 10:1–2).[36]

Moreover, a biblical-theological tracing of the Bible's story line shows that Israel is thematically and intertextually linked not just to the patriarchs but to Adam, corporately recapitulating his status and roles. Israel is another "Adam," called God's son as Adam was (Luke 3:38); and the themes of blessing, fruitfulness, and multiplication first directed to Adam are repeated to the patriarchs and advanced through Israel (Gen 47:27; Exod 1:7; Lev 26:3–13; Deut 7:13; Ps 107:38; Isa 51:2).[37] In fact, these blessings to Israel, echoing the early chapters of Genesis, are projected into the future when the Genesis commission is fulfilled (Ezek 34:25–31; cf. Jer 3:16–17). Just as Adam enjoyed the presence of God in the arboreal temple of Eden, so Israel had the tabernacle and later the temple as the place where God's presence was supremely manifested.[38] Additionally, the significant offices of

---

[36] See also Isa 27:2–6; Jer 2:21; 12:10–11; Ezek 15:1–8; Hos 14:7.

[37] Gentry and Wellum, *KTC*, 226–28; N. T. Wright, *The Climax of the Covenant* (Minneapolis: Fortress, 1991), 21–23; idem, *The New Testament and the People of God*, 262–64. Wright observes that at crucial turning points in the story line, "Abraham's call, his circumcision, the offering of Isaac, the transition from Abraham to Isaac and from Isaac to Jacob, and in the sojourn in Egypt—the narrative quietly insists that Abraham and his progeny inherit the role of Adam and Eve. There are, interestingly, two differences which emerge in the shape of this role. The command ('be fruitful . . .') has turned into promise ('I will make you fruitful . . .'), and possession of the land of Canaan, together with supremacy over enemies, has taken the place of Adam's domin-ion over nature" (263). Cf. Bruce K. Waltke, *An Old Testament Theology: An Exegetical, Canonical, and Thematic Approach* (Grand Rapids: Zondervan, 2007), 297.

[38] J. V. Fesko, *Last Things First: Unlocking Genesis 1–3 with the Christ of Eschatology* (Fearn, Ross-shire, Scotland: Mentor, 2007), 125–26 helpfully summarizes: "God placed Adam in the garden, which was a source of sustenance and the location of the temple, and so too God placed Israel, his son, in a land flowing with milk and honey (Exod. 13:5). . . . G. K. Beale notes that 'Israel's land is explicitly compared to the Garden of Eden (see Gen. 13:10; Isa. 51:3; Ezek. 36:35; 47:12; Joel 2:3) and is por-trayed as very fruitful in order to heighten the correspondence to Eden (cf. Deut. 8:7–10; 11:8–17; Ezek. 47:1–12).' The promised land was also the ultimate resting place of

prophet, priest, and king exemplified within Israel's leadership structure go back to Adam. These offices coalesce in another son of God, another Adam, and a significant representative of Israel—David.[39] Lastly, Israel as a nation cannot be understood theologically apart from its being the means by which the promised seed (Gen 3:15) would emerge and reverse the effects of the fall and triumph over the serpent through a royal deliverer.

Therefore, theologians have to address more than the usage of the term *Israel* and must attend to the redemptive-historical development of Israel's identity, roles, and vocation when seeking to derive conclusions regarding Israel's relation to Jesus and, subsequently, the church. In other words, the titles, metaphors, and imagery of Israel, as well as Israel's service to the Lord and identity through covenant structures (the law, tabernacle/temple, priestly-sacrificial system, feasts, Sabbath, circumcision, etc.) have to be taken into account through the progress of revelation (developed through the covenants: creation, Noahic, Abrahamic, Mosaic, Davidic, and new) to the person and work of Christ if proper theological conclusions are to be drawn with respect to his relationship to Israel. The case to be demonstrated is that Jesus really is the "true Israel" in that he not only represents Israel but also fulfills Israel's identity, calling, and promises in inaugurating the new age, ratifying the new covenant, and bringing forth the dawning of the eschatologically restored Israel—the church.

---

the once ambulatory desert tabernacle—the place where Israel met with, served, and offered sacrifices to God. When the ultimate goals of the covenant made with Israel are considered, the same protological elements reappear. . . . Israel was to take the redemptive knowledge of God to the ends of the earth in the same way that Adam was to spread the image and worship of God throughout the earth (Isa. 49:6)." The scholarly literature on Eden as a garden-temple with abundant links to the tabernacle and the Jerusalem temple is overwhelming, e.g., Beale, *The Temple and the Church's Mission*, 66–80; T. Desmond Alexander, *From Eden to the New Jerusalem: Exploring God's Plan for Life on Earth* (Nottingham, UK: InterVarsity, 2008), 13–60.

[39] Priestly functions are attributed to David when he brings the ark to Jerusalem (2 Sam 6:14, 17–18; cf. 8:18), and he exercised the gift of prophecy as well (e.g., 2 Sam 23:1–7; Psalm 22; Acts 2:30). See Bruce, *This Is That*, 72.

Christ as the True Israel: Israel in Typological Perspective

In examining how Jesus Christ recapitulates Israel's role and purpose, I will explore themes associated with Israel that were embedded with eschatological and restoration elements. Most notably, the typological pattern of sonship emerges. The NT unequivocally presents Jesus as the divine Son, but he is also what God's sons anticipated. Jesus is presented as the antitypical Adam (Rom 5:12–21; cf. 1 Cor 15:21–22, 45–49), the covenantal head of the new humanity, restoring them to the dignity and the role for which they were created by undoing the curse (Heb 2:5–18; cf. Psalm 8). Furthermore, Christ is the true seed of Abraham (Gal 3:16)[40] and the promised, ideal David (Acts 2:24–36; 13:32–37; Rom 1:3–4; Heb 1:1–14; 5:5). The correspondence is not just in terms of identity, for he fulfills the eschatological goals and promises associated with each of these covenantal figures. For example, already in Matthew's genealogy (Matt 1:1–17) and the opening chapter of Luke's Gospel (e.g., Luke 1:32–33, 54–55, 67–79), the reader receives significant clues that the climax of Israel's story, the end of exile, the promises to Abraham and David, are being fulfilled through Jesus (cf. Rom 15:8–13).[41] Likewise, the nation of Israel belongs to the stream of sonship (see above) that culminates in Christ.

---

[40] This important theme will not be examined here; see DeRouchie's chapter.

[41] For the theme of fulfillment in the structure of Matthew's genealogy, see R. T. France, *The Gospel of Matthew*, NICNT (Grand Rapids: Eerdmans, 2007), 28–33; Joel Kennedy, *The Recapitulation of Israel: Use of Israel's History in Matthew 1:1–4:11*, WUNT 2/257 (Tübingen: Mohr Siebeck, 2008), 72–100. For an overview of Luke 1, see Richard B. Hays, "The Liberation of Israel in Luke-Acts: Intertextual Narration as Countercultural Practice," in *Reading the Bible Intertextually*, ed. Richard B. Hays, Stefan Alkier, and Leroy A. Huizenga (Waco, TX: Baylor University Press, 2009), 103–6. Luke's nativity narrative "forms a bridge between the Old Testament age of promise and the age of fulfillment which will run as a connecting thread throughout the whole of Luke-Acts" (Mark L. Strauss, *The Davidic Messiah in Luke-Acts: The Promise and its Fulfillment in Lukan Christology*, JSNTSup 110 [Sheffield, UK: Sheffield Academic, 1995], 86).

Christ as the Son out of Egypt

Perhaps the most direct typological correspondence between Israel and Christ is found in Matthew 2:15, where Hosea 11:1 ("Out of Egypt I called my son") is fulfilled upon Jesus' departure and return from Egypt to avoid Herod. The citation seems obscure since Hosea 11:1 seems to merely recollect Israel's original exodus (cf. Exod 4:22); however, when the broader context of Hosea 11 is considered, Hosea himself not only recalls Israel's exodus, idolatry, and God's judgment, but he also anticipates a future restoration, a new exodus from "Egypt" (Hos 11:10–11).[42] Moreover, the corporate identification of the people of Israel with a single individual representative, Jesus, is connected to the prophecy of the future king of Israel coming out of Egypt (Num 24:7–9, 17–19), which is echoed in Hosea 11:10–11 (cf. Num 23:22, 24; 24:8–9).[43] In sum, Matthew's citation of Hosea 11:1 with reference to Jesus' flight to Egypt, which can only be understood in light of the broader context of Hosea 11, serves two purposes. First, Matthew identifies Jesus as God's Son—the true Israel who recapitulates and embodies Israel's history. Second, this Son ushers in a new exodus, commencing the restoration of Israel: "Matthew believed that the return from exile promised in Hosea ultimately became a reality with the true son of Israel, Jesus Christ."[44]

The Gospels further present Jesus as the antitypical Israel and the One who inaugurates Israel's new exodus promises. The messianic forerunner,

---

[42] For a convincing analysis of the use of Hos 11:1 in Matt 2:15, see Beale, *A New Testament Biblical Theology*, 406–12; idem, "The Use of Hosea 11:1 in Matthew 2:15: One More Time," *JETS* 55 (2012): 697–715; cf. Schreiner, *New Testament Theology*, 73–75; Holwerda, *Jesus and Israel*, 37–40.

[43] Ibid., 407–10; idem, "The Use of Hosea 11:1," 700–703; cf. France, *The Gospel of Matthew*, 80–81. The link between the people of Israel and a representative leader is also found in Hos 1:10–11.

[44] Schreiner, *New Testament Theology*, 75. Israel's eschatological future included the nations flowing to Israel. Matthew's genealogy with the mention of Gentile women already hinted at Jesus' role extending beyond Israel, but the magi coming and offering gifts (Matt 2:1–12) is the initial fulfillment of Isa 60:3, 5–6, 10–11, 14 (Beale, *A New Testament Biblical Theology*, 389). For more on how Matthew 2 shows Israel's history recapitulated in Jesus with the predominant backdrop of the exodus motif, see Kennedy, *The Recapitulation of Israel*, 103–53.

John the Baptist, appears in the wilderness preaching about the arrival of the kingdom, preparing the way of the Lord.[45] The eschatological Elijah has appeared (Mal 3:1; 4:5; cf. Matt 17:10–13), and Jesus' baptism and the accompanying divine approval (Matt 3:15–17; cf. Mark 1:10–11; Luke 3:21–22) also point to Jesus Christ as the true representative of Israel, the Servant of the Lord, and agent of Israel's new exodus.[46] With the backdrop of the exodus description of Isaiah 63:11–15; 64:1 (cf. 1 Cor 10:1–4), where the Spirit brings Israel out of the water and gives them rest, Matthew 3:15–17 portrays a greater reenactment: Jesus identifies with his people, goes through the waters, and the Spirit descends upon him (see Isa 11:2; 42:1; 61:1).[47] Jesus' "baptism in the waters of the Jordan represents a new exodus (he, so to speak, crosses the Jordan into the land), and the descent of the dove signifies the onset of new creation (cf. Gen. 1:2; 8:8–12, which fits with Isa 32:15; 44:3, linking the Spirit to the new creation work of God)."[48] Further, God's perspective of Jesus in the announcement, "This is my beloved Son" (Matt 3:17; Luke 3:22), recalls the sonship of Israel, echoing Exodus 4:22; Hosea 11:1; Jeremiah 31:9 (and possibly Jer 38:20 LXX [= Jer 31:20] where Ephraim is called "my beloved son"), the messianic enthronement psalm of a Davidic king (Ps 2:7), and possibly Isaac (Gen 22:2, 12). The voice out of heaven confirms Jesus as the unique Son of God, the true Israel and true king, summing up all that these previous sons anticipated.

---

[45] See Isa 40:3 in Matt 3:3; and Isa 40:3; Mal 3:1; Exod 23:20 in Mark 1:2–3; and Isa 40:3–5 in Luke 3:4–6. These passages are significant for understanding the arrival of Israel's restoration in the gospel of Christ. See Rikk E. Watts, "Mark," in *Commentary on the New Testament Use of the Old Testament*, ed. G. K. Beale and D. A. Carson (Grand Rapids: Baker, 2007), 113–20; and for the interpretative framework of Isa 40:3–5 in Luke-Acts, along with the link of the "Way" terminology in Acts as designating the church as the true heir and reconstitution of Israel, see David W. Pao, *Acts and the Isaianic New Exodus* (Grand Rapids: Baker, 2002), 37–69; cf. Schnabel, *Acts*, 290.

[46] For further in-depth analysis of Jesus' baptism in relation to Israel, see Holwerda, *Jesus and Israel*, 42–44; Beale, *A New Testament Biblical Theology*, 412–17; Kennedy, *The Recapitulation of Israel*, 175–84.

[47] Beale, *A New Testament Biblical Theology*, 414–15; Watts, "Mark," 120–22.

[48] Thomas R. Schreiner, *The King in His Beauty: A Biblical Theology of the Old and New Testament* (Grand Rapids: Baker, 2013), 436.

Christ as the True Servant

Another important feature with the Spirit's descent upon Jesus is that God declares this is the Son in whom he is well pleased. A clear allusion to Isaiah 42:1 is present in Matthew 3:16–17, thereby identifying Jesus as the Isaianic Servant. Alongside the servant named Jacob/Israel in Isaiah (41:8–9; 42:19; 43:10; 44:1–2, 21, 26; 45:4; 48:20; 49:3), there is another servant, a faithful Israel anointed by the Spirit who accomplishes Israel's salvation and restoration (Isa 42:1–7; 49:1–7; 50:4–9; 52:13–53:12). The Servant is the true Israel (Isa 49:3) who accomplishes God's promises of deliverance to Israel. Not just in the narrative of Jesus' baptism, but throughout the NT Jesus is presented as the eschatological Servant (e.g., Matt 12:18–21; Luke 22:37; Acts 3:26; 8:28–37; Phil 2:7; 1 Pet 2:21–25).[49] Moreover, Jesus fulfills the Servant-Israel's mission by his atoning death (Isaiah 53; cf. Rom 4:23–25; 8:32; Gal 1:4), in cleansing and restoring Israel, and also in Israel's task to the nations (Isa 49:6; cf. 42:6–7) as indicated by Luke 2:32 and Acts 26:23 (cf. John 1:4; 8:12; 9:5; 12:46), for Jesus is the light of the nations.[50] Therefore, Jesus does not restore the nation of Israel in order to bless the nations in the future; he accomplishes this task in his first coming.[51]

---

[49] For further discussion of the servant theme in the NT, see Dempster, "The Servant of the Lord," 165–77; Schreiner, *New Testament Theology*, 265–68; 295–97. See also Robin Routledge, "Replacement or Fulfillment? Re-applying Old Testament Designations of Israel to the Church," *STR* 4 (2013): 147–51.

[50] Beale, *A New Testament Biblical Theology*, 683–84, points out that Paul, as Christ's follower, also participates in the commission of the Servant (Acts 13:47; 26:18). Cf. Alan J. Thompson, *The Acts of the Risen Lord Jesus: Luke's Account of God's Unfolding Plan*, NSBT 27 (Downers Grove, IL: InterVarsity, 2011), 118–20.

[51] Contra Vlach, "What Does Christ as 'True Israel' Mean?," 49–50, and Saucy, *The Case for Progressive Dispensationalism*, 191. Rightly, P. Chase Sears, *Heirs of Promise: The Church as the New Israel in Romans* (Bellingham, WA: Lexham, 2015), 29–32; cf. Jonathan Menn, *Biblical Eschatology* (Eugene, OR: Resource, 2013), 25–26. Just as the corporate solidarity of the Israel-Servant relationship is fulfilled in Christ, so also the Son of Man theme as Daniel 7 presents this figure in individual and corporate terms. See R. T. France, "Old Testament Prophecy and the Future of Israel," *TynBul* 26 (1975): 67; Beale, *A New Testament Biblical Theology*, 393–401, 652; Schreiner, *The King in His Beauty*, 437–39.

A similar theme in a different context is found in the overflow of blessings described in Paul's eulogy in Ephesians 1:3–6. This passage has lexical
and conceptual parallels to Isaiah 44:1–5: God's election of Israel (vv. 1–2),
the future outpouring of the Spirit on his offspring (v. 3), and God's faithfulness to the Abrahamic promises (vv. 3–5) where Gentiles join themselves to
Israel. Each of these thematic elements unites in Ephesians 1:3–6.[52] Paul
praises the Father for his blessings, among them being election and adoption, which come by being "in the beloved"—Christ. As we have already
seen, Isaiah 44:1 refers to Israel as God's servant, but Israel is also identified as *Yeshurun* (Isa 44:2; cf. Deut 32:15; 33:5, 26), a term of endear-
ment meaning "Upright One" but translated in the LXX of Isaiah 44:2 as
"beloved" (ἠγαπημένος). This is the same word Paul uses to identify Jesus
Christ, for he is the "beloved" in Ephesians 1:6. Therefore, given the background of Isaiah 44:1–5 in Ephesians 1:3–6, Paul understood Christ to be
Yeshurun, Israel; and through him, the eschatological presence of the Spirit
(Eph 1:3; cf. 1:13–14), the blessings of the Abrahamic promises, have come
to fruition. The Ephesian Christians (Jew and Gentile) are loved, adopted,
and chosen by being united in the "beloved," the true Israel.

Christ as the Obedient Son in the Wilderness

The Israel-Christ typology is further evident in the wilderness temptation
(Matt 4:1–11; Luke 4:1–13).[53] Having identified with Israel in his baptism,
this son is led into the wilderness for forty days to be tempted by Satan,
thereby mirroring Israel's wandering in the wilderness for forty years. Jesus
answers each temptation from Deuteronomy (6:13, 16; 8:3), each citation
coming from Moses's rehearsal of Israel's history of sin and failure. Unlike

---

[52] The following is based on the observations and excellent analysis by Joshua
Greever, "Will the True Israel Stand Up? Jesus as the True Israel in Ephesians 1:3–
6" (paper presented at the annual meeting of the Evangelical Theological Society,
Baltimore, MD, 19 November 2013).

[53] See France, *Jesus and the Old Testament*, 50–53; Holwerda, *Jesus and Israel*,
44–47; LaRondelle, *The Israel of God*, 64–65; Kynes, *A Christology of Solidarity*, 28–35.
Beale, *A New Testament Biblical Theology*, 417–22, also rightly notes the presence of
Moses and Adam typology in the temptation narrative.

Israel, however, Jesus is the obedient Son. "As the messianic king and Son of God (2 Sam. 7.14; Ps. 2.7; 89.27; 4QFlor), Jesus represents the nation and fulfills the task of eschatological Israel in the wilderness."[54] By his obedience and later vindication through resurrection, Jesus gains far more than what Satan had offered as all authority in heaven is bestowed upon him (Matt 28:18–20). Indeed, as the true, loyal Israel and messianic king, he decrees his followers to make disciples of all nations, to the ends of the earth (Acts 1:8), thus marking the eschatological gathering of the nations to Zion, a reality that pointed to Christ himself (Isa 2:2–5; 45:20–22; 55:5; 56:6–7; Mic 4:1–5; Zech 2:11; 8:20–23; cf. Gal 4:21–31; Heb 12:18, 22–24).[55]

Christ as the True Vine

Finally, another example of the Israel-Christ relationship is found in John 15:1. John presents Jesus as the "true vine" as opposed to the false, apostate vine, Israel (see OT references above). The most important OT allusion or intertext that backgrounds John 15 is Psalm 80 where the symbol of the vine (= Israel) is bound up with the psalmist's cry for restoration, his recall of the exodus, and his plea for God to raise up his eschatological Son of Man.[56] The prophecy of the restoration of the vine through a son, the king, is fulfilled in Jesus. Up to this point in John's Gospel, Jesus has "superseded the temple, the Jewish feasts, Moses, various holy sites; here he supersedes

---

[54] Strauss, *The Davidic Messiah*, 216.

[55] Kynes, *A Christology of Solidarity*, 182–84, 189–91; Menn, *Biblical Eschatology*, 31–32; Eckhard J. Schnabel, "Israel, the People of God, and the Nations," *JETS* 45 (2002): 46–47; Andreas J. Köstenberger and Peter T. O'Brien, *Salvation to the Ends of the Earth: A Biblical Theology of Mission*, NSBT 11 (Downers Grove, IL: InterVarsity, 2001), 106, 129–31, 135–37. "In Jesus' vindication on the Mountain of Commissioning . . . we see the fulfilment of the hopes of the restoration on Mount Zion: it was to Jesus . . . as the restored Son Israel—that the Gentiles were to gather to participate in eschatological salvation" (Terence L. Donaldson, *Jesus on the Mountain: A Study in Matthean Theology*, JSNTSup 8 [Sheffield, UK: JSOT, 1985], 200; cf. 182–88).

[56] See Andrew Streett, *The Vine and the Son of Man: Eschatological Interpretation of Psalm 80 in Early Judaism* (Minneapolis: Fortress, 2014), 209–21; cf. D. A. Carson, *The Gospel according to John*, PNTC (Grand Rapids: Eerdmans, 1991), 513–14.

Israel as the very locus of the people of God."[57] According to John 15:1–8, only those who are organically united with the true vine, incorporated as branches bearing fruit, are participants in Jesus, the true Israel.

The above survey demonstrates that Jesus Christ embodies what Israel was meant to be as a loyal and obedient son. More importantly, however, Jesus does not just identify with Israel and assume her role; he is the fulfillment of Israel's eschatological hopes in accomplishing the new exodus, drawing the nations to himself, and ratifying the promised new covenant (Jer 31:29–40; Ezek 36:24–38; Luke 22:20; 1 Cor 11:25; 2 Cor 3:3–18; Hebrews 8–10). As the Davidic son and Servant-Israel, Christ is the covenant of the people (Isa 42:6; 49:8). Through Jesus Christ, the Savior of Israel and the nations, the eschatological, renewed Israel has emerged—the church.

The Church as the New, Restored Israel in Jesus

Progressive covenantalism understands the Israel-church relationship as *indirect*—the church is the fulfillment of Israel *only* in Christ, the true Israel. On the one hand, there is danger in collapsing the church into Israel depending on how one puts the covenants together and interprets the many titles and designations of Israel that are directly applied to the church in the NT.[58] On the other hand, the error of dispensationalism is to keep Israel and the church so separate that the implication is that there are two peoples of God given God's distinct plans for Israel and the church. Alternatively, for dispensationalists who maintain that there is one people of God, the problem remains. How Jewish Christians can be recipients of OT nationalistic promises apart from Gentile Christians in a future

---

[57] Carson, *John*, 513; cf. Andreas J. Köstenberger, *A Theology of John's Gospel and Letters*, BTNT (Grand Rapids: Zondervan, 2009), 502–3.

[58] OT designations of Israel applied to the church include, among others, assembly, the people of God, the elect, children of Abraham, the flock of God, circumcision, priesthood, vineyard, and bride/wife. See Paul S. Minear, *Images of the Church in the New Testament* (Louisville: Westminster John Knox, 1960); Beale, *A New Testament Biblical Theology*, 669–79.

millennial stage is confounded by the fact that *all* believers have their identity in Christ (1 Cor 12:12–13; Gal 3:26–29) and *all* the promises and the inheritance are theirs through him (Rom 4:12–17; 2 Cor 6:16–7:1; Eph 1:11–23; Heb 9:15), as is fitting for adopted sons of God (Rom 8:15–17; Gal 4:4–7).[59] Ecclesiology must emerge from Christology: the church is the new, eschatological Israel because Christ, the last Adam, is the new covenant head of his people, the one who reconstitutes the true people of God through his cross work.[60] More specifically, it is because Jesus is the antitype of OT Israel that his disciples are deemed the true circumcision (Phil 3:3; Col 2:11), inward Jews (Rom 2:28–29), and Abraham's seed (Rom 4:16–18; Gal 3:7–9).

One passage that highlights how the church is the antitype of Israel through Jesus is 1 Peter 2:4–10. From the beginning of the epistle, Peter identifies his primarily Gentile audience with language of exile and diaspora, imagery of OT Israel now applied to the eschatological people of God and foreseen by the prophets (1 Pet 1:10–12).[61] In 1 Peter 2:4–10, the identity and function of the church are presented as the new Israel through Christ. Jesus, the resurrected Messiah, is the "living stone" and the cornerstone laid in Zion (cf. Ps 118:22; Isa 28:16). Those conjoined to him are "living stones" and are being built up as God's true temple, serving as priests and offering spiritual sacrifices (1 Pet 2:5; cf. Eph 2:20–22). "The temple in Jerusalem is no longer the center of God's purposes; rather, the church of Jesus Christ,

---

[59] See David I. Starling, "The Yes to All God's Promises: Jesus, Israel and the Promises of God in Paul's Letters," *RTR* 71 (2012): 185–204.

[60] While not explored here, the OT itself demonstrates that Gentiles/nations would become incorporated into eschatological Israel (e.g. Isa 56:3–8; 66:18–25; Psalm 87). See Gentry and Wellum, *KTC*, 445–61; Beale, *A New Testament Biblical Theology*, 656–69; Schnabel, "Israel, the People of God," 39–42.

[61] First Peter 1:14, 18, 21; 4:2–4 indicate the readers are predominantly Gentile, and yet the exilic language associates them with Israel as does the term *Gentiles* which refers to non-Christian outsiders in 1 Pet 2:12, so Richard Bauckham, "James, 1 Peter, Jude, and 2 Peter," in *A Vision for the Church: Studies in Early Christian Ecclesiology in Honour of J. P. M. Sweet*, ed. Marcus Bockmuehl and Michael B. Thompson (Edinburgh: T&T Clark, 1997), 160–61; cf. Ray F. Van Neste, "The Church in the General Epistles," in *The Community of Jesus*, 137–38.

composed of believers, . . . constitutes the temple of God."[62] Through union in Christ, God's new temple of believers takes on Israel's identity and role in a heightened, eschatological sense. The church is now made up of God's priests who communicate God's glory to the nations (1 Pet 2:9) and mediate God's blessings in the world (cf. v. 5).

The church is also God's chosen race, royal priesthood, holy nation, special possession, and constituted people through his remarkable mercy (2:9–10). This language alludes to Exodus 19:6; Isaiah 43:20–21; and Hosea 2:23. Exodus 19:6 is Israel's charter statement when it was constituted as God's people following the exodus and as such features the divine goal of the covenant relationship: if Israel obeys God's covenant, then they would be God's treasured possession, a kingdom of priests, and a holy nation. Peter applies these designations to the church because they are the people of the new exodus.[63] The Israel and exodus typology is also developed from Isaiah 43:20–21 (cf. Isa 43:16–19), as God's chosen race is depicted coming out of the Babylonian exile with overtones of new creation. Regardless of ethnic background, the church is now the true race that God redeems through the lamb of the greater exodus (1 Pet 1:19; cf. Isa 53:7; 1 Pet 1:2 with Exod 24:6–8). Lastly, Peter's use of Hosea 2:23 (cf. Hos 1:9–11) in 1 Peter 2:9–10 indicates that the church is beginning to fulfill Hosea's restoration prophecies. In the context of Hosea, God has disowned Israel because of her spiritual adultery and idolatry. Israel is "not my people," becoming just like a Gentile nation, cut off from the promises. In Hosea 2:23, however, God mercifully promises to restore this faithless, Gentile-like nation. According to Peter, the prophecy regarding God's "Gentile" people returning and becoming his people once again is taken typologically as his mercy is extended to the church, including those who

---

[62] Schreiner, *New Testament Theology*, 744. Beale, *A New Testament Biblical Theology*, 741, notes that the "building of the latter-day temple was to occur in conjunction with other restoration promises and was one of the telltale signs that the restoration was commencing."

[63] Bauckham, "James, 1 Peter," 161; D. A. Carson, "1 Peter," *Commentary on the New Testament Use of the Old Testament*, 1030–31; Schreiner, *New Testament Theology*, 743.

really are Gentiles.[64] Throughout this passage Peter makes clear that "the privileges belonging to Israel now belong to Christ's church. The church does not replace Israel, but it does fulfill the promises made to Israel; and all those, Jews and Gentiles, who belong to Christ are now part of the new people of God."[65]

On a final note, it is important to observe that Peter identifies the church as a holy (singular) nation (1 Pet 2:9). The old covenant nation of Israel pointed forward to a singular, multiethnic nation of the redeemed— the church. Moreover, although the language of "nations" is employed in Revelation 21–22, such does not establish that separate national identities or entities will continue throughout the consummated eternal state.[66] The people of God are depicted as coming from all nations and people groups who persevere and overcome through Christ (Rev 21:7; cf. 5:9; 7:9) in contrast to the faithless who are designated for eternal destruction (Rev 21:8;

---

[64] Carson, "1 Peter," 1031–32. The usage of Hos 1:10; 2:23 is applied by Paul in Rom 9:23–26 in a similar manner. For discussion, see Beale, *A New Testament Biblical Theology*, 705–8. For general discussion of typology in 1 Pet 2:4–10, see Goppelt, *Typos*, 153–55.

[65] Thomas R. Schreiner, *1, 2 Peter, Jude*, NAC, vol. 37 (Nashville, TN: B&H, 2003), 115. Contra, W. Edward Glenny, "The Israelite Imagery of 1 Peter 2," in *Dispensationalism, Israel, and the Church*, 156–87. Curiously, Glenny recognizes the typological patterns in 1 Pet 2:4–10 including the element of escalation and advancement instrinsic to typological relationships, but then he nullifies these typological links when he concludes that these typological patterns do "not negate the future fulfillment of the national, political, and geographic promises . . . made to Israel in these [OT] contexts" (187). If so, Peter's usage of these texts is purely analogical *not* typological. As I have argued, these OT texts featuring Israel's national/political identity and role, which Peter directly applies to the church through Christ, are typological because of the fulfillment accomplished by Christ as he establishes the prophesied true temple (the church) and new exodus. Glenny is also inconsistent, for Christ can be the final fulfillment of the typological patterns of 1 Pet 2:6–8, but the church is only the initial fulfillment of the pattern of 1 Pet 2:9–10 (186). This is unconvincing, for if Christ, the living stone and cornerstone laid in Zion, is the end of the road for these typological patterns, why would this not be the case for those conjoined to this eschatological stone, the living stones—the church—in these last times (1 Pet 1:20)?

[66] Contra, for example, Blaising and Bock, *Progressive Dispensationalism*, 50–51. See their quotation in note 5 earlier. While national distinctions will come to an end in the eschaton, this does not deny that ethnicities may continue.

20:15). "[T]he 'nations' and their kings who enter the gates of the New Jerusalem in 21:24–26 are identified by John in 22:14 with those 'who wash their robes' and thus obtain 'the right to the tree of life and may enter the city by the gates.' . . . In other words, they are those who continue to be faithful to their original commitment to Jesus Christ and his saving work."[67] The consummated state of Revelation 21–22 is a vision where the city of God is the people of God, where God dwells among all his saints.[68]

Conclusion

In summary, progressive covenantalism understands national Israel as a typological pattern not unlike other OT persons, institutions, and events. Individual persons in the OT typologically foreshadowed Jesus, the chief antitype, and likewise God used a corporate Adam, the Israelite nation, to point to a greater Son, Jesus, and to a faithful community, the church. Israel is related to the church secondarily as the typological relationship is directed through Christ. Since Christ is the antitypical and true Israel, the agent of restoration who brings to fruition Israel's promises and fulfills the covenants, the church, through him, is the one and only new covenant community (Jer 31:26–40; Ezek 36:22–36).[69] All followers of Jesus have

---

[67] Eckhard J. Schnabel, "John and the Future of the Nations," *BBR* 12 (2002): 267 (and see his whole discussion, pp. 265–70). Cf. Menn, *Biblical Eschatology*, 304–7; Robert H. Gundry, "The New Jerusalem: People as Place, Not Place for People," *NovT* 29 (1987): 254–64.

[68] Gundry, "The New Jerusalem," 257, notes that God takes up his abode with the saints (Rev 21:3). Just as God had tabernacled with Israel, in the future "he will make the saints, who are the church, his abode. . . . [T]he plural 'peoples' [Rev 21:3] . . . [emphasizes] the internationality of the church, made up as it is of the redeemed from the pagan nations as well as from Israel. As peoples, the church will be God's city."

[69] Contra Bruce A. Ware, "The New Covenant and the People(s) of God," in *Dispensationalism, Israel, and the Church*, 68–97, who splits the spiritual aspects of the new covenant as being implemented "now" in the church from the physical/territorial aspects that are "not yet" fulfilled to the nation of Israel. Besides a questionable use of inaugurated eschatology, Ware misses how Israel is typological of an eschatological, restored Israel through Christ, which does not entail "a strict identity of Israel and the church" (92). Jeremiah already depicts Gentiles among a restored people of

direct knowledge of the Lord, being taught by God (cf. Isa 54:3; John 6:45; 1 Thess 4:9; 1 John 2:20, 27), possess the gift of the eschatological Holy Spirit with the law written on the heart, and look back to the finality of the forgiveness of sins through the cross (Jer 31:31–34). These new covenant promises, like the typological aspects of national Israel, are channeled through Christ to God's end-time people, Jew and Gentile alike. Thus, the church does not replace or absorb OT Israel; rather Israel was a type of Jesus and, derivatively, of a new and regenerate covenant community. In this way the Israel-Christ-church relationship in typological and redemptive-historical perspective avoids the direct unification of Israel and the church as promulgated in covenant theology, while also evading the significant separation of Israel and the church with each having distinct plans as portrayed in dispensational theology.

God (e.g. 4:2; 12:14–17; 16:14–18), and the NT authors can naturally apply the new covenant promises to the church due to the work of Christ. See Gentry and Wellum, *KTC*, 484–516; Wellum, "Beyond Mere Ecclesiology," 195–209; and note also David G. Peterson, *Transformed by God: New Covenant Life and Ministry* (Nottingham, UK: InterVarsity, 2012).

CHAPTER 3

The Mosaic Law, Theological Systems, and the Glory of Christ[1]

Jason C. Meyer

Introduction: The Procrustean Bed and Theological Systems

In Greek mythology Procrusteus was the son of Poseidon. He had an iron bed that he offered to weary travelers. He used hospitality as a torture trap. If travelers were too short for the bed, he would stretch out their bodies to fit the bed. If they were too tall for the bed, he would cut off the excess length of their legs.

Theological systems can become a Procrustean bed. If the text does not satisfy our system, we can stretch the text to say what we want. If the text says more than what comfortably fits our system, we can cut off what we wish it would not say.

I am not denigrating theological systems. On the contrary, theological systems can *sharpen* our understanding of the whole counsel of God, but only if they do not first *determine* our understanding of God's Word.

---

[1] Special thanks to Tom Schreiner, Jason DeRouchie, and Andy Naselli, who took time to read an earlier draft of this essay and provided excellent feedback.

Therefore, theological systems should always be paired with theological self-awareness. We must be up front with our theological commitments, taking them to Scripture. The Bible does not belong *on* the bed; the Bible *is* the bed. The Bible alone has the authority to serve as the Procrustean bed for all our thinking. If we love the Bible more than our theological systems, we will be eager to measure our systems with the scriptural standard.

In this chapter I endeavor to do two things: First, examine how theological systems influence our approach to the Mosaic law today. Second, unpack a progressive covenantal understanding of the law.

A Spectrum Analysis of Theological Systems and the Mosaic Law

Theological systems influence our reading of the Mosaic law because of their built-in biases. Some theological systems stress the shared similarities (i.e., continuity) between the Mosaic law and NT ethics. Other systems want to stress the differences between the two (i.e., discontinuity).

Is there a way to visualize how various theological systems approach the Mosaic law? It is exceedingly difficult to summarize these systems in a compact way without oversimplification; however, it is worth the risk in order to help readers navigate through the different options.[2]

One way to diagram different views on a comparative spectrum is to give each theological system a specific place along a continuum that measures continuity and discontinuity. How much carryover is there between an Israelite living under the old covenant and a Christian living under the new covenant? The following continuum organizes the views according to most carryover to the least carryover.

---

[2] For example, new covenant theology is not placed on this diagram due to its close relationship to progressive covenantalism, although slight differences remain between the two views.

Road of Continuity/Discontinuity

⟵ Continuity			Discontinuity ⟶
Theonomy	Covenant Theology	Progressive Covenantalism	Forms of Dispensationalism
			Progressive Revised Classical

Theonomy and Covenant Theology

The first two systems of theology stress continuity with respect to the law and NT ethics. Theonomy has distinguished itself on the far left of the continuity divide because it sees the most carryover from the OT law to NT ethics.[3] It stresses continuity and keeps discontinuity to a minimum. Covenant theology is positioned to the right of theonomy on the continuity/discontinuity divide.[4] Covenant theology stresses more discontinuity than theonomy but still maintains an overall commitment to continuity. Covenant theology is not monolithic in its views on the law, but adherence to the tripartite division is a common denominator.[5]

Both theonomy and covenant theology use the tripartite division of the law consisting of the three categories—moral, civil, and ceremonial. This division has a venerable pedigree in the history of Christian theology. It

---

[3] See, for example, Greg L. Bahnsen, "The Theonomic Reformed Approach to Law and Gospel," in *Five Views on Law and Gospel*, ed. Wayne Strickland (Grand Rapids: Zondervan, 1993), 93–143.

[4] On the treatment of the law from a covenant theologian, see Knox Chamblin, "The Law of Moses and the Law of Christ," in *Continuity and Discontinuity: Perspectives on the Relationship Between the Old and New Testaments*, ed. John S. Feinberg (Wheaton, IL: Crossway, 1988), 181–202.

[5] For example, there is a debate over whether the Mosaic law is a "republication" of the covenant of works. Advocating this view is Bryan D. Estelle, J. V. Fesko, and David VanDrunen, eds., *The Law Is Not of Faith: Essays on Works and Grace in the Mosaic Covenant* (Phillipsburg, NJ: P&R, 2009). For a work arguing against the republication view, see Andrew M. Elam, Robert C. Van Kooten, and Randall A. Bergquist, *Merit and Moses: A Critique of the Klinean Doctrine of Republication* (Eugene, OR: Wipf and Stock, 2014).

dates back at least to Aquinas and possibly to Tertullian.[6] Perhaps the most concise formulation is found in the Westminster Confession of Faith.

> 3. Besides this law, commonly called moral, God was pleased to give the people of Israel, as a Church under age, ceremonial laws, containing several typical ordinances, partly of worship, prefiguring Christ, his graces, actions, sufferings, and benefits; and partly, holding forth divers instructions of moral duties. All which ceremonial laws are now abrogated, under the New Testament.

> 4. To them also, as a body politic, he gave sundry judicial laws, which expired together with the State of the people; not obliging any other, now, further than the general equity thereof may require.

> 5. The moral law doth forever bind all, as well justified persons as others, to the obedience thereof; and that, not only in regard of the matter contained in it, but also in respect of the authority of God the Creator who gave it. Neither doth Christ in the gospel any way dissolve, but much strengthen this obligation.[7]

While the tripartite division is common to both theonomy and covenant theology, its application is different.

Theonomists contend that the moral and civil laws are still binding today (continuity), while the ceremonial laws are no longer binding because of Christ's sacrifice (discontinuity). Covenant theologians hold that the moral law is binding (continuity), but both the civil and the ceremonial laws are abrogated (discontinuity).[8]

---

[6] Richard N. Longenecker, "Three Ways of Understanding Relations Between the Testaments: Historically and Today," in *Tradition and Interpretation in the New Testament: Essays in Honor of E. Earle Ellis for His 60th Birthday*, ed. Gerald F. Hawthorne with Otto Betz (Grand Rapids: Eerdmans, 1987), 24.

[7] WCF 19:3–5.

[8] For more details on how covenant theology differs from theonomy, see William S. Barker and W. Robert Godfrey, eds., *Theonomy: A Reformed Critique* (Grand Rapids: Zondervan, 1990).

Perhaps the simplest way to distinguish all the views on the spectrum is to note that theonomy and covenant theology use the tripartite division of the law, while the other theological systems do not. The other four systems of thought all say the Mosaic law has come to its end. Christians are under the binding authority of the law of Christ, not the law of Moses. The law of Christ is "the demand of God that is binding on Christians since the coming of Christ."[9] The law of Christ includes the demands and teachings of Christ and his apostles. Parts of the law of Moses carry over but only because they now are part of the law of Christ.

Progressive Covenantalism

Progressive covenantalism provides a middle way between covenant theology and dispensationalism. The defining document is Gentry and Wellum's book, *Kingdom Through Covenant*.[10] Progressive covenantalism has affinity with the theological movement that has been called "new covenant theology,"[11] but there are also some differences. For example, progressive covenantal theologians make the case for a creation covenant, whereas some within new covenant theology do not.[12] Like covenant theologians, they stress the organic unity of the Scriptures but reject the paedo-baptism of covenant theology, which takes the genealogical principle as a promise for the children of believers.[13] Progressive covenantalism's approach to the Mosaic law tilts toward more discontinuity and is closer to progressive dispensationalism, yet for different reasons.

---

[9] Douglas J. Moo, "The Law of Moses or the Law of Christ," in *Continuity and Discontinuity*, 215.

[10] Peter J. Gentry and Stephen J. Wellum, *Kingdom Through Covenant: A Biblical-Theological Understanding of the Covenants* (Wheaton, IL: Crossway, 2012).

[11] The best popular treatment is Tom Wells and Fred Zaspel, *New Covenant Theology: Description, Definition, Defense* (Frederick, MD: New Covenant Media, 2002).

[12] Michael J. Vlach, "New Covenant Theology Compared with Covenantalism," *TMSJ* 18 (2007): 206.

[13] Gentry and Wellum, *Kingdom Through Covenant*, 694–703.

Dispensationalism

Dispensational theology has gone through various revisions in its history. Classic dispensationalism stresses discontinuity and began in the nineteenth century with theologians such as John Nelson Darby and Lewis Sperry Chafer. This system of thought became prominent and popular through the *Scofield Reference Bible*.

Revised dispensationalism made some important changes to classic dispensationalism. Key theologians include Charles C. Ryrie and John Walvoord. Revised dispensationalism represents dispensational thinking during the 1950s through the 1980s.[14] Progressive dispensationalism is a further revision that became more prominent beginning in the 1980s and 1990s with the defining book by Craig Blaising and Darrell Bock.[15]

What does each branch of dispensationalism teach? Classic dispensationalism made a distinction between two types of humanity and two types of salvation. The earthly humanity (Israelites alive at the return of Christ) will experience an earthly salvation, while heavenly humanity will experience the resurrection and heavenly salvation. Different dispensations provide different rules to govern the people living under each time period or epoch.[16] In this system, the dispensation of the Mosaic law ended with God's program for Israel and a dispensation of grace for the church began. Accordingly, they stress discontinuity between the age of law and the age of the church.

Revised dispensationalism kept the seven distinct dispensations of the *Scofield Reference Bible* intact but abandoned the "eternal dualism of heavenly and earthly peoples,"[17] distancing themselves from classic

---

[14] See Charles C. Ryrie, *Dispensationalism Today* (Chicago: Moody, 1969).

[15] Craig S. Blaising and Darrell L. Bock, *Progressive Dispensationalism* (Grand Rapids: Baker, 1993). See also Robert L. Saucy, *The Case for Progressive Dispensationalism* (Grand Rapids: Zondervan, 1993).

[16] Classic dispensationalism typically distinguishes seven distinct stewardship arrangements: innocence (prefall), conscience (Adam until Noah), government (Noah to Babel), promise (Abraham until Moses), law (Moses to Christ), grace (Pentecost to the rapture), and the millennium.

[17] Blaising and Bock, *Progressive Dispensationalism*, 31.

dispensationalism's implication that law and grace were two different ways of salvation.[18]

Progressive dispensationalism allows for more continuity, stressing a "holistic and unified view of eternal salvation."[19] Israel and the church are still distinct, but they have been brought together in the sense that the church already enjoys the blessings promised to Israel *in part*. In the next dispensation all the blessings of the new covenant will be realized, including a literal fulfillment of the promises to ethnic Israel.

The differences between progressive covenantalism and progressive dispensationlism are more complicated. One of the key differences is hermeneutical. Progressive dispensationalism adopts a so-called complementary hermeneutic that exists alongside a literal hermeneutic. Therefore, they claim that the way the NT authors read the OT is somewhat incomplete. The apostles take the original promises and make complementary changes to them *without exhausting the original promises*. They find their spiritual fulfillment in the church and their more literal fulfillment in Israel's future (usually in the millennium). For example, progressive dispensationalists say that the original promise of land still awaits "literal" fulfillment for ethnic Israelites. Those in the progressive covenantal camp observe that the OT itself intertextually interprets the land promises as pointers to the new

---

[18] Statements made in the original Scofield Reference Bible contributed to that overall impression. "The point of testing is no longer legal obedience as the condition of salvation, but acceptance or rejection of Christ with good works as a fruit of salvation." See C. I. Scofield, ed., *The Scofield Reference Bible* (New York: Oxford University Press, 1917), 115n1. In other words, God dealt with Israel under the law covenant in terms of legal obedience as a condition for salvation, while God deals with the church in terms of acceptance of Christ as the condition for salvation (with good works as a fruit of salvation). Charles Ryrie stated that early dispensationalists made many such statements, but they never intended to teach two ways of salvation (*Dispensationalism Today*, 112). Robert Saucy points out that subsequent expressions of dispensationalism have consistently and carefully affirmed that salvation has always been by grace through faith (*The Case for Progressive Dispensationalism*, 14–15), which is reflected in the revised notes in the New Scofield Reference Bible.

[19] Blaising and Bock, *Progressive Dispensationalism*, 47.

creation, not the land of Canaan.[20] They believe the NT authors have correctly read the original sense of the promises. There is no need to supplement their reading with a more "literal" fulfillment in the future. Most importantly, progressive covenantalism differs from dispensationalism in placing a more pronounced stress on the progressive unfolding of the biblical covenants and their final fulfillment in Christ.

It is important to resist exaggerating the differences between these views. It surprises some to see the extent to which they share a common core of ethical content. All the views say Christians are called to obey God's commands. They do not differ from one another as much in terms of *what* a Christian is called to do but in terms of *how* one reaches that conclusion, which is specifically illustrated in the ongoing application of the Sabbath command.[21]

An Attitude Check: An Exercise in Theological Self-Awareness

The Sabbath debate represents a definite practical difference, but it is not the defining difference. Instead, as Bruce Waltke argues, the defining difference is the respective *attitudes* toward the Mosaic law.[22] Here is how

---

[20] Gentry and Wellum, *Kingdom Through Covenant*, 607. The promise of rest in Psalm 95 is given centuries after Joshua. The promise of rest that remains for "today" (Ps 95:7–8) does not point back to Canaan but forward to the new creation (cf. Heb 4:8). Some progressive covenantalists do affirm a future for ethnic Israel in Paul's treatment of the issue in Rom 11:25–32, and some take a historic premillennialist reading of Revelation 20, but they do not claim the millennium is necessary to fulfill the original "land" promises. Classic dispensationalism says that OT promises were *not* "spiritually" fulfilled in the church. These promises will find a "literal" fulfillment later with ethnic Israel. Progressive dispensationalism acknowledges that the NT writers often present OT promises as spiritually fulfilled in the church. They simply go further by saying this NT fulfillment does not exhaust the entirety of the promise. It still awaits further fulfillment by ethnic Israel in the future (Blaising and Bock, *Progressive Dispensationalism*, 103–4). See also Darrell Bock, "Summary Essay," in *Three Views on the Millennium and Beyond*, ed. Darrell L. Bock (Grand Rapids: Zondervan, 1999), 292.

[21] See the essay by Thomas Schreiner in this volume.

[22] See Bruce K. Waltke, "Theonomy in Relation to Dispensational and Covenant Theologies," in *Theonomy: A Reformed Critique*, 69.

Waltke explains the difference in attitude: "Dispensationalists, concentrating on its spiritually debilitating effects through man's sinfulness, negate it; Reformed theologians, moving beyond its weakness to its spiritual value in conjunction with the Spirit, validate it. Dispensationalists pit law against Spirit; Reformed theologians combine them."[23] If attitude is a "fundamental difference," one must ask how attitude can be measured. It is best measured by comparing our attitude toward the law with the plumb line of the NT authors as the standard of comparison. Perhaps I can make this point most clearly through a more personal narrative. Consider this approach an attempt at practicing a little theological self-awareness.

I started my theological studies with a strong preference for continuity. I had studied covenant theology and dispensationalism and chose the continuity of the former over the discontinuity of the latter due to the negative statements I read about the law in classic dispensationalism. My paedo-baptist background in a Dutch Reformed Church gave me an early *preference* for continuity. I had also read O. Palmer Robertson's *Christ of the Covenants*, and he persuaded me that covenants structure the Scriptures, not dispensations.[24] I later studied theology at a Baptist church, and I began to see that I had merely assumed paedo-baptism all my life. I studied both paedo-baptism and believer's baptism. It was a painful process, but in the end I became more persuaded that the case for believer's baptism had the most scriptural support.

This new conclusion forced me to reckon with my prior preference for continuity. I needed to be more aware of my proclivity toward continuity with respect to passages about the Mosaic law. In seminary this search led me to my dissertation, where I ran into difficulties in determining if my exegetical conclusions fit with any of the existing theological systems.[25] It felt like a Goldilocks dilemma: I was looking for not too hot, not too cold,

---

[23] Ibid.

[24] O. Palmer Robertson, *The Christ of the Covenants* (Phillipsburg, NJ: P&R, 1980), 190–99.

[25] Jason C. Meyer, *The End of the Law: Mosaic Covenant in Pauline Theology* (Nashville, TN: B&H Academic, 2009).

but just right. Some systems seemed overly negative (too cold) toward the law while others seemed overly positive (too hot) toward the law.

Too Cold

I had already found classic dispensationalism too cold with respect to the law. I did, however, discover an attitude toward the law that still felt lukewarm at times and cold as ice at other times in so-called new covenant theology. For example, this statement troubled me: "We simply must see that Law can only measure and punish outward acts of behavior. It cannot deal with the heart and inward motives."[26]

Simply put, the perspective advanced was that the old covenant law was a legal code and as such had to be *merely external* to legislate morality and convict lawbreakers. The author went further in stating that the problem with the Ten Commandments is that the "laws on the Tablets of Stone are *not high and spiritual enough* for a full-fledged son of God living under the New Covenant."[27] I take it to mean that "not spiritual enough" is another way of highlighting the mere externality of the law. Also stated was that "the Law of Moses could not deal with the heart or with motives simply because that is beyond the ability of a purely objective law."[28]

Two problems arise from these statements. First, Paul did not say that the problem with the law was that it was not spiritual enough. He says the opposite. "For we know that the law is spiritual, but I am made out of flesh, sold into sin's power" (Rom 7:14).[29] The problem was not the nature of the law but the nature of sinful humanity. Paul says the same thing later: the law "was limited by the flesh" (Rom 8:3). The law could not serve as the solution to our sin problem. Only God could decisively deal with sin through the sacrifice of Christ (Rom 8:3).

---

[26] John G. Reisinger, *But I Say unto You* (Southbridge, MA: Crowne, 1989), 20.

[27] Ibid., 21 (emphasis in original).

[28] Ibid., 19.

[29] All Scripture references in this chapter are from the HCSB unless noted otherwise.

Second, reading the Ten Commandments as merely external misses their *structure*. The first commandment (idolatry) and last commandment (covetousness) address profoundly internal issues. How can one limit covetousness to mere legislation? If the first and the last have an internal and spiritual dimension, then we should read all of them as "spiritual."

Others in the camp of new covenant theology may say things differently, but I have not read any open challenges to John Reisinger's claims on this specific point. Furthermore, one must also show caution in lumping all adherents of a system into a group and expect that there is unanimous agreement on every point.[30] My only point here is that I detected an attitude toward the law that did not equate with the attitude I found in Romans 7. We should robustly join Paul in affirming that the law is spiritual (Rom 7:14), holy, just, and good (Rom 7:12). The law should be a delight. The inner man can delight or "joyfully agree" in the law (Rom 7:22). Systems of theology that stress discontinuity have to reckon with those clear affirmations.[31]

Too Hot

I have seen the opposite problem in some of my reading of theologians within the Reformed tradition. They seemed zealous to almost equate the old covenant and the new covenant. The impulse is to affirm that the Mosaic covenant is the same in "essence and substance" with the new covenant.[32] When I sought out key passages as standards of comparison, they did not seem to allow that kind of equating. Two passages (2 Corinthians 3; Hebrews 8) stand out as important plumb lines.

The Glory of the New Covenant. In 2 Corinthians 3, Paul says two things about the old covenant and its ministry: (1) it was glorious, and (2) the greater glory of the new covenant has brought the old to an end. The glory

---

[30] The later work of Tom Wells and Fred Zaspel was more balanced in its approach. Wells and Zaspel, *New Covenant Theology.*

[31] Waltke agrees on this point. He says that dispensationalists "tacitly" acknowledge Rom 7:12 but give it "inadequate attention" in practice. See his "Theonomy in Relation to Dispensational and Covenant Theologies," 65.

[32] Jochem Douma, *The Ten Commandments: Manual for the Christian Life*, trans. Nelson D. Kloosterman (Phillipsburg, NJ: P&R, 1996), 5.

of the new eclipses and brings an end to the glory of the old. In terms of attitude, those committed to continuity are quick to affirm the glorious nature
of the Mosaic covenant but slower to stress the eclipse of the old covenant
because of the greater glory of the new covenant. Those who prefer discontinuity stress the superiority of the new covenant over the old covenant but
downplay the goodness and glory of the old covenant. The text will not allow
for a false dichotomy. The Mosaic covenant was a glorious covenant that
now has come to an end because of the greater glory of the new covenant.
Let us look at some of the details.

The word "glory" takes center stage in this passage, which is clear from
the fact that it shows up ten times in just five verses (v. 7 [2x], v. 8, v. 9 [2x],
v. 10 [3x], v. 11 [2x]). Paul ascribes glory to both the old covenant and the
new covenant, but he does not portray them as equally glorious because
he *compares and contrasts* them. The Mosaic law came with great glory,
but the glory of the new covenant outshines the glory of the law covenant.
Paul makes three comparisons between the old and the new: (1) logical,
(2) qualitative, and (3) temporal.

First, the logical comparison comes in 2 Corinthians 3:7–9. Paul's "if,
then" argument moves from the lesser to the greater. If the lesser is true,
then the greater is even more certainly true. The facts of the matter are
clear in the comparison: the ministry of the law brought death and condemnation; the ministry of the new covenant brings life and saving righteousness. Paul puts these facts into an inescapable conclusion: if the ministry
of the old covenant that led to many "not so glorious" effects (i.e., death)
came with glory, then it is even more certain that the new covenant is more
glorious because its ministry leads to more glorious effects.

Second, the qualitative comparison shows up in verse 10: "In fact, what
had been glorious is not glorious now by comparison because of the glory
that surpasses it." Covenantal glory has been recalibrated with the coming
of Christ. Paul Barnett nicely captures the nuance here in saying that the
glory of the new covenant "outglorified" and thus "deglorified" the glory of
the old covenant.[33] Scripture calls the sun and the moon the two great lights

---

[33] Paul Barnett, *The Second Epistle to the Corinthians*, NICNT (Grand Rapids:
Eerdmans, 1997), 187.

(Gen 1:16), but the moon is still classified as a "lesser light," and the sun is the "greater light" (Gen 1:16). In the same way, the glory of the old covenant is great and bright when considered on its own; nevertheless, when it is compared to the greater and brighter light of the new covenant, the old covenant pales *in comparison*.

Third, Paul makes his temporal point most clearly in 2 Corinthians 3:11; "For if what was fading away was glorious, what endures will be even more glorious." Verse 11 provides the foundation for verses 9–10. His point is not to denigrate the old but to provide a support for its eclipse: it has come to an end, and the new remains. The new has eclipsed the old because it remains while the old fades away. No future covenant will eclipse the new covenant.

These three comparisons show how difficult it is to maintain that the old and the new are equal in essence and substance. Some try to shield the old covenant from the force of Paul's contrasts by saying that what comes to an end is not the *existence* of the old covenant but its *effects*.[34] The clearest indicator that Paul is thinking of the existence of the old covenant is the parallelism of the contrast in verse 11. As argued above the term "endures" shows that Paul is making a point about the existence: the old ends, and the new endures. Paul is *not* comparing effects: the effects of the old covenant have come to an end while the effects of the new covenant endure.

Paul's other word choices must also be taken seriously. He uses the words "abound" (v. 9 NASB, NRSV) and "surpassing" (v. 10 NIV), which signify "amount of glory," not "certainty of glory." Paul's logic in verse 10 also requires a *comparison* of greater glory and lesser glory. Any attempt to say the covenants are equal in glory causes Paul's point in verse 10 to cease to make any sense.

---

[34] The debate hinges in part on whether one reads the Greek word καταργέω in the sense of "nullify" or "come to an end." Does the action relate to the *effects* or the *existence* of the old covenant? Scott J. Hafemann makes the best case for the "effects" interpretation in *Paul, Moses, and the History of Israel: The Letter/Spirit Contrast and the Argument from Scripture in 2 Corinthians 3*, WUNT 81 (Tübingen: Mohr Siebeck, 1995), 309. I appreciate Hafemann's view, but I find it unsatisfactory because it does not make the best sense of the context. For a detailed case against that reading, see Meyer, *The End of the* Law, 90–93.

The Superiority of the New Covenant. These same comparisons are prominent in Hebrews 8. I will present only a few pointers. There is no question that Hebrews presents the new covenant as a superior covenant. "But as it is, Christ has obtained a ministry that is as much more excellent than the old as the covenant he mediates is better, since it is enacted on better promises" (Heb 8:6 ESV). Hebrews does not shrink back from using terms like "superior" and "better" to describe the new covenant. If the new covenant is "superior," then what fault does the author find with the old covenant? Hebrews shows that the old covenant was not designed to change the heart. Indeed, the old covenant's lack of ability to change the heart points to the rationale for a new covenant. "For if that first covenant had been faultless, there would have been no occasion for a second one" (Heb 8:7). The fault is then identified with the people (Heb 8:8). The new covenant has the power to take out the heart of stone, unlike the old covenant. After quoting Jeremiah 31, the author of Hebrews then draws out the implication for the end of the old covenant. The Mosaic covenant is called "old," and that means it must give way to the "new." "By saying, *a new covenant*, He has declared that the first is old. And what is old and aging is about to disappear" (Heb 8:13, emphasis mine).

The above points are a challenge to covenant theology. One cannot, however, lump all covenant theologians into the same camp on this question. Some differ on how to understand the newness of the new covenant. It is refreshing to read covenant theologian Michael Horton admit that some within covenant theology have stressed continuity at the expense of the newness of the new covenant. He is just as right to point out that some covenant theologians have held to the qualitative newness of the new covenant.

> I'll grant that especially in anti-Anabaptist polemics, Calvin and his heirs have sometimes so stressed continuity within the one Abrahamic covenant of grace that the newness of the new covenant is insufficiently appreciated. Long ago, Voetius and Cocceius represented the wideness of the spectrum in covenant theology on that question, and more recent Reformed scholars (e.g., Vos, Ridderbos, Murray, Kline, Gaffin, et al.) have explored the qualitatively new blessings in the new covenant. So while I

definitely think this criticism keeps us on our toes, there's enough out there to qualify the charge that we see the Spirit's work as "basically the same across redemptive history."[35]

One other text that exemplifies the exegetical struggle that takes place when one has a preference for continuity or discontinuity is John 1:16. John speaks of two graces, and he connects them together with a preposition (ἀντί). Two issues must be settled when approaching these three words. First, how does one pinpoint the identity of the first grace and the second grace? Second, how do the two graces relate to each other?

First, verse 17 provides the key for defining the graces because the word "for" shows the tight connection between verses 16 and 17: "For the law was given through Moses, grace and truth came through Jesus Christ." The law given through Moses was a grace, and what has come through Jesus Christ is also a grace. There can be no false dichotomy. Both are graces.

Second, how do the two graces relate to each other? The preposition defines the relationship between them. Unfortunately the translations go different directions. The HCSB says "grace after grace." The ESV renders it "grace upon grace." The 1984 version of the NIV says "one blessing after another," but the latest revision has "grace in place of grace already given." I favor the latter translation and the case made by commentators like D. A. Carson.[36]

These three words are a good test case for a theological system. This text holds two things together that some systems want to make mutually exclusive: (1) the Mosaic law was a *grace*, and (2) the grace of the gospel of Jesus has *replaced* the grace of the law. Systems of continuity are quick to affirm that the law was a grace but are slower to embrace the idea of replacement. Systems of discontinuity quickly and loudly say amen to replacement but are slow to say a similar amen to the fact that the Mosaic law was a "grace."

---

[35] Michael Horton, "Kingdom Through Covenant: A Review by Michael Horton," The Gospel Coalition, accessed August 23, 2015, http://thegospelcoalition.org/article /kingdom-through-covenant-a-review-by-michael-horton.

[36] D. A. Carson, *The Gospel According to John*, PNTC (Grand Rapids: Eerdmans, 1991), 132.

Readers of Scripture should robustly say amen to both: the Mosaic law was a grace that has now been fulfilled and replaced.

Some may object to the most natural reading of the grammar for theological reasons. The term ἀντί really never means one thing stacked upon something else. Yet Reformed theologians like Herman Ridderbos reject the natural reading of substitution because "John's Gospel does not understand the relation of the old and the new, Moses and Christ in that way."[37] Ridderbos is one of my favorite authors, but his argument here is entirely unconvincing. One of the strongest arguments for the substitution reading of the text is the way John presents the relation between old and new. John 1:16–17 becomes programmatic for the rest of John's Gospel. As is well known, John shows that Jesus replaces the temple and the feasts of Passover, Unleavened Bread, and Booths.[38]

What shall we say in response to these texts? Minimally they keep us on our theological toes so the grace of the old covenant and the newness of the new covenant are *both sufficiently* stressed and appreciated. Let us now apply this attitude check to the way theological systems approach the law.

The Ditches of Continuity or Discontinuity

The New Testament writers stress both continuity and discontinuity between Christians and the Mosaic law. Therefore, any theological system that fails to stress the grace of the old covenant or the newness of the new covenant is in a theological ditch. I grew up driving on a country road in South Dakota that had two deep ditches on either side. It was imperative to stay out of both ditches. The road was narrow enough at times that if you started veering toward one ditch, it was easy to overcorrect and end up going into the opposite ditch.

---

[37] Herman N. Ridderbos, *The Gospel of John: A Theological Commentary* (Grand Rapids: Eerdmans, 1997), 56.

[38] See Frank Thielman, *The Law and the New Testament* (New York: Crossroad Publishing, 1999), 96–105.

Christians must avoid drifting into either of these theological ditches. Our dislike for one ditch may actually make it easier for us to drift into the other ditch. Listen to C. S. Lewis make this point about pairs of errors.

> I feel a strong desire to tell you—and I expect you feel a strong desire to tell me—which of these two errors is the worse. That is the devil getting at us. He always sends errors into the world in pairs—pairs of opposites. And he always encourages us to spend a lot of time thinking which is the worse. You see why, of course? He relies on your extra dislike of the one error to draw you gradually into the opposite one. But do not let us be fooled. We have to keep our eyes on the goal and go straight through between both errors.[39]

If we return to the original spectrum, we can change the labels to fit the ditch analogy.

Road of Continuity/Discontinuity					
Ditch of Continuity			**Ditch of Discontinuity**		
Theonomy	Covenant Theology	Progressive Covenantalism	Forms of Dispensationalism		
			Progressive	Revised	Classical

Scanning this spectrum quickly will show that I label two theological systems as ditches: theonomy and classic dispensationalism. I believe covenant theology, progressive covenantalism, and progressive dispensationalism are more viable systems of theology than the systems occupying the poles of the spectrum. Nevertheless, at times a preference for continuity or discontinuity may leave a theological system vulnerable to what Lewis warned against: an "extra dislike of the one" may gradually lead those who hold to one system to overcorrect and move too far in the opposite direction. Some biblical texts are like rumble strips that warn about the danger of getting too close to certain ditches.

---

[39] C. S. Lewis, *Mere Christianity* (New York: Simon & Schuster, 1996), 161.

Theonomy's overemphasis on continuity does not sufficiently stress the newness of the new covenant. Classic dispensationalism's overemphasis on discontinuity has left it open to the charge that grace is not stressed sufficiently.[40]

I agree with Douglas Moo's assessment that revised dispensationalism does not sufficiently stress continuity. In comparing his view to that of dispensationalist Wayne Strickland, Moo gives the following summary: "While I heartily endorse his stress on the basic discontinuity between the law of Moses and the New Testament Christian, I miss what I think are some necessary perspectives on the continuity between the two."[41] Moo says the two views are close, but it is like listening to a familiar symphony that is slightly off tune. He concludes that the difference in pitch is owing to dispensationalism's greater tilt toward discontinuity, which flows from the stress that the system puts on the separation between Israel and the church. Moo does not share this sharp wedge of separation:

> I think that God pursues one program throughout salvation history. The church today is the recipient not only of the blessings, but of the true fulfillment of both the Abrahamic covenant and of the Mosaic covenant. Consequently, while the law of Moses may no longer be a *direct and immediate* authority for the Christian, its teaching remains indirectly applicable to us through the "fulfillment" of that law in Christ and his law.[42]

Progressive covenantalism agrees with Moo in affirming that God has one program and purpose that unites all of salvation history rather than breaking up the Bible into different programs. Progressive covenantalism stands closer to covenant theology in terms of its emphasis on the organic unity of the Bible than classic dispensationalism. Progressive and revised dispensationalism have moved further from classic dispensationalism on

---

[40] See C. I. Scofield, *Rightly Dividing the Word of Truth* (Findlay, OH: Fundamental Truth, 1940), 5.

[41] Douglas Moo, "Response to Wayne G. Strickland," in *Five Views on Law and Gospel*, 315.

[42] Ibid. (emphasis in original).

this point, even though the distinctions between Israel and the church have not been eliminated altogether. I do not place progressive and revised forms of dispensationalism in a theological ditch because neither form teaches that law and grace are two separate ways of salvation.

My own views on the law align most closely with progressive covenanta-lism. In what remains I will reflect on my differences with covenant theology on the relationship of the Mosaic law to new covenant believers.

The Law of Moses and the Glory of Christ: Progressive Covenantalism and the Law

Numerous factors influence whether one adopts a progressive covenantalist approach or a covenant theology approach to the Mosaic law. I discuss four factors in question form in what follows. I also suggest that love for neighbor is the primary lens through which the Christian views the law of Moses. The love of Christ is the primary lens through which the Christian views the law of Christ.

Issues Separating Covenant Theology and Progressive Covenantalism

1. *Tripartite division: rightly dividing the law?* Covenant theologians view the law of Moses as directly binding on a believer because it uses the tripartite division of the law to distinguish aspects of the law that have ended and aspects of the law that remain in force. The Westminster Confession of Faith says the "moral law doth forever bind all to the obedience thereof."[43] Therefore, these theologians have a confessional commitment to the continuity of the Ten Commandments from the OT to the NT. They would argue that the moral law remains directly and eternally in effect because it reflects the character of God. The character of God does not change, and thus the moral law cannot change.

---

[43] WCF, 19.5.

I do not think the tripartite division of the law is the best starting point, though it has some attractive features. First, Jesus himself made a distinction within the law by identifying "weightier" and "lighter" matters in the law (Matt 23:23). Second, if God's moral commands are based on his character, then it makes sense that the moral commands would be unchanging because God's character is unchanging. Third, Paul clearly treats at least some of the Ten Commandments as authoritative, and thus they perhaps fit into the category of moral law.[44]

These attractive features are not, however, satisfactory arguments because they are offset by numerous difficulties. First, the NT does not explicitly establish a tripartite division and only speaks of the law as a totality or *singular entity* (see especially Gal 3:10–11). Thus, it is illegitimate to read these distinctions into the NT. Second, the law in its Mosaic form is so intricately connected that trying to isolate and untangle one thread within the law from the others is often a frustrating exercise in futility. It is difficult to determine what things are moral and what things are not moral. Third, even the Ten Commandments are not automatically binding because many see the Sabbath command as abrogated under the new covenant.[45] Fourth, this approach actually prevents the law from speaking to us in its entirety. Relegating something in the law as "civil" rather than "moral" can inadvertently cause us to turn a deaf ear to the wise guidance certain commands give us today.

Others in the Reformed stream acknowledge some of these same difficulties. Jerram Barrs at Covenant Theological Seminary acknowledges that the tripartite divisions "are not hard and fast."[46] He continues: "For example, many of the ceremonial laws include moral and civil aspects. Many of the civil laws include moral aspects. A problematic consequence of this view, if it is held with systematic rigor, is that the beauties of the ceremonial and

---

[44] Paul quotes the fifth command as prescriptive in Eph 6:2. He also refers to the sixth, seventh, eighth, and tenth commandments in Rom 13:9.

[45] See Thomas Schreiner's essay in this volume.

[46] Jerram Barrs, *Delighting in the Law of the Lord: God's Alternative to Legalism and Moralism* (Wheaton, IL: Crossway, 2013), 314.

civil aspects of the law become lost to us during this present age."[47] The NT writers were not blind to the beauty of the ceremonial and civil aspects of the law. For example, Paul sees ministerial beauty displayed in the details of priestly service in the temple (see 1 Cor 9:13–14).

2. *What does it mean to be no longer under the law?* The NT writers stress that believers are no longer under the law of Moses. Christians are "not under the law" (Gal 5:18; cf. Rom 6:14–15). They are "released from the law" (Rom 7:6). The law had a beginning and an end. It came into the world "430 years" after the promise to Abraham (Gal 3:17). The law had an end because it remained in force only "until the Seed to whom the promise was made would come" (Gal 3:19). In other words, the law was added 430 years after the promise, and it came to an end with the fulfillment of the promise—the coming of Christ (the promised Seed). Galatians 3–4 shows a shared structure of thought with regard to the temporary nature of the law:

3:19: When the "Seed" comes, the authority of the law comes to an end.

3:23–24: When the "faith" era comes, the authority of the guardian comes to an end.

4:1–4: When the time came to completion (the time set by the father), the authority of the guardians and managers came to an end.

Covenant theologians make a crucial distinction when they interpret these texts. They say the believer is no longer under the law of Moses in its *condemning* function, but the believer is under the law in its *guiding* function.[48] Richard Gaffin says the law in its *"specific codification"* at Sinai "has been terminated in its entirety by Christ in his coming," but the moral core of the Mosaic law "specifies imperatives that transcend the Mosaic economy."[49]

---

[47] Ibid.

[48] Herman N. Ridderbos, *Paul: An Outline of His Theology* (Grand Rapids: Eerdmans, 1975), 282–83.

[49] Richard B. Gaffin Jr., *By Faith, Not by Sight: Paul and the Order of Salvation*, 2nd ed. (Phillipsburg, NJ: P&R, 2013), 36 (emphasis in original).

Gaffin clarifies: "In its central commands, the law given at Sinai, notably the Decalogue, reveals God's will as that which is inherent in his person and therefore incumbent on his image-bearing creatures as such, regardless of time and place, whether Jew or non-Jew."[50]

The problem with this view is not what it affirms but what it denies. Release from the law surely means the believer is set free from the penalty of condemnation that the law brings to bear on us in terms of its capacity to curse and condemn. But it is incorrect to say Paul restricts his phrase "under the law" to its condemning function alone. Moo has what is perhaps the best response to this line of reasoning. The problem is that the contexts of these texts cannot be restricted to the *"penalty* of sin" through the law because Paul stresses freedom from the *"power* of sin" through the law.[51] Context is king in interpretation. I will attempt to show which view the context favors in what follows.

3. *How does a believer bear fruit for God in sanctification?* I believe a clear answer emerges as one studies the contexts of Galatians 5 and Romans 7. The context of Gal 5:18 ("But if you are led by the Spirit, you are not under the law") includes a discussion on the fruit of the Spirit (5:22–23) and the call to keep in step with the Spirit (5:25). The net result of this call is that the Christian will produce behavioral qualities that are acceptable in the sight of God. The Spirit-empowered fruit of Christian obedience will accord with any law code of conduct, not just the Mosaic law (Gal 5:23). Moo's conclusion is judicious: "It is difficult to avoid the conclusion, then, that life in the Spirit is put forward by Paul as the ground of Christian ethics, *in contrast to* life 'under law.'"[52]

Paul's approach to behavioral fruit bearing in Romans 7 is similar to Galatians 5. The believer bears fruit for God *only after* being released from the law. The law is powerless to produce fruit bearing for God; it can bear fruit only for death (Rom 7:5). Release from the law enables the believer to escape the oldness of letter and serve in the new way of the Spirit (Rom 7:6). Verse 6 bears witness to this shift with a clear redemptive-historical

---

[50] Ibid.

[51] Moo, "The Law of Moses or the Law of Christ," 211.

[52] Ibid., 215 (emphasis in original).

turning point: "But now." This new way of the Spirit produces fruit for God—something the old way of the letter could never do. "Ironically and paradoxically, those who live under the law bear fruit resulting in sinful passions, transgression of the law, and death, while those who have died to the law bear fruit that amounts to the law's fulfillment."[53] Paul emphasizes that Christians "fulfill" the law (Rom 8:4; 13:8, 10; Gal 5:14), while at the same time stressing that they are no longer "under the law" (Rom 6:14–15; Gal 5:18).[54]

The simple fact is that these contexts do not stress what covenant theology would want Paul to stress: the law's fruitfulness for sanctification. Thus, it seems illegitimate to introduce distinctions into the discussion that Paul did not make. He speaks of the law as a whole.

4. Mode matters: indirect or direct relation to the Mosaic law? The best way to summarize the evidence thus far is to say that the economy of the Mosaic law has come to an end *as a whole* and the Mosaic law *as a whole* continues to serve as a helpful, yet indirect guide. Paul relates to the law in terms of the entirety of its guiding wisdom, not as a direct and binding legal code. This approach is preferable because one can interact with the entirety of the Mosaic system rather than neatly trying to distinguish between moral, civil, and ceremonial.

I agree with Moo that the law of Moses is "indirectly applicable to us through the 'fulfillment' of that law in Christ and his law."[55] What does "indirect" mean? One must distinguish between the law of Moses as Scripture and the law of Moses as a law code. The law of Moses has direct authority as *Scripture* and indirect authority as *law*; therefore, the law has an *indirect application* to our lives today. In other words, the mode in which the law of Moses operates today makes all the difference in this discussion. Mode matters. Covenant theology makes the mode more direct for the Christian, while progressive covenantalism makes the mode less direct.

---

[53] Meyer, *The End of the Law*, 283.

[54] This dynamic is perhaps best spelled out by Stephen Westerholm, *Perspectives Old and New on Paul: The "Lutheran" Paul and His Critics* (Grand Rapids: Eerdmans, 2004), 431–39.

[55] Moo, "Response to Wayne G. Strickland," 315.

The new covenant Christian meets the Mosaic law in a distinctly different mode of existence from the old covenant Israelite. Under the old covenant the complete Mosaic law-covenant had direct authority as a complete legal code; however, it no longer functions in that way under the new covenant.[56] It is completely authoritative as revelation, but now we are directly dependent on Christ and his apostles for guidance in how to approach all past revelation (including the law of Moses).

Another contrast comes in the form God's commands take in the old covenant documents and the new covenant letters. The old covenant law code was detailed and specific. Numerous case studies prescribe specific ways of living and specific punishments if those ways are not followed. The NT takes a different approach. There are few detailed case studies on what to do and what the punishment should be if one transgresses a command. Paul certainly prescribes Christian behavior in his letters, but it is striking how little he prescribes behavior *with reference to the Mosaic law*. There are specific commands about divorce, immorality, greed, and many other topics; however, in discussions of the Mosaic law, Paul normally *describes* the "fruit" of Christian obedience with a retroactive reference to the way that it conforms to the law and thus amounts to its "fulfillment." This distinction should not be pressed too far so that it is overstated. One can find exceptions to this general rule. For example, Paul seems to prescribe direct obedience to Exodus 20:12 in Ephesians 6:1–3.[57] What is

---

[56] Brian Rosner rightly argues that we relate to the specific commandments in the law not as binding because they belong to the Mosaic system, but as wisdom for believers living in the new covenant age. Believers "do not read the law *as law-covenant*, but rather *as prophecy* and *as wisdom*" (emphasis in original). See his *Paul and the Law: Keeping the Commandments of God*, NSBT 31 (Downers Grove, IL: InterVarsity, 2013), 218. D. A. Carson distinguishes between the law as law-covenant and the law as prophecy (D. A. Carson, "Atonement in Romans 3:21–26," in *The Glory of the Atonement: Biblical, Historical and Practical Perspectives: Essays in Honor of Roger Nicole*, ed. Charles E. Hill and Frank A. James III [Downers Grove, IL: InterVarsity, 2004], 139.)

[57] Rosner does not see this text as an exception. He would deny the prescriptive nature of Paul's appeal. Rather, he thinks Paul appeals to the commandment of the Mosaic law "not as law (Eph. 6:1–2), but as advice concerning how to walk in wisdom (cf. Eph. 5:15)." *Paul and the Law*, 208. This distinction is difficult to maintain. I prefer to see it as an exception to Paul's general pattern.

striking is how little Paul takes this approach. It is the exception and not the general rule.

This point raises a related question. If the Mosaic law has continuing relevance as an *indirect* guide, then what is the primary lens through which a Christian should read it? Is there a consistent theme one should look for in the commands of the Mosaic economy that put the spotlight on its primary relevance today? The answer is love.

The Lens of Love: Love and the Law of Moses

The Mosaic law is part of God-breathed Scripture (2 Tim 3:16). No one should denigrate it or treat it as irrelevant. No one can read Psalm 119 without being confronted with the fact that the law is a delight for the redeemed. Therefore, the law of Moses is not just *relevant* for our lives; it is *refreshing* to our souls. It stirs up our hearts as a thing of delight to meditate upon day and night (Ps 1:2).

The Mosaic law remains perpetually relevant as an indirect guide, but this does not mean it is unimportant! The greatest guidance the law gives is in the area of love. The word *love* is too often a squishy, sentimental word that lacks specific moral content in our culture. The law of Moses fills up the word *love* with God-breathed content.

Paul demonstrably approached the OT law in this way. He quotes the love command of Leviticus 19:18 in both Romans 13:9 and Galatians 5:14. The varied commands in the Mosaic law give us a concrete expression of what love looked like in one specific cultural setting. We have to take the principle of love found in the command and apply it to our current cultural setting. Therefore, one can now ask, "How does this command guide us in love for neighbor?" The difference in cultural context between an OT Israelite and a NT Christian will often preclude a direct transfer.

My colleague, Jason DeRouchie, gives a great example about how the law speaks of love for neighbor. Moses commands the people to have a parapet or railing around their roof. "If you build a new house, make a railing around your roof, so that you don't bring bloodguilt on your house if someone falls from it" (Deut 22:8). It would be wrong to approach this law by asking what parts of it are moral, civil, or ceremonial. It serves as an indirect guide for us today in terms of how we love our neighbor. In those days the roof was flat, and it was a place where one would entertain guests. In Minnesota, where I live, there is no way we are going to host gatherings on my roof. Nevertheless, I have a deck where people come and sit with us. This text says that love for neighbor means I will care about their safety and will put a protective railing around my deck. We could extend it further. If a family brings over a small child that could fall down a flight of stairs, then I should put up a protective gate.

The Mosaic law also serves as a guide when it comes to the opposite of love. One can see the relevance of the Mosaic law when talking about breaking the covenant of marital love. Jesus addresses the issue of divorce in cases when "sexual immorality" is present (Matt 5:32). But what specific acts are included? The word for "sexual immorality" (*porneia*) is a general term that does not specify the types of acts in view. The Mosaic law gives the most helpful interpretive backdrop that can provide needed specificity. Therefore, the NT's silence on "bestiality" does not imply that it has suddenly become morally acceptable. This example shows that it does not work to say that whatever is not explicitly reaffirmed in the NT is no longer binding for believers.

I have surveyed some of the ways the Mosaic law serves as an indirect guide in the call to love one another. If the law of Moses is indirect, then how does the law of Christ function as our direct guide? The most direct guide for loving one another is the law of Christ, not the law of Moses, because the new standard for love is Christ's cross.

Escalation: The Law of Christ and the Glory of Christ

Here is the distinction I believe matters most: a progressive covenantalist approach stresses the escalation of progressive revelation with respect to the move from the Mosaic law to the law of Christ. In the progress of redemption, the "old" anticipates the new; but when the new comes on the scene, it replaces the old because the new both fulfills and eclipses the old.

How does the law of Christ eclipse the Mosaic law? The law of Christ is a progressive advancement over the Mosaic law in one important respect: the law of Christ more directly and explicitly ties the believer to Christ's cross. The law of Christ has a greater gospel shape than the law of Moses. The law of Moses was a grace from God and a law of love, but its standard of love falls short of the heights of love found in the sacrifice of Christ.

There is a direct connection between the law of Christ and the cross of Christ. The law of Christ is defined in Galatians 6:2: "Carry one another's burdens; in this way you will fulfill the law of Christ." Here Paul draws a direct line between the cross of Christ (Christ carried our sins on the cross) and the law of Christ that calls us to carry one another's burdens. Christ's law cannot be emptied of other commands from Christ and his apostles. But its emphasis on the love of Christ gives it a greater gospel shape than the Mosaic law because the cross is the new standard of love. I could point to other examples of this same dynamic, but two more will suffice: the love command and the idea of tithing today.

First, the new commandment is one of the best examples of how Christ recalibrates the whole law of Moses. Jesus refers to obedience to his own commandments as a measure of covenantal love. He does not appeal to the Mosaic law. "If you love Me, you will keep *My commands*" (John 14:15; emphasis added). One chapter earlier Jesus labels the love commandment as a "new" commandment, even though the command to love is not unheard of in the OT. This command is new in one specific sense in that it is tied to Jesus: "As I have loved you" (John 13:34). The new standard (i.e., "as I have loved you") soars to new heights far above the former standard (i.e., as you love yourself).

John expounds further on the uniqueness of this love in his letters. First John 3:23–24 urges believers to keep God's commandments. When John unpacks the meaning, he stresses a singular commandment in two parts: believe in the gospel and love one another. Why do these two things not form a plural instead of a singular commandment? The love of Christ and loving one another are so intertwined that John does not separate them. John's first letter offers a sterling example of how our love for others can no longer be separated from Christ's love for us. Christ's love is the new standard or definition of love. "This is how we have come to know love: He laid down His life for us. We should also lay down our lives for our brothers" (1 John 3:16–17).

The gospel shape of love in the new covenant connects the love of Christ and loving like Christ. The "new" commandment is only one example of this point. Let us now consider the love of Christ and tithing.

Second, despite popular ideas of stewardship today, no NT text commands believers to give 10 percent of their income to the church. The tithe commandment came from a paradigm relating to the twelve tribes of Israel. The Levites did not own land like the rest of the eleven tribes, and thus the tithe was an essential part of ensuring that they could continue to survive and minister. Nehemiah 13:10–12 highlights an example of how much the Levites depended on the tithe. The Christian lives under a new paradigm. Paul addresses financial themes frequently, but he never specifies an amount or percentage. He calls the Corinthians to set something aside to give "in keeping with how he prospers" (1 Cor 16:2). But Paul does not make reference here to a new paradigm. What is the standard of giving? The most sustained exposition of stewardship in the NT (2 Corinthians 8–9) says that the grace of Christ's sacrifice is the new point of reference.

The Macedonians went well beyond a tithe. They gave sacrificially ("beyond their ability" [2 Cor 8:3]) and willingly ("on their own" [2 Cor 8:3]) despite "deep poverty" and a "severe testing by affliction" (2 Cor 8:2). Paul declares that "grace" (2 Cor 8:1) came down and it produced "abundance of joy" in the Macedonians (2 Cor 8:2). God's grace comes first, and then joy springs up in the heart and overflows in "the wealth of their generosity" (2 Cor 8:2). Seven verses later comment further on this "grace." Sacrificial giving is grounded in the "grace" of Christ's sacrifice, which is spelled out in financial imagery. "For you know the grace of our Lord Jesus Christ: Though He was rich, for your sake He became poor, so that by His poverty you might become rich" (2 Cor 8:9). As noted earlier, Paul can look back at the priests as a reference point that supports why Christian ministers should get their living from the gospel (1 Cor 9:13–14). But that example does not become the central reference point or the paradigm for all giving. All giving is recalibrated around the new paradigm of Christ's sacrifice.

Conclusion: A Final Plea

I do not want to imply for a moment that this issue is easy. It is not. Jonathan Edwards agrees: "There is perhaps no part of divinity attended with so much intricacy, and wherein orthodox divines do so much differ as stating the precise agreement and differences between the two dispensations of Moses and Christ."[58] The difficult nature of the Mosaic law and the Christian requires that we listen intently to the text and to one another. I confess that I not only *want* to read books from these other theological perspectives, but I *need* to read them because they often stress an aspect or emphasis of the text that I am prone to gloss over too quickly. No system of thought is perfect. We all see through a glass dimly. No theological system will fully arrive before Jesus' return.

We must avoid the temptation to have fantasy arguments with others in which we always win. Usually these fantasies come to a climax when our "opponents" are compelled to change their minds in light of our superior arguments and inescapable reasoning. We must also avoid the temptation to ignore the best arguments and the best advocates of a view and set up straw arguments in their place. For example, we should avoid throwing around the word *antinomian* in a cavalier way. Saying believers are not under the Mosaic law is not sufficient evidence for the charge of antinomianism. Paul can flatly say that he is not "under the law," even though he can live as though he does for the evangelistic purpose of winning those under the law (1 Cor 9:20). What is most instructive is when Paul relates to Gentiles. He says he lives as one "without the law"; this does not mean he operates in a lawless sphere. Whether he acts as one with or without the law of Moses, he is never "without God's law but within Christ's law" (1 Cor 9:21).

The believer is emphatically not released from all manifestations of law. We are never without God's law but within Christ's law (1 Cor 9:21).

---

[58] Jonathan Edwards, "Inquiry Concerning Qualifications for Communion," in *The Works of President Edwards*, 8th ed. (New York: Leavitt & Allen, 1858), 1:160. Cited by Daniel P. Fuller, *Gospel and Law: Contrast or Continuum?* (Grand Rapids: Eerdmans, 1980), 5–6.

Ultimate continuity exists throughout the ages in terms of the Creator-creature distinction. The creature is always bound by the Creator's demands (continuity). There is discontinuity in terms of the *content* of those demands and what we should *call* the system of demands (Mosaic law or the law of Christ). This type of distinction is the only way to make sense of how Paul can distinguish the Mosaic law from the law of God/law of Christ in 1 Corinthians 9.

Bias cuts two ways: (1) others become victims of our bias, and (2) we become victims of our bias. Others become victims of our bias when we are harsh, critical, and mean-spirited toward those with whom we disagree. We become victims of our own bias by uncritically adopting what others in our own camp are saying just because they are in *our* camp. A preference for continuity or discontinuity can make us hair-trigger critics that are quick to throw theological stones at one another.

Perhaps we should be happy when we incur criticism that comes not just from one side or the other but from *both* sides. Martyn Lloyd-Jones believed two-sided criticism could be a sign of balanced thinking if you occupy the space between two polarities. One of the biggest temptations in theological debates is to so stress one side of the spectrum that other things are almost denied. In other words, something is stressed so strongly on one side that something else gets virtually excluded on the other side. For example, listen to what he says about the symmetrical union between doctrine on the one side and experience on the other.

> It seems to me that we have a right to be fairly happy about ourselves as long as we have criticism from both sides. . . . For myself, as long as I am charged by certain people with being nothing but a Pentecostalist and on the other hand charged by others with being an intellectual, a man who is always preaching doctrine, as long as the two criticisms come, I am very happy. But if one or the other of the two criticisms should ever cease, then,

I say, is the time to be careful and to begin to examine the very foundations.[59]

I can relate to these words at an experiential level. When I have said "positive" things about the law, I have sometimes been accused of being a covenant theologian. When I have said "negative" things about the law, I have been accused of being a dispensationalist. Sometimes I have quoted something from Psalm 119 about delighting in the law only to have someone else feel the need to qualify that "delight" to death. Sometimes I have quoted something from Paul about the end of the old covenant, and someone will hear it as a call to arms to defend the old covenant from some kind of inferiority complex.

My great desire in these discussions is that Scripture serves as our attitude check toward the Mosaic law. I also care deeply about the way we carry out these discussions. The bitter irony is that arguing over the commands of God can create conflict that causes us to break those commands (like the call to love one another; John 13:34). Overall agreement on these matters should not be a prerequisite to love one another. My *greatest* desire in these discussions is that the glory of Christ would shine most brightly. I believe the law of Christ more explicitly and directly ties the believer to the riches of Christ's love found in the cross of Christ.

---

[59] D. Martyn Lloyd-Jones, *The Love of God: Studies in 1 John* (Wheaton, IL: Crossway, 1993), 18.

CHAPTER 4

Covenantal Life with God from Eden to Holy City

ARDEL B. CANEDAY

Introduction: On Covenant Stipulations

Disagreement on whether God's covenants are conditional or unconditional is rooted in debates over the law-gospel contrast including the divine-human correlation variously expressed: promise-requirement, grace-command, divine favor-human response, and covenant provisions-covenant stipulations. Many object that God's covenant of promise to Abraham is fulfilled in Christ Jesus and is conditioned upon repentance, faith, love, and obedience. They represent the Abrahamic covenant and the gospel as *unconditional* but the Mosaic covenant as *conditional*. This essay challenges this as too stark and simplistic.

Peter Gentry and Stephen Wellum agree.[1] Yes, the law covenant entails numerous stipulations requiring obedience: "Do this, and live" or "If you obey, I will bless you." Yet they insist that "conditional" does not account for the Lord's gracious initiating act of redeeming Israel from slavery in Egypt as grounding the law covenant to bring about his promise of ultimate eschatological redemption in Jesus Christ (cf. Exod 19:4–6).[2] The law covenant

---

[1] Peter J. Gentry and Stephen J. Wellum, *Kingdom Through Covenant: A Biblical-Theological Understanding of the Covenants* (Wheaton, IL: Crossway, 2012), 608.
[2] Ibid., 638.

becomes obsolete and old because its purpose reaches fulfillment with the new covenant established by Christ's endless priesthood (Heb 8:7–13). For when the priesthood changes, the covenant must also change (7:11–12).

Gentry and Wellum affirm that the blending of God's sovereign promise making and covenant keeping with the conditional stipulations of obedience is integral to the biblical story line beginning in Eden and reaching consummation in the Holy City. This blending poses "a deliberate tension within the covenants" that intensifies as Scripture's story line with its "covenants progress toward their fulfillment in Christ."[3]

To identify the law covenant's distinguishing feature as *conditional* and to label other covenants *unconditional* introduces confusion as though God's other covenants do not entail conditions. Is fulfillment of a covenant jeopardized if it entails conditionally expressed stipulations? Did the law covenant fail to accomplish God's redemptive-historical purpose for it because Israel failed to observe all the Lord stipulated? Does not Scripture's unfolding mystery show that the Lord designed Israel's unfaithfulness to foreshadow typologically the faithfulness of Jesus Christ just as Adam's disobedience typologically anticipated the obedience of Christ?[4]

If we use *unconditional*, should it not refer to God's establishment of all his covenants with humans? Was not God's choosing of Abraham and of Isaac not Ishmael, and of Jacob not Esau, *unconditional* (cf. Rom 9:6–24)? As for *conditional*, the term refers to the *covenantal stipulations* placed upon humans with whom God enters covenant and which do not jeopardize fulfillment of any of God's covenants. God obligates humans to obey what he stipulates in his covenants, and all whom he desires to enable do obey. Adam was covenantally required to obey by caring for the garden and by eating fruit from every tree except one (Gen 2:15–16). God's covenant obligated Abraham and his seed to walk blamelessly with God while observing the covenant sign, circumcision (Gen 17:1–2, 14).

---

[3] Ibid., 609.

[4] See Ardel B. Caneday, "The Faithfulness of Jesus Christ as a Theme in Paul's Theology in Galatians," in *The Faith of Jesus Christ: Exegetical, Biblical, and Theological Studies*, ed. Michael F. Bird and Preston M. Sprinkle (Milton Keynes, UK: Paternoster; Peabody, MA: Hendrickson, 2009), 185–205.

Imperatival or conditional stipulations do not imperil fulfillment of God's covenants concerning either their jurisdiction over covenant members or their eschatological purposes. God's unfolding purpose administered through covenants that entail conditional stipulations is not jeopardized, thwarted, rendered meritorious, or based on human obedience.[5]

This chapter disavows the notion that all of Scripture consists of two isolatable messages: *law*, consisting of God's demands, and *gospel*, composed of God's gracious giving. Instead, it argues that the *formulation* of covenant stipulations remains the same across the covenants while the content of stipulations changes. The difference between old and new covenants is not that the former is conditional and the latter is not. Rather, because the old was purposefully temporary in anticipation of its fulfillment and completion in the new covenant, it stipulated obedience that featured earthly shadows of God's heavenly kingdom. The new covenant features Christ Jesus as the law's replacement, for he is the one who cast the shadows of the former covenant which, in all of its aspects, foreshadowed Messiah, the coming One. True, God unconditionally established his various covenants with humans, but each covenant entails provisions with stipulations that both promise blessings to all who obey (remaining in saving covenant relationship with God) and announce curses upon the disobedient.[6]

Revelation 22 illustrates this essay's thesis. "The Alpha and the Omega, the First and the Last, the Beginning and the End" announces, "I am coming soon!" (22:13, 12).[7] He forewarns, "My reward is with me, and I will give to each person according to what they have done" (22:12). His forewarning entails covenant blessing and curse embedded with provision and stipulations: *Blessing* to "the one who keeps the words of the prophecy written in this scroll" (22:7) and to "those who wash their robes, that they may have the right to the tree of life and may go through the gates into the city" (22:14). *Curse* of exclusion from both the tree and the city belong to the

---

[5] Cf. Gentry and Wellum, *Kingdom Through Covenant*, 609.

[6] Other OT covenants—the Noahic, Abrahamic, and Davidic—deserve attention, but space restricts our focus to the relationship between the old and new covenants.

[7] Unless otherwise indicated all Scripture citations are from the New International Version 2011.

evil, disobedient ones (22:15). Covenant *stipulations* indicate who receives the blessing of access to the tree and the holy city—only those who abide by the prophecy's words and also wash their robes. The covenant *provision*, which grounds the blessing and authorizes the stipulation, is less explicit but foundational, for mention of the washed robes alludes to freedom from sin's guilt by the sacrificial death of the Lamb (1:5; 7:14).[8] Only those who wash their robes in the blood of the Lamb, which makes them white and free from guilt, have access to the tree of life and the city (22:14; 7:14; and 1:5).[9]

The covenant provision expressed here as "washed robes" with its allusion to Christ's atoning sacrificial death, which is the legal ground of salvation expressed by Paul as the obedience of Christ (Rom 5:12–19), is not disputed. At issue are *covenant stipulations* that identify who receives access to the tree of life and to the holy city, the access Adam surrendered by disobedience. Using conventional covenantal stipulation formulation—"if . . . then"—the prophet warns everyone: "If anyone adds anything to them, God will add to that person the plagues described in this scroll. And if anyone takes words away from this scroll of prophecy, God will take away from that person any share in the tree of life and in the Holy City, which are described in this scroll" (Rev 22:18–19). Though some invert John's threat into a test of authentic faith, the warning is plainspoken grammatically.[10] It issues a future-oriented covenantal stipulation that warns against incurring eternal loss; John does not present a covenantal threat that states if someone augments or detracts from the prophecy, this one was never truly redeemed. That is not the function of this passage, which entails a warning.

---

[8] Take note of the variant in Rev 1:5: λούσαντι (washed) in the Byzantine text tradition but λύσαντι (liberated) in the critical text. Both 7:14 and 22:14 use πλύνω. That an early scribe, by using a synonym for πλύνω, attempted to bring 1:5 into conformity with 7:14 and 22:14 seems evident. Also see Bruce M. Metzger, *A Textual Commentary on the Greek New Testament*, 2nd ed. (Stuttgart: Deutsche Bibelgesellschaft, 1994), 662.

[9] The oxymoronic imagery of blood as the cleansing agent, a purposefully offensive concept, ought to have its proper arresting effect. Lamentably, the expression and concept have become much too formulaic and pedestrian.

[10] On inverting warnings, see Thomas R. Schreiner and Ardel B. Caneday, *The Race Set Before Us: A Biblical Theology of Perseverance and Assurance* (Downers Grove, IL: InterVarsity, 2001), 150–57.

John expressly directs his threat to believers who have "washed robes," lest we perish.

Inheriting God's promises is always conditional, for he grants his covenant blessings to those who, by his own grace, observe stipulations that require persevering, obedient belief. From Adam's habitation of the Edenic garden with access to the tree of life to inheritance of our eternal habitation, God's holy city, with free access to the tree of life, covenantal life with God always entails stipulations expressed as commands or conditionals. The Lord commanded Adam, "You are free to eat from any tree in the garden; but you must not eat from the tree of the knowledge of good and evil, for when you eat from it you will certainly die" (Gen 2:16–17). Likewise, the Lord's prophet mirrors this warning in Revelation 22:18–19.

The Law and the Gospel: An Exaggerated Contrast

Many classical dispensationalists and covenant theologians agree that the Mosaic law was a covenant of works that demanded perfect obedience resulting in eternal life. Many from both systems tend to filter NT exhortations, admonitions, and threats through their respective hermeneutical grids lest obedience be assigned a role in our salvation. Consequently, they interpret exhortations and warnings that issue in either salvation or condemnation as retrospective tests of faith's genuineness. Their respective hermeneutical templates come to the same conclusion. They invert covenant stipulations so that "the one who perseveres to the end will be saved" becomes "the one who is saved will persevere to the end."[11] This reading of NT admonitions and threats is not unlike the Lutheran law-gospel hermeneutic.

Louis Berkhof observes that, like the Lutheran view, some early "Reformed theologians represented the law and the gospel as absolute opposites." They conceived of the "law as embodying all the demands and commandments of Scripture, and of the gospel, as containing no demands whatsoever, but only *unconditional* promises; and thus excluded from it all

---

[11] See the discussion in ibid., 150–54.

requirements."[12] Against this stark contrast others "correctly maintained that even the law of Moses is not devoid of promises, and that the gospel also contains certain demands. They clearly saw that man is not merely passive, when he is introduced into the covenant of grace, but is called upon to accept the covenant actively with all its privileges, though it is God who works in him the ability to meet the requirements."[13]

Recently, Mark Jones has offered a historical overview of the debate among Reformed theologians concerning those who define the gospel narrowly, as virtually synonymous with justification, so as to exclude from it commands, admonitions, exhortations, and warnings.[14] He states, "Often, any 'threatening' is understood as a 'law threatening,' and so the 'gospel' is held out to believers as a means of escaping such a threatening."[15] His concern is that both Scripture and historic confessions, such as the Canons of Dort, testify that the gospel threatens believers with eternal perdition for their good "in order that they may persevere to the end in renewed obedience to the one who is both lawgiver and rewarder."[16]

Prominent within this in-house Reformed dispute is the question whether the Mosaic law is a "republication" of the Adamic covenant of works. This bears heavily upon the place and role of NT admonitions and warnings. Disagreement concerning these warnings entails divergent views within Reformed churches. On the one hand, Federal Vision advocates regard NT warnings as addressed to covenant members, some of whom will actually apostatize and perish.[17] Antithetical to this view is the so-called Escondido Theology, which features a deep divide "between law and gospel,"

---

[12] Louis Berkhof, *Systematic Theology* (Grand Rapids: Eerdmans, 1939), 612.

[13] Ibid., 613.

[14] Mark Jones, *Antinomianism: Reformed Theology's Unwelcome Guest?* (Phillipsburg, NJ: P&R, 2013), 45–47.

[15] Ibid., 50.

[16] Ibid. Jones features Canons of Dort 5.14, "Of the Perseverance of the Saints."

[17] See E. Calvin Beisner, ed., *The Auburn Avenue Theology, Pros and Cons: Debating the Federal Vision* (Fort Lauderdale, FL: Knox Theological Seminary, 2004). Cf. Thomas R. Schreiner, *Run to Win the Prize: Perseverance in the New Testament* (Wheaton, IL: Crossway, 2010), 90–92, who distinguishes between the Federal Vision and Arminian views on apostasy.

a view "more characteristic of Lutheran than of Reformed theologians."[18] For example, Michael Horton affirms:

> Thus, the Law condemns and drives us to Christ, so that the Gospel can comfort without any threats or exhortations that might lead us to doubt. . . . The Gospel acts without threats, it does not drive one on by precepts, but rather teaches us about the supreme goodwill of God towards us. . . . While the Gospel contains no commands or threats, the Law indeed does and the Christian is still obligated to both "words" he hears from the mouth of God.[19]

Believing that threats of eternal perishing and exhortations to obedience and works incite doubt, some relegate all of these to the law. So Tullian Tchividjian claims, "The Gospel contains no threats at all, but only words of consolation. Wherever in Scripture you come across a threat, you may be assured that the passage belongs in the Law."[20] Does such a construal accurately account for stipulations that punctuate God's covenants within Scripture, including the new covenant?

From the beginning Scripture is replete with covenant language even where the Hebrew or Greek words for covenant (בְּרִית or διαθήκη) are not present within contexts of either the OT or NT. Thus, just as the concept of covenant is evident within Revelation 22, though διαθήκη is not in the context, so we have warrant to consider the Creator's relationship with Adam as covenantal in nature. For, though בְּרִית is not used in Genesis 1–3, it is right to infer a covenant framework for understanding the obligations God places on Adam and Eve. This inference is confirmed by the obligations

---

[18] John Frame, *The Escondido Theology: A Reformed Response to Two Kingdom Theology* (Lakeland, FL: Whitefield Media Productions, 2011), 2.

[19] See Michael Horton, "The Law and the Gospel" (http://whitehorseinn.gor/free-articles/thelaw-the-gospel-by-michael-horton.html). Cf. Charles P. Arand and Michael Horton, "Does the Covenant of Works/Covenant of Grace Schema Confuse the Law/Gospel Distinction?: A Lutheran/Reformed Conversation—The Reformed View," *Modern Reformation* 9, no. 4 (July/August 2000): 24–27.

[20] See Tullian Tchividjian, "Law and Gospel: Part 3" (http://liberate.org/2012/06/29/law-and-gospel-part-3-tullian-tchividjian). See also idem, *One Way Love: Inexhaustible Grace for an Exhausted World* (Colorado Springs: David C. Cook, 2013).

and conditions for obedience with sanctions for disobedience disclosed in Genesis 2:16–17.[21] The text stipulates: "And the LORD God commanded the man, 'You are free to eat from any tree in the garden; but you must not eat from the tree of the knowledge of good and evil, for when you eat from it you will certainly die.'" The force of two infinitive absolutes emphasizes the fullness of divinely authorized permission to eat from God's abundant provision of food but also the terror of transgressing this permission.

So God's covenant stipulation consists of a probationary test that features a divine command to eat fruit from all but one tree, which was not evil in itself (1:31). Nothing inherent within the tree stipulated God's prohibition, because Genesis presents the woman's assessment that the tree's fruit was good for food, appealing, and desirable for acquiring wisdom without dispute (3:3). Only God's prohibition and threat for disobedience forbade eating the fruit of one tree and established Adam's probationary covenantal test. Sustenance and appetite could be satiated with fruit from the abundance of trees in the garden except one. Adam was to learn that he would not live by food alone but by every word that comes from the Lord's mouth (cf. Deut 8:3; Matt 4:1–4).[22] God's word, entailing promise and threat, required Adam to believe, to trust the Lord, in order that he might obey God and receive his covenant blessing with full and unrestricted access to the trees of life and of knowledge of good and evil.[23]

Thus, we properly acknowledge that God's covenant with Adam during his probationary period entails his primal duty to retain dominion over himself lest sin intrude with death in tow. In other words, the Creator situated Adam in paradise and endowed him to reign, but first he must possess dominion over his own passions by obeying God's covenant stipulation. God's warning commandment, however, became a provocation to covet wisdom, signified by the tree of the knowledge of good and evil. Thus, Adam abdicated his Creator-endowed reign over both sin's allurement and

---

[21] Cf. Gentry and Wellum, *Kingdom Through Covenant*, 613.

[22] Cf. O. Palmer Robertson, *The Christ of the Covenants* (Phillipsburg, NJ: P&R, 1980), 83–85.

[23] Cf. William N. Wilder, "Illumination and Investiture: The Royal Significance of the Tree of Wisdom in Genesis 3," *WTJ* 68 (2006): 56.

his passions, invoking the covenant curse, death for himself and his descendants (cf. Rom 5:12–19; 7:7–13).[24] By his disobedience he forfeited access to the tree of life and relinquished dominion over creation itself, which became subjected to the Creator's curse (Gen 3:17–19; Rom 8:19–22). Redemption from this curse for both Adam's descendants and creation comes in the last Adam alone.

Much about the Adamic covenant is under debate, including its nomenclature and its nature. Within Reformed theology, "covenant of works" tends to dominate. Some, such as O. Palmer Robertson and John Murray, avoid the notion of works lest it exclude grace by opting for "covenant of creation."[25] Whether the covenant entails merit sustains debate within confessional Reformed groups. Yet, as indicated above, more intensive is the persistent intramural debate within Presbyterian and Reformed churches, which focuses on whether the Mosaic law is a "republication" of the covenant of works.[26] Though some from both sides of this dispute view the Adamic covenant as a covenant of works, the dispute focuses on whether the Sinai covenant repeats or republishes the Adamic covenant construing it as a covenant of works.[27] In this tortuous intramural debate, challengers of republication accuse defenders of lacking precision and exhibiting inconsistency throughout their argument.[28]

---

[24] See A. B. Caneday, "Already Reigning in Life Through One Man: Recovery of Adam's Abandoned Dominion (Romans 5:12–21)," in *Studies in Paul's Letters: A Festschrift for Douglas J. Moo*, ed. Jay E. Smith and Matthew Harmon (Grand Rapids: Zondervan, 2014), 27–43.

[25] See, e.g., Robertson, *The Christ of the Covenants*, 55–56. Cf. John Murray, "The Adamic Administration," in *Collected Writings of John Murray*, 4 vols. (Carlisle, PA: Banner of Truth Trust, 1977), 2:47–59.

[26] See, Bryan D. Estelle, J. V. Fesko, and David VanDrunen, eds., *The Law Is Not of Faith: Essays on Works and Grace in the Mosaic Covenant* (Phillipsburg, NJ: P&R, 2009). See also, James T. Dennison Jr., Scott F. Sanborn, and Benjamin W. Swinburnson, "Merit or 'Entitlement' in Reformed Covenant Theology: A Review," *Kerux* 24 (2009): 3–152.

[27] See Murray, "The Adamic Administration," 50. Dennison et al. defend Murray's position concerning the Mosaic covenant while Estelle et al. reject Murray's construal.

[28] See Dennison et al., "A Review," 30.

Contrary to the republication debate, much about Murray's and Robertson's presentations is commendable concerning the nature of the "covenant of creation" as gracious and not entailing merit. Though the garden covenant is not insignificant to this chapter, the nature of the law covenant and its correlation with the new are crucial. Without becoming embroiled in the intra-Reformed debate, my concern is to argue, contrary to some in the Reformed tradition, that the Mosaic covenant is not to be construed as entailing merit in any sense.

Continuity between the Law Covenant and the New Covenant

Scripture constrains acknowledgment of a contrast between the new covenant and the old, one that is redemptive-historical in nature, entailing foreshadow and fulfillment, mystery and disclosure. Yet lacking is the severe "law-gospel" contrast that is a hallmark of Lutheranism as an interpretive principle for reading the Scriptures. Instead, from Scripture's testimony concerning the nature of the old covenant in relation to the new, four converging lines of evidence emerge: (1) conditional covenant formulations; (2) full obedience required by the law covenant; (3) repeated expressions of God's grace—election and covenant faithfulness; and (4) divinely designed ineffectuality—accounting for the NT's view of the law. These lines of evidence continue to persuade that however we are to characterize the law covenant, Scripture compels us to acknowledge that it entails grace. The apostle John indicates in his Gospel's prologue: "Out of his fullness we have all received grace in place of grace already given. For the law was given through Moses; grace and truth came through Jesus Christ" (John 1:16–17).

Conditional Covenant Formulations

Four features of the new covenant constitute its "newness," for every member of the covenant: (1) knows the Lord, (2) is a recipient of forgiveness of sins, (3) belongs to the people of God, and (4) has God's laws engraved upon their hearts (Jer 31:29–34; Heb 8:8–12). How one construes these properties of the new covenant in distinction from the old, as provided by the OT prophet and the NT preacher, diverges within Christian traditions. For the believers' church tradition, the newness implies some dimension of *discontinuity* between the two covenants. Nevertheless, unity in the posited "covenant of grace" leads advocates of covenant theology to affirm *continuity* of the two covenants.

Both traditions divide even further. The believers' church tradition includes dispensationalists (both classical and progressive) but also others appreciative of and owing much to Reformed theology with elements of continuity, who accent discontinuity as to their views on Israel and the church. Some adopt the self-designation "new covenant theology" (NCT).[29] Others distinguish their view from NCT with the proposed designation "progressive covenantalism."[30] How we construe the new covenant's structure and nature in correlation with earlier biblical covenants is paramount.[31]

Covenant Stipulations, Old and New

Concerning their content, new covenant stipulations of repentance, faith, obedience, or doing good are distinctively different from old covenant stipulations. The new, with the law engraved upon the heart, stipulates obeying Christ Jesus as Lord; the old, etched in stone tablets, stipulates obeying God's covenant commandments that feature a panoply of heavenly shadows and copies. Though the content of stipulations differs, their form does not, for both new and old covenants employ variously formatted stipulations including imperatives and conditionals: "If you obey, then I will bless you" or "Do this, and you will live." Thus, to claim that the stipulations of the new covenant are different formulations structurally—"Do because you are blessed" versus "Do this in order to be blessed"—is not

---

[29] See, for example, Tom Wells and Fred Zaspel, *New Covenant Theology: Description, Definition, Defense* (Frederick, MD: New Covenant Media, 2002) and Steve Lehrer, *New Covenant Theology: Questions Answered* (by the author, 2006).

[30] Cf. Gentry and Wellum, *Kingdom Through Covenant*, and this volume.

[31] Cf. Gentry and Wellum, *Kingdom Through Covenant*, 64–65.

accurate and does not address the new covenant's true superiority over the old (Heb 8:8–12).

Four factors are noteworthy concerning the argument in Hebrews that the old covenant with its stipulations and ordinances was passing away (8:13). First, each of the preacher's five urgent warnings employs the same covenantal stipulation form or structure found throughout the old covenant. Where receiving God's salvation or wrath is at issue, new covenant stipulations have binding force that promises either covenant blessings or curses formulated like stipulations of the old covenant. Second, the reasoning is often *a fortiori*. If failure to heed the law covenant was severe, how much more severe will be punishment for disobeying the gospel announced by the Lord Jesus (cf. Heb 2:2–4). Third, the sermon builds with new covenant stipulations crescendoing with greater urgency as five passages warn lest (1) we *neglect* so great a salvation (2:1–4), (2) we *harden* our hearts (3:5–4:13), (3) we *fall away* (6:4–12), (4) we *sin willfully* (10:26–31), and (5) we *refuse to hear* (12:14–29). Fourth, Hebrews emphatically presents the gospel as threatening us with perdition unless we persevere in loyalty to Christ.

The two most forceful warnings make this obvious.[32] Consider the fourth warning:

---

[32] In their extensive critical review of *Kingdom Through Covenant*, Jonathan M. Brack and Jared S. Oliphint claim that Gentry and Wellum abandon any concept of a visible church, a "mixed" body within the church of the New Testament. They contend that Gentry and Wellum "have to reckon with the many NT apostasy passages," but they "do not provide a detailed analysis of NT apostasy texts" (210–11). Gentry and Wellum do address the so-called apostasy passages, but their multiple-point explanation of these texts does not satisfy Brack and Oliphint, who treat passages such as those in Hebrews as if they were indicative descriptions of apostates, passages explained by virtue of a "mixed" church. A point that seems to be missed by Brack and Oliphint is that Gentry and Wellum understand these passages to be *warnings lest believers apostatize and perish*. While they acknowledge that "the 'mixed' community interpretation of these texts is a *possible* reading," even as many other nonpaedo-baptists understand them, Gentry and Wellum are persuaded of a better way to understand the passages as *urgent threats against apostasy*, which "does better justice to *all* of the scriptural data." For their understanding of the warnings of Hebrews and of passages like these, they direct readers to *The Race Set Before Us* by Schreiner and Caneday, a point not addressed by the reviewers. See Brack and Oliphint, "Questioning the Progress in Progressive

If we deliberately keep on sinning after we have received the knowledge of the truth, no sacrifice for sins is left, but only a fearful expectation of judgment and of raging fire that will consume the enemies of God. Anyone who rejected the law of Moses died without mercy on the testimony of two or three witnesses. How much more severely do you think someone deserves to be punished who has trampled the Son of God underfoot, who has treated as an unholy thing the blood of the covenant that sanctified them, and who has insulted the Spirit of grace? For we know him who said, "It is mine to avenge; I will repay," and again, "The Lord will judge his people." It is a dreadful thing to fall into the hands of the living God (10:26–31).

This urgent warning does not present the tepid notion that this passage's purpose is to define apostasy or to notify Christians that "apostasy happens" in the church, a "mixed" body of believers and unbelievers.[33] Indeed, apostasy from Christ occurs in the confessing church, but conveyance of this information is hardly the function of warnings. The passage warns us lest we apostatize from Christ. The passage is not introspective but Christ centered, focused on Christ Jesus, the prize to be won (cf. Heb 12:1–3). Warnings do not call for retrospective review of faith's authenticity but for prospective laying hold of the inheritance of salvation in Christ. They warn lest we follow a course that irrevocably leads to perdition. They urgently juxtapose salvation as the assured blessing for heeding the gospel's warning antithetically to perdition as the unalterable curse for ignoring the gospel's threat.

The climactic warning in Hebrews is an emphatic argument from the lesser to the greater that appeals to an envisioning of Mount Sinai with fear-inducing displays of God's presence, so terrifying that even Moses declared,

---

Covenantalism: A Review of Gentry and Wellum's *Kingdom Through Covenant*," *WTJ* 76 (2014): 189–217.

[33] As they argue their case against Gentry and Wellum, Brack and Oliphint appeal to Heb 10:26–29 but treat it as if it were a retrospective test that exposes apostates rather than receive it as it is, a future-oriented warning lest believers apostatize (Brack and Oliphint, "Questioning the Progress in Progressive Covenantalism," 214).

"I am trembling with fear" (12:21). In his fifth warning, against the disclosure of God's awesomeness, the preacher says,

> You have come to God, the Judge of all, to the spirits of the
> righteous made perfect, to Jesus the mediator of a new covenant,
> and to the sprinkled blood that speaks a better word than the
> blood of Abel. See to it that you do not refuse him who speaks.
> If they did not escape when they refused him who warned them
> on earth, how much less will we, if we turn away from him who
> warns us from heaven? (12:23–25).

The five ascendingly urgent warnings neither call believers to doubt their "confession of hope" nor to question whether "he who has promised is faithful" to secure us unto salvation in the day that is approaching. The preacher commingles appeals for bold confidence and intense threats, doing so without any hint of contradiction, for both serve the same objective, our loyalty to Christ. He simultaneously proclaims assured confidence in God's steadfast covenant promise and the urgent imperative to persevere in faithfulness to Christ.[34] For this messianic era God's appointed means of preserving believers in faithfulness to Christ entails preaching the gospel that fuses together forceful warnings, lest believers perish by deliberately refusing to heed Jesus Christ, and assurances of God's steadfast promise of salvation to everyone who believes in his Son (cf. 6:4–20; 10:19–39). The preacher more succinctly juxtaposes these two aspects when he proclaims, "Therefore, do not throw away your confidence, which possesses a great reward. For you have a need of perseverance, in order that when you have done the will of God, you may receive what was promised" (10:35–36, my translation).[35]

Despite classic Reformed theology's affirmation that the warnings provide believers the means to persevere unto final salvation, some Reformed

---

[34] Numerous witnesses from the Reformed tradition testify to this commingling of threat and assurance without mutual destruction. For example, see William Cunningham, *Historical Theology: A Review of the Principal Doctrinal Discussions in the Christian Church Since the Apostolic Age*, vol. 2 (London: Billing & Sons, 1862; repr., London: Banner of Truth, 1969), 500–501.

[35] Schreiner and Caneday, *The Race Set Before Us*, 192–204.

theologians find this objectionable. For example, concerning the admonition, "Make every effort to live in peace with everyone and to be holy; without holiness no one will see the Lord" (Heb 12:14), R. Scott Clark reasons that "if we express this truth as a condition that the believer who is united to Christ, *sola gratia, sola fide* must meet then how much holiness is enough?"[36] Because he believes stipulations would jeopardize the covenant and introduce works righteousness, Clark argues that the

> solution for this problem is to recognize the difference between "if . . . then" and "do . . . because." The medieval and Romanist schemes set up deadly conditionals: obey in order to gain (or keep) favor. The Protestants set up grace-wrought consequences. We Protestants seek to obey, in the grace of Christ, in union with Christ, *because* we've been redeemed and because we've been given new life.[37]

Clark's solution excludes from consideration the classic Reformed understanding of gospel warnings as vital to God's appointed means by which he preserves his own. Clark supposes that covenant stipulations—"if . . . then" or "do . . . in order to"—necessarily entail accruements of merits (Romanist) and put believers in jeopardy of perishing (Arminian).

Thus, concerning NT passages that entail threats, Clark concludes, "The key to unlocking the warning passages is the distinction between the covenants of works and grace. This is not a formula for making the passages go away. It is the biblical way of reading these passages in context and applying them fruitfully toward conformity to Christ."[38] He distinguishes between what he calls "antecedent conditions" (if . . . then), which reflect the "covenant of works," which he says "Christ kept by his active obedience," and "consequent conditions" (do . . . because), which are of the "covenant of grace," which he claims "are consequent to faith." Accordingly, new covenant warnings entail "evangelical obedience," which is a "consequent

---

[36] R. Scott Clark, "How Should We View the Warning Passages?" (http://rscottclark.org/2013/10/how-should-we view-the-warning-passages).
[37] Ibid.
[38] Ibid.

condition of the covenant of grace—not something we must perform; rather it is a condition met in us, not by us, but by the Holy Spirit."[39]

Against Clark but in accord with Bavinck, Berkhof, Cunningham, and many others in the classical Reformed tradition, including the Canons of Dort, the NT frequently administers gospel warnings expressed by conditionals with real and inviolable consequences.[40] These warnings neither imperil believers nor subject them to meriting God's favor. Rather, they are an *effective means* to preserve Christ's own. The preacher's culminating threat directs believers to contemplate the dread Moses felt on the mountain in the Lord's presence and to ponder how much more dreadful it is to come to Mount Zion, the city of the living God, the heavenly Jerusalem (Heb 12:25).

How does the language structure of new covenant stipulations differ from old covenant stipulations? It is manifest that what is stipulated has changed because we reside under the new covenant, not the old. Nevertheless, the language structure or form suited for stipulations that promise blessings or threaten curses has not changed.

Grammatically, how the old and new covenants express stipulations as well as blessings or curses does not differ. Consider Leviticus 18:5: "Keep my decrees and laws [covenant stipulation], for the person who obeys them will live by them [covenant blessing]. I am the LORD." Now ponder Paul's stipulation to Timothy: "Watch your life and doctrine closely [covenant stipulation]. Persevere in them, because if you do [covenant stipulation], you will save both yourself and your hearers [covenant blessing]" (1 Tim 4:16).

Again, consider how Paul formulates his covenantal appeals in Romans 8:11–17.

> And if the Spirit of him who raised Jesus from the dead is living in you, he who raised Christ from the dead will also give life to your

---

[39] R. Scott Clark, "Heidelcast: Conditions and the Covenant of Grace (Part 2)," accessed August 24, 2015, http://rscottclark.org/wp-content/audio/heidelcast-47-nov-3-2013.mp3.

[40] Concerning Heb 2:1; 3:14; 6:11; etc., Berkhof states, "They do not prove that any of those addressed will apostatize, but simply that the use of means is necessary to prevent them from committing this sin. Cf. Acts 27:22–25 with verse 31 for an illustration of this principle" (*Systematic Theology*, 548).

mortal bodies because of his Spirit who lives in you [covenant provision].

Therefore, brothers and sisters, we have an obligation—but it is not to the flesh, to live according to it [covenant stipulation]. For if you live according to the flesh [covenant stipulation], you will die [covenant curse]; but if by the Spirit you put to death the misdeeds of the body [covenant stipulation], you will live [covenant blessing].

For those who are led by the Spirit of God are the children of God. The Spirit you received does not make you slaves, so that you live in fear again; rather, the Spirit you received brought about your adoption to sonship [covenant provision]. And by him we cry, "*Abba*, Father." The Spirit himself testifies with our spirit that we are God's children [covenant provision]. Now if we are children, then we are heirs—heirs of God and co-heirs with Christ [covenant blessing], if indeed we share in his sufferings [covenant stipulation] in order that we may also share in his glory [covenant blessing].[41]

The difference between the old and new covenants is not how the stipulations are grammatically structured or formed or that the former stipulates obedience and the new does not. Nor is the difference that the law covenant threatens divine curses and promises divine blessing with conditional stipulations but that the grace covenant in Christ issues no stipulations. Clearly the New Testament is filled with gospel threats and promises addressed to believers, which if heeded inviolably lead to eternal life but if ignored will end in condemnation.

Full Obedience Required by the Law Covenant

The first reference to the law covenant made at Sinai is framed by divine mercy, namely, redemption from slavery in Egypt, and formulated in terms

---

[41] Cf. Scott J. Hafemann, *The God of Promise and the Life of Faith: Understanding the Heart of the Bible* (Wheaton, IL: Crossway, 2001), 123.

of obedience to God's commandments and of keeping the covenant. The Lord instructs Moses to tell the people of Israel,

> "You yourselves have seen what I did to Egypt, and how I carried you on eagles' wings and brought you to myself [covenant provision]. Now if you obey me fully and keep my covenant [covenant stipulation], then out of all nations you will be my treasured possession [covenant blessing]. Although the whole earth is mine, you will be for me a kingdom of priests and a holy nation [covenant blessing]." These are the words you are to speak to the Israelites. (Exod 19:4–6)

The Israelites respond, "We will do everything the LORD has said" (Exod 19:8). From this some have argued that these are not the terms of a gracious covenant through which the Lord designed to deal graciously with his people. Rather, it is often claimed, the covenant stipulations entail merit, a covenant of works, not grace. Historically such a reading of the Mosaic covenant has been apparent within both covenant theology and classical dispensationalism, though not all in either viewpoint share this conclusion. For example, Geerhardus Vos contends that inheritance of life promised to all who observe the law is "no less emphatically" grounded in "grace alone" than is the salvation promised in the new covenant and that any notion of a meritorious connection between the two skews the relationship.[42]

Does the old covenant demand "perfect obedience" because it calls for "full obedience"?[43] Again, Vos argues that God's favor toward Israel was not suspended upon perfect obedience but rather,

---

[42] Geerhardus Vos, *Biblical Theology: Old and New Testaments* (Grand Rapids: Eerdmans, 1948), 127.

[43] The point of the question is not to suggest that God as Creator and Lord of the covenant does not demand perfect obedience since failure to render perfect obedience to him incurs his wrath and invokes death and condemnation. Rather, because from the beginning God purposed to provide his righteous Son as the perfectly obedient one as an atoning sacrifice, he does not demand perfect obedience of his people in order to remain in covenant relationship with him. God does require obedience from the heart.

we find that there was real gospel under the theocracy. The people
of God of those days did not live and die under an unworkable,
unredemptive system of religion, that could not give real
access to and spiritual contact with God. Nor was this gospel-
element contained exclusively in the revelation that preceded,
accompanied, and followed the law; it is found *in the law itself.*
That which we call "the legal system" is shot through with strands
of gospel and grace and faith.[44]

In addition, covenant promise of Israel's possession and continuance in the
land stipulated obedience (Deut 4:1–2, 39–40); and individual Israelites,
such as Caleb and Joshua, fully obeyed the law but not perfectly. The Lord
confirms his oath to Moses that he would not bring into the promised land
the generation of Israelites who rebelled against him by refusing to take the
land. "Because they have not followed me wholeheartedly, not one of those
who were twenty years old or more when they came up out of Egypt will see
the land I promised on oath to Abraham, Isaac and Jacob—not one except
Caleb son of Jephunneh the Kenizzite and Joshua son of Nun, for they followed the LORD wholeheartedly" (Num 32:11–12; cf. 14:24; Josh 14:8–9).

Likewise, Scripture testifies concerning David that he "had done what
was right in the eyes of the LORD and had not failed to keep any of the
LORD's commands all the days of his life" (1 Kgs 15:5).[45] This mention of
David's full obedience contrasts with the moral failure of Abijah, Jeroboam's
son, who "committed all the sins his father had done before him; his heart
was not fully devoted to the LORD his God, as the heart of David his fore-
father had been" (1 Kgs 15:3), of whom Samuel presages as "a man after
[God's] own heart" (1 Sam 13:14; Acts 13:22).

In view here is not perfect obedience but wholehearted obedience
called for in the *Shema*: "Love the LORD your God with all your heart and
with all your soul and with all your strength" (Deut 6:5). David called for
this covenant obedience when he solemnly charged Solomon "to follow all

---

[44] Ibid., 127–29 (emphasis in original).

[45] It is true that the verse adds "except in the case of Uriah the Hittite." Yet this
qualification does not diminish the fullness of David's obedience but magnifies God's
grace.

the commands of the LORD your God" (1 Chr 28:8). David added, do this "with wholehearted devotion and with a willing mind, for the LORD searches every heart and understands every desire and every thought. If you seek him, he will be found by you; but if you forsake him, he will reject you forever" (28:9).

Likewise, the NT portrays Zechariah and Elizabeth: "Both of them were righteous in the sight of God, observing all the Lord's commands and decrees blamelessly" (Luke 1:6). Blamelessly, not perfectly, they obeyed what the law stipulated: "You must be blameless before the LORD your God" (Deut 18:13). Yet, as members of a nation that broke covenant with the Lord, many, including Daniel and his friends, went into exile, the curse of the covenant. Others, such as Zechariah and Elizabeth as well as Simeon and Anna, because they too were members of a nation that violated the covenant, endured the curse of exile as slaves even within their own land (cf. Ezra 9:8–9; Neh 9:36; Luke 2:67–75).[46]

Repeated Expressions of God's Grace, Election, and Covenant Faithfulness

The Pentateuch speaks of God's gracious choosing of Israel as the foundation of the covenant he made with the nation and as the leading argument and motivation for Israel to reciprocate with covenant loyalty and wholehearted obedience to the covenant stipulations. Thus, the Lord's formulation of the covenant at Sinai features God's great redemptive act in bringing his people out of slavery in Egypt as an act of love and of mercy. Based on this, the Lord instructs Moses to set before Israel the general covenant stipulations.

> *"You yourselves have seen what I did to Egypt, and how I carried you on eagles' wings and brought you to myself.* Now if you obey me fully and keep my covenant, then out of all nations you will

---

[46] Cf. James M. Scott, "For as Many as Are of Works of the Law Are Under a Curse (Galatians 3.10)," in *Paul and the Scriptures of Israel*, ed. Craig A. Evans and James A. Sanders, JSNTSup 83 (Sheffield, UK: JSOT, 1993), 198–213.

be my treasured possession. Although the whole earth is mine, you will be for me a kingdom of priests and a holy nation. These are the words you are to speak to the Israelites" (Exod 19:4–6; emphasis added).

Likewise, even the words of Leviticus 18:5—"Keep my decrees and laws, for the person who obeys them will live by them"—are set in a context encased in grace and mercy. "Speak to the Israelites and say to them: '*I am the* LORD *your God*. You must not do as they do in Egypt, where you used to live, and you must not do as they do in the land of Canaan, where I am bringing you. Do not follow their practices. You must obey my laws and be careful to follow my decrees. *I am the* LORD *your God*'" (Lev 18:2–4; emphasis added). These verses emphatically remind the Israelites of their God of grace and mercy. The same reminder completes the instructions at 18:30. Mention of Egypt reminds Israel of the depravity of that nation and to recall the Lord's redemption of them from slavery.

Moses explicitly warns the Israelites against putting confidence in the flesh and exhorts them to worship the Lord by obeying him because of his mercy (Deut 8:10–18). Again he emphasizes that the law covenant entails grace, for the Lord goes before them, as promised, to drive out the land's inhabitants. The Lord acts on their behalf not because of their righteousness but on account of his own promise to dispossess the land's inhabitants.[47]

> After *the* LORD *your God has driven them out before you*, do not
> say to yourself, "*The* LORD *has brought me here to take possession
> of this land* because of my righteousness." No, it is on account
> of the wickedness of these nations that *the* LORD *is going to drive
> them out before you*. It is not because of your righteousness or your
> integrity that you are going in to take possession of their land;
> but on account of the wickedness of these nations, *the* LORD *your
> God will drive them out before you, to accomplish what he swore to
> your fathers, to Abraham, Isaac and Jacob*. Understand, then, that
> it is not because of your righteousness that the LORD your God

---

[47] The great Shema and its surrounding context also demonstrate that Israel's obligations to obey the Lord do not stand contrary to grace. See Deuteronomy 6.

is giving you this good land to possess, for you are a stiff-necked people (Deut 9:4–6; emphasis added).

Ineffective by Design—Accounting for the New Testament's View of the Law

The law covenant's flaw was *not* its conditional stipulations *but its divinely embedded ineffectuality, temporality, and obsolescence.* As Hebrews affirms, if the law covenant had something wrong with it, the fundamental flaw was not with the covenant itself but with the people (Heb 8:7–8). The entire law-covenant was a copy, a shadow of the good things to come in the one to whom it typologically pointed (10:1–4). Just as the nation and all their recorded experiences from Egypt to exile and return was given typologically (cf. 1 Cor 10:1–13), God infused Israel's experiences, events, places, institutions, worship, prophets, priesthood, kingship, tabernacle, temple, land, and the whole law itself with typological significance. All who resided under the law's jurisdiction are instructed to look for him who would come to coalesce all the foreshadows in himself, fulfilling them all and bringing the law covenant to its designed climactic end for us upon whom the ends of the ages have come (10:11).

God designed the law covenant to be subordinate to both the promise it sustained and the new covenant it foreshadowed, which would render it obsolete. Thus God designed the law covenant to command wholehearted obedience that it could not secure (Ps 51:16–17), to require circumcision of hearts that it was powerless to circumcise (Deut 10:6; 30:6), to promise eternal life that it could not deliver (Lev 18:5; Rom 7:10), to demand righteousness that it was not able to impute (Gal 3:21), and to require remission of guilt that it was impotent to accomplish (Heb 10:11).[48] Under the

---

[48] Cf. Gentry and Wellum, *Kingdom Through Covenant*, 639. They agree that "the old covenant has a built-in *tension*. God demands obedience from Israel, yet they disobey. The law holds out life, but due to sin it cannot ultimately save. There is nothing in the law-covenant that changes the human heart, which is what the people desperately need. In fact, as the history of Israel unfolds, the law-covenant brings greater condemnation because it reveals more and more of Israel's sin; it increases sin quantitatively by

law covenant, were there any Israelites whose sins were remitted, who were righteous, who received eternal life, whose hearts were circumcised, who received the Spirit, who obeyed the Lord wholeheartedly? Yes, indeed! But obeying the Lord, receipt of the Spirit, heart circumcision, reception of eternal life, justification, and forgiveness of sins were extrinsic to that covenant of shadows.

Every such circumcision of heart, called for by the law covenant, was a foreshadow and foretaste of the promised new covenant Messiah who would give the blessing of Abraham, the promise of the Spirit (Gal 3:14). He is the one who delivers the promised covenant life, who secures covenant obedience, who declares individuals righteous, and who grants remission of sins. Many Israelites did obey the law because their hearts were circumcised, and they were recipients of the Spirit and of eternal life but not by any power of the old covenant. For the law covenant was powerless to effect the change of heart necessary or to bestow the Spirit or the life it promised. Rather, the law, functioning typologically, pointed away from itself as it testified to the coming One who alone could offer himself as the effective sacrifice to take away sin and to give the Spirit who would circumcise hearts unto obedience and enliven with eternal life (Rom 3:21).

Conclusions

Though all Christians abide under the jurisdiction of God's new covenant in Christ Jesus, there are several aspects about the covenant over which we disagree with one another. One of these concerns the nature and role of covenant stipulations. We find ourselves susceptible to the same errors to which our forebears were subject, whether throughout church history or

---

defining explicitly what is contrary to God's character and demands (Rom. 5:20); and it imprisons Israel under sin's power and condemnation (Rom. 3:19–20; Gal. 3:10, 13; Col. 2:14). Even God's provision of a sacrificial system, because it was only typological and provisional, functioned as a 'reminder of sins' (Heb. 10:3), pointing forward to the need for a new covenant which would bring transformation of heart and the full forgiveness of sin. Yet the old covenant, as part of God's unfolding plan, is the means by which God's initial promise of redemption will take place" (emphasis in original).

as the patriarchal forebears were during the historical periods of the earlier covenants. Thus, we must avoid repeating their misunderstandings and
failings. We must guard against misconstruing new covenant stipulations
as Eve, whose husband followed her lead, misconstrued the stipulation of
the first covenant, or as many of Abraham's descendants did when they
presumed covenant blessings by virtue of bearing its sign in their flesh, or
as Israelites did supposing that possession of the law insulated them from
God's judgment. We also need to guard against misconstruing new covenant
stipulations as though the imperatives or the various forms of conditionals
either raise doubts about our covenant membership in Christ or beguile us
to suppose that obedience entails meriting our continued covenantal stand-
ing with God.

From the beginning, according to Scripture, by unbelief humans have
misconstrued the Lord's covenant stipulations. When the serpent incited
doubt, Eve exaggerated the covenant stipulation, claiming that the Lord
threatened death for touching the tree of the knowledge of good and evil.
Though Adam was present with her, by failing to rebuke her distortion, he
rendered Eve susceptible to the serpent's deception. Doubt, deception, and
distortion led to disbelief and transgression when she took, ate, and gave
some fruit to Adam who deliberately disobeyed when he joined his wife in
covenant transgression (cf. 1 Tim 2:14). By abdicating dominion over his
passions concerning the allurement of one token tree in the garden, Adam
invoked the curse of death upon himself and upon the entirety of God's created order. Consequently, Adam's offspring, conceived in his sinful likeness
and image, persist in unbelief and disobedience as they misconstrue and
transgress stipulations of the Lord's subsequent covenants.

Israelites misconstrued the Abrahamic and Mosaic covenants, for
not all of Israel were truly of Abraham, whose true parentage is of all who
believe. Instead, they presumed that the covenant blessings promised to
Abraham were theirs simply by possessing circumcision, the stipulated sign
of the covenant in their flesh. For them earthly circumcision was an end
in itself rather than a signifying token of the heavenly gift of a circumcised
heart. They also misconstrued the Mosaic covenant, for when they received
the law covenant they presumed that the blessings of the law covenant were

theirs simply by possessing the law with its stipulated covenant sign, the Sabbath, etched in stone tablets, rather than by observing it as commanded (Rom 2:12–29). Despite the Lord's warnings, after the Israelites entered the promised land they failed to observe the Lord's covenant stipulations but became proud as though their own strength established them in the land (cf. Deut 8:10–18). They regarded their own righteousness as the basis for their possession of the land (cf. 9:4–6). Passover ritual rebuked their hollow observance. Their children were trained to ask, "What is the meaning of the stipulations, decrees and laws the LORD our God has commanded you?" (6:20). And they were to reply,

> We were slaves of Pharaoh in Egypt, but the LORD brought us out of Egypt with a mighty hand. . . . But he brought us out from there to bring us in and give us the land he promised on oath to our ancestors. The LORD commanded us to obey all these decrees and to fear the LORD our God, so that we might always prosper and be kept alive, as is the case today. And if we are careful to obey all this law before the LORD our God, as he has commanded us, that will be our righteousness. (6:21, 23–26)

So, as we ponder God's covenants initiated by his will of purpose, Scripture persuades us to acknowledge that when he established his covenants with humans, his will was unconditional, without constraints from anything outside his own purpose. Nevertheless, as we consider the stipulation of God's will of command within his covenants, Scripture convinces us to affirm that he deals with humans conditionally, as created persons made in his image. Divine revelation makes clear that every human covenantal relationship with God is established and initiated by God's invariable covenant provision. Only because God unconditionally takes the initiative to bless us with his saving mercies and endow us with the Spirit do we obey his covenant stipulations or conditions. The apostle John succinctly expresses this—"This is love: not that we loved God, but that he loved us and sent his Son as an atoning sacrifice for our sins" (1 John 4:10). God's covenant provision of unconditional love grounds the response he stipulates in order that we might receive the covenant blessing of life. Thus, John states, "Beloved, if God loved us in this manner, we also ought to love one another" and again, "We love because he first loved us" (4:11, 19, my translation).[49] Augustine embraced the Lord's stipulations rightly when he prayed, "My whole hope is in thy exceeding great mercy and that alone. Give what thou commandest and command what thou wilt."[50] And so it is that if we obey God's stipulations proclaimed in and through his new covenant in Christ Jesus, God's Word assures us that we shall have access to the tree of life in God's Holy City. But if we do not heed God's threatening stipulations, we will be cast outside, and our share in the tree of life and in the Holy City will be taken from us.[51]

---

[49] Scripture requires that we distinguish between God's unconditional love and conditional love. See D. A. Carson, *The Difficult Doctrine of the Love of God* (Wheaton, IL: Crossway, 2000), 16–24.

[50] Saint Augustine, *Confessions and Enchiridion*, trans. and ed. Albert C. Outler, The Library of Christian Classics (Philadelphia: Westminster, 1955), 195.

[51] Publication of Brad G. Green, *Covenant and Commandment: Works, Obedience and Faithfulness in the Christian Life*, NSBT 33 (Downers Grove, IL: InterVarsity, 2014), came too late to include as a resource.

CHAPTER 5

Circumcision of Flesh to Circumcision of Heart: The Typology of the Sign of the Abrahamic Covenant[1]

JOHN D. MEADE

Introduction

The topic of circumcision in the Bible has raised no small discussion in scholarly literature.[2] In this chapter I intend to contribute to this discussion

---

[1] I wish to thank Peter Gentry and Stephen Dempster for reading an earlier draft of this paper. Their comments saved me from many errors and stimulated my thinking on this topic in significant ways.

[2] Michael V. Fox, "The Sign of the Covenant: Circumcision in Light of the Priestly'*ôt* Etiologies," *RB* 81 (1974): 557–96; John Goldingay, "The Significance of Circumcision," *JSOT* 88 (2000): 3–18; Jason S. DeRouchie, "Circumcision in the Hebrew Bible and Targums: Theology, Rhetoric, and the Handling of Metaphor," *BBR* 14 (2004): 175–203; Robert G. Hall, "Circumcision," in *The Anchor Bible Dictionary*, ed. David Noel Freedman (New York: Doubleday, 1992), 1,025–31; Frans Jonckheere, "La circonsion [*sic*] des anciens égyptiens," *Centaurus* 1 (1951): 212–34; Philip J. King, "Circumcision: Who Did It, Who Didn't and Why," *BAR* 32 (2006): 48–55; Meredith G. Kline, "Oath and Ordeal Signs—I," *WTJ* 27 (1964–65): 115–39; idem, "Oath and Ordeal Signs—II," *WTJ* 28 (1965–1966): 1–37; William H. C. Propp, "Circumcision: The Private Sign of the Covenant," *BRev* 20 (2004): 22–29; idem, "The Origins of Infant Circumcision in Israel," *HAR* 11 (1987): 355–70; Jack M. Sasson, "Circumcision in the Ancient Near

in two ways. First, the meaning of the biblical rite of circumcision will be explained against the background of the ancient Near East. A complete discussion of circumcision in ancient Near Eastern cultures is not possible, so I will summarize the results of a previous study. Second, once the significance of circumcision has been clarified, I will then explain the typological development of circumcision through the biblical canon as it moves from external to internal heart (un)circumcision. Focus will be placed on the Deuteronomic vision for a people who will be covenantally faithful from an internal devotion. This is taken up as part of the future hope of the prophets—Jeremiah and Ezekiel—and finally in the NT, which attests that this eschatological heart circumcision has already been realized in the new covenant community. The former topic has received far less treatment than the latter, but a clear understanding of the original meaning and significance of circumcision will contribute to the overall biblical-theological presentation. Once the background and theme of circumcision in the OT are treated, attention will shift to the NT and a subsequent theological formulation of circumcision as it pertains to ecclesiology and baptism.[3]

East," *JBL* 85 (1966): 473–76; Richard C. Steiner, "Incomplete Circumcision in Egypt and Edom: Jeremiah (9:24–25) in the Light of Josephus and Jonckheere," *JBL* 118 (1999): 497–505; Maurice Stracmans, "Un rite d'initiation a masque d'animal dans la plus ancienne religion egyptienne?" *Annuaire de l'Institut de Philologie et d'Histoire Orientales et Slaves*, XII (1952): 427–40; idem, "A propos d'un texte relatif à la circoncision égyptienne (1re période intermédiaire)," *Mélanges Isidore Lévy* (1955): 631–39; idem, "Encore un texte peu connue relative à la circoncision des anciens égyptiens," *Archivo Internationale di Etnografia e Preistoria*, 2 (1959): 7–15.

[3] For the question of circumcision's relationship to baptism, see C. John Collins, "What Does Baptism Do for Anyone? Part I," *Presbyterion* 38, no. 1 (2012): 1–33; Idem, "What Does Baptism Do for Anyone? Part II," *Presbyterion* 38, no. 2 (2012): 74–98; David Gibson, "Sacramental Supersessionism Revisited: A Response to Martin Salter on the Relationship Between Circumcision and Baptism," *Themelios* 37 (2012): 191–208; Martin Salter, "Does Baptism Replace Circumcision? An Examination of the Relationship Between Circumcision and Baptism in Colossians 2:11–12," *Themelios* 35 (2010): 15–29.

Summary of the History and Significance of Circumcision

Circumcision is first mentioned in the Bible in Genesis 17 at the confirming/upholding of the Abrahamic covenant, previously initiated in Genesis 15.[4] After rehearsing the promises for seed (17:6; cf. 15:4) and land (17:7; cf. 15:18), verse 9 introduces further information about the already existing covenant relationship. Yahweh commands Abram to keep (שׁמר) "my covenant." Verse 10 clarifies that the covenant Abraham will keep is the circumcision of every male offspring. The text includes several details concerning the rite: (1) the act of circumcising the flesh of the foreskin (v. 11a); (2) circumcision will be a sign of the covenant between Yahweh and Abraham and his descendants (v. 11b); (3) every male (including offspring and anyone bought with money from a foreigner) shall be circumcised on the eighth day (v. 12a); (4) Yahweh's covenant in Abraham's flesh will be an eternal covenant (v. 13b); and (5) the one who has not undergone circumcision shall be cut off from the people; he has broken Yahweh's covenant (v. 14). Even though this text contains details about circumcision, it does not provide the meaning of the rite. Only appeal to extrabiblical sources reveals the significance of the rite.

Based on the biblical text, Egypt is the most probable religious-cultural milieu to locate Abraham. Both Abraham and later Israel share this common milieu and would probably understand their rite in light of Egypt's own rite.

Evidence of circumcision in Egypt exists from the fourth millennium BC to the Roman period. Egyptians practiced an incomplete circumcision of the foreskin.[5] The rite was applied to some young males (ages 6–14) not

---

[4] For the argument that God made *one* covenant with Abraham, which was upheld with him in Genesis 17, and the rest of the patriarchs, see Peter J. Gentry and Stephen J. Wellum, *Kingdom Through Covenant: A Biblical-Theological Understanding of the Biblical Covenants* (Wheaton, IL: Crossway, 2012), 275–80. For a similar view see also Jeffrey J. Niehaus, "God's Covenant with Abraham," *JETS* 56 (2013): 249–71.

[5] See Jonckheere, "Circoncision," 228, who describes two procedures of incomplete circumcision.

for the purpose of a prenuptial or puberty rite as some suppose,[6] but, significantly, the best evidence indicates that circumcision was an initiation rite for those who would serve in the court of Pharaoh as priests.[7]

Many aspects of Egyptian circumcision can be compared and contrasted with Israel's practice of circumcision.

Comparisons. The technique of circumcision is applied to the male prepuce in both cultures. Since mutilations of the body could occur in a number of different places, it is significant that both cultures circumcised the same part of the body.

Contrasts. First, each culture used a different technique for circumcision. Second, while in Egypt circumcision was applied to males between the ages of 6 and 14, in Israel the rite of circumcision was applied to males when they were eight days old. Third, and most significant, the rite was specifically reserved for royalty and clergy in Egypt, while it was applied *generally* to every male in Israel.

Conclusions. The similarities and differences between the cultures provide grounds for understanding the theology of circumcision in Israel. First,

---

[6] Jonckheere, "Circoncision," 232; Sasson, "Circumcision," 474. Sasson says, "In Egypt, however, texts, sculptures, and mummies seem to support, the conclusion that babies never underwent the operation; it was reserved for either a period of prenuptial ceremonies or, more likely, for initiation into the state of manhood." The evidence only confirms the first part of Sasson's statement concerning babies; it does not confirm his positive proposal.

[7] For scholars who conclude that circumcision was a specific rite for priests and royalty, see George Foucart, "Circumcision (Egyptian)," in *ERE*, 3:674a-b, 675b; Aylward M. Blackman, "Priest, Priesthood (Egyptian)," in *ERE*, 10:293–302 (esp. 299b–300a); cf. also the articles by Maurice Stracmans in note 2. For scholars who only question but do not seek to answer whether circumcision was general/specific and obligated/voluntary in Egypt, see Jonckheere, "Circoncision," 231; and Sasson, "Circumcision in the Ancient Near East," 474 (cf. n.10). Unfortunately, other scholars do not even seem to be aware of the question when they attempt to understand the significance of circumcision in the OT, see Fox, "The Sign of the Covenant," 592; Goldingay, "The Significance of Circumcision," 3–18; Hall, "Circumcision," 1026; Roland de Vaux, *Ancient Israel: Its Life and Institutions*, trans. John McHugh (New York: McGraw Hill, 1961), 47; Adolphe Lods, *Israel: From Its Beginnings to the Middle of the Eighth Century*, trans. S. H. Hooke (London: Routledge & Kegan Paul, 1932), 198; King, "Circumcision: Who Did It, Who Didn't and Why," 48–55.

from her origins Israel was called to be a kingdom of *priests* and a *holy* nation (Exod 19:6); that is, Israel was specially called to be devoted to Yahweh and his rule and reign.[8] Therefore, given the Egyptian background of circumcision of royalty and clergy, it was fitting for every Israelite male to undergo the general rite of circumcision, which identified them as Yahweh's devoted priests (cf. Gen 17:12). The sign of circumcision matched and reinforced the identity they subsumed at Sinai. Second, *every* Israelite male underwent circumcision at eight days old, indicating that from birth each son of Abraham was devoted to the service of Yahweh.

In God's providence and wisdom, he chose to reveal the special relationship Abraham and his family would have with him through the already familiar cultural and religious category of Egyptian circumcision of royalty and priesthood. The sign of circumcision was intended to show devotion to the service of Yahweh and his kingdom. Such a sign was perfect for this covenant people whom God would use to extend his blessing to the nations (Gen 12:1–3). In actual practice, however, the sign of circumcision led to tensions, which anticipated a better circumcision to come. Genesis 17:23–27 reports that Abraham circumcised himself, Ishmael, and all the males of his household. And herein lies the tension created by the external sign of circumcision: the sign of devotion and consecration is applied to all of the biological children of Abraham, even those not chosen to continue the family of Abraham such as Ishmael and later Esau (cf. Mal 1:2–3). Furthermore, even the true biological seed of Abraham, who underwent circumcision (i.e., the descendants of Jacob/Israel), would become rebellious and would be no more devoted to Yahweh and his rule than the rest of the nations (cf. Jer 3:17; 9:25–26). The external sign of devotion to Yahweh was not indicative of the internal reality of the people's wicked, stubborn hearts (e.g., Jer 7:24). Yet this external sign of circumcision foreshadowed the internal circumcision of the heart that Deuteronomy employs in its description of the people of God after they return from exile.

---

[8] See the careful exegesis in Gentry and Wellum, *Kingdom Through Covenant*, 312–27. For the meaning of "holy" as "devoted" or "consecrated" see also Peter J. Gentry, "Sizemore Lectures I: Isaiah and Social Justice," *MJT* 12 (2013): 1–15; idem, "Sizemore Lectures II: No One Holy like the Lord," *MJT* 12 (2013): 17–38.

Typological Development of Circumcision in Deuteronomy

The first place one encounters circumcision of the heart in Scripture is in Deuteronomy.[9] First, I will analyze the genre of Deuteronomy in order to understand its message properly. Second, I will describe the Deuteronomic vision of a loyal people, who are covenantally faithful to Yahweh from a devoted heart. Third, I will place heart circumcision in the context of a loyalty covenant expecting faithfulness from a devoted heart.

The Literary Form of Deuteronomy

The book of Deuteronomy shares the literary form of a covenant or treaty, particularly, the form employed by the Hittites from the fifteenth to the thirteenth centuries BC.[10] Understanding Deuteronomy as a vassal treaty is crucial because literary form and poetics contributes to the overall meaning of the text.[11] The actual form of the book reveals that Yahweh is the great King and Israel is the vassal who is swearing loyalty and allegiance to Yahweh alone.[12] The book details a loving, loyal covenant relationship

---

[9] Although Lev 26:41–42 contains an important reference to "their uncircumcised heart," space constraints require its omission from discussion. I address it in the following: John D. Meade, "Circumcision of the Heart in Leviticus and Deuteronomy: Divine Means for Realizing the Deuteronomic Vision," *SBJT* 18 (2014): 59–85, accessed August 23, 2015, http://www.sbts.edu/resources/category/journal-of-theology/sbjt-183-fall-2014.

[10] For more information on the suzerain vassal treaty or covenant structure as influenced by other cultures, see Kenneth Kitchen, *On the Reliability of the Old Testament* (Grand Rapids: Eerdmans, 2003), 283–89.

[11] Adele Berlin, *Poetics and Interpretation of Biblical Narrative* (Sheffield: Almond, 1983; repr., Winona Lake, IN: Eisenbrauns, 1999), 17, states, "In simpler words, poetics makes us aware of how texts achieve their meaning. Poetics aids interpretation. If we know *how* texts mean, we are in a better position to discover *what* a particular text means" (emphasis in original).

[12] For these themes in the Hittite texts, see Gary Beckman, *Hittite Diplomatic Texts*, 2nd ed. (Atlanta: Scholars, 1999), 2.

between Yahweh and Israel in which the people should be devoted to Yahweh from the inside out, that is, from the heart.

The Deuteronomic Vision for Covenant Loyalty from the Heart

The word "heart" (לְבָב/לֵב) is used 858 times in the Hebrew Bible according to the study by Hans Walter Wolff.[13] His study concluded that the word is used in six different ways: (1) placement of the organ of the heart (e.g., Jer 23:9), (2) feelings (e.g., Prov 15:13; 17:22), (3) wish as desire or longing (e.g., Ps 21:2 [EV 21:3]), (4) reason (e.g., Deut 29:3 [EV 29:4]), (5) decisions of the will (e.g., Prov 16:9), and (6) heart of God (e.g., 1 Sam 2:35). Of these usages, Wolff's analysis shows that 400 of these occurrences refer to the reason and intellect of man, that is, what one would call the mind. The heart is the control center of the human being according to the OT. It is not simply the place where one feels, but more often it is the place where one understands and wills. If one's heart was devoted to Yahweh, the whole person—intellect, dreams, and emotions—would then be devoted to him.

Devotion from the heart. As a covenantal text Deuteronomy exhorts and commands its readers to be loyal to Yahweh from the heart because of the grace shown to them in the past and the future blessing of life in the land. In Deuteronomy the texts that contain לֵב as an object of the preposition בְּ "in, with" when describing the verbs "to love" (6:5; 13:4; 30:6), "to serve" (10:12; 11:13), "to do" (26:16), "to obey" (30:2), and "to seek" (4:29) demonstrate the goal for a people to be devoted to Yahweh with all their heart.[14]

In addition to these verbs modified by בְּ, Moses also calls the people "to set" "my words" (11:18) or "all the words" (32:46) on (עַל) their heart.

---

[13] Hans Walter Wolff, *Anthropology of the Old Testament*, trans. Margaret Kohl (Philadelphia: Fortress, 1974), 40.

[14] These references usually contain the full phrase: "with all your heart and with all your soul," though 6:5 contains the additional בְּכָל־מְאֹדֶךָ, usually translated "with all your might." In the course of my research, I was glad to see a similar study done by Jason C. Meyer, *The End of the Law: Mosaic Covenant in Pauline Theology* (Nashville, TN: B&H Academic, 2009), 239.

The verb שִׂים functions as a command in 11:18 and in 32:46, which communicates that it is desirable for the people to place or set Moses' instructions on their heart and soul, that is, for them to internalize the Torah or instruction of Moses. In 6:6, the verb form of הָיָה ("to be") indicates that the words Moses commanded the people *shall* be upon (עַל) their hearts. The people are to place the Torah on the part of them that controls their feelings, reason, desires, and will. Moses envisions nothing less than a people fully constrained and controlled by the Torah from the heart.

Heart circumcision attains the Deuteronomic vision. Deuteronomy presents heart circumcision as important for attaining the Deuteronomic vision of loyalty from a devoted heart. The root מוּל ("to circumcise") occurs only twice in Deuteronomy, and both instances relate to circumcision of the heart (10:16; 30:6). עָרְלָה ("foreskin") occurs only once as the object of מוּל in 10:16. We will treat the matter systematically as follows: (1) interpret the metaphor in 10:16, (2) interpret the metaphor in 30:6, and (3) synthesize the inner Deuteronomic development and draw preliminary conclusions.

Deuteronomy 10:16

Deuteronomy 10:12–22 is a unit of discourse contained in the general stipulation section of Deuteronomy 4:45–11:32 (see the covenant structure below). This whole section is unified by the central theme of loyalty to Yahweh in covenant relationship. The basic outline of the general stipulation is as follows:

General Stipulation: 4:45–11:32[15]

A. Basic Principle of Covenant Relationship	4:45–6:3
B. Measures for Maintaining Covenant Relationship	6:4–25
C. Implications of Covenant Relationship	7:1–26
D. Warnings Against Forgetting Covenant Relationship	8:1–20
E. Failures in Covenant Relationship	9:1–10:11
F. Restoration to Covenant Relationship	10:12–22
G. Choices Required by Covenant Relationship	11:1–32

---

[15] Adapted from Steven W. Guest, "Deuteronomy 26:16–19 as the Central Focus of the Covenantal Framework of Deuteronomy" (PhD diss., The Southern Baptist Theological Seminary, 2009), 56.

In 10:12–22 Moses exhorts the people to maintain covenant loyalty by balancing exhortations with statements about the character of Yahweh in episodic fashion. The literary structure of 10:12–22 establishes heart circumcision as the central concern in Deuteronomy:

A¹ Exhortation to Loyal Devotion: <u>Fear</u>, Walk, <u>Love</u>, <u>Serve</u>, Keep   12–13
    B¹ Yahweh Is Praised: Sovereign Creator and Redeemer   14–15
A² Exhortation to Loyal Devotion: Circumcise and Do Not Stiffen   16
    B² Yahweh Is Praised: Supreme God and Faithful to Weak   17–18
A³ Exhortation to Loyal Devotion: <u>Love</u>, <u>Fear</u>, <u>Serve</u>, Cling, Swear   19–20
    B³ Yahweh Is Praised: Faithful God of the Patriarchs and Exodus   21–22

The statements about Yahweh's character (B sections) become the grounds for the earnest pleas to be devoted to Yahweh (A sections). The theme of loyal devotion prompts the origination of the reference to heart circumcision. The *center* of the exhortation sections (A²) contains the only positive command, which calls the people to an *internal* action, i.e., to circumcise their hearts. As indicated by the literary structure, the *central* concern is the *internal* condition of the human heart. The second half of the verse confirms this interpretation by commanding them to stop stiffening their necks by recalling their past rebellions (cf. 9:6, 13).

Circumcision identifies and devotes a person to loyal service of God, i.e., indicates one is a priest. If this meaning is correct, then it would also be true in this context where circumcision is now applied internally to the center of the human being's thoughts, volition, reason, and desires. A circumcised or devoted heart would then manifest itself in covenant loyalty to Yahweh (A¹ and A³).

In this context the metaphor of heart circumcision reveals a development in God's plan for creating a covenant people who would be loyal to him and love him from a devoted heart brought about by circumcision.

Deuteronomy 30:6

The second instance of circumcision in Deuteronomy comes at 30:6: "And Yahweh will circumcise your heart and the heart of your descendants [lit. "seed"] in order that you might love Yahweh, your God, with all your heart and with all your soul so that you might live" (my translation). The reference

to heart circumcision in 30:6 as the response to impending covenant treach-
ery mirrors the usage in 10:16 where it functioned as the central response
to covenant breaking. Therefore both units (4:45–11:32 and 29:1–30:20)
use heart circumcision as the key to resolving covenant infidelity, and thus
heart circumcision is a theme that binds the book together.

Deuteronomy 30:1–10 expounds the blessing and the curse with an
emphasis on the blessing. The syntax and structure of the first section is
notoriously difficult. Based on discourse grammar, the following structure
for 30:1–10 emerges:[16]

I. Temporal Scheme of Return	1–3
A. Protasis: The people return	1–2
B. Apodosis: Yahweh restores the people	3
II. Scope of Return	4–7
A. Protasis: Difficult circumstances	4a
B. Apodosis: Yahweh's power to restore	4b–7
A^1 Geographical return	4bc
B^1 Blessings	5
A^2 Internal transformation	6
B^2 Blessing: Safety from enemies	7
III. Results of Return	8–10
A^1 Obedience	8
B Blessings	9
A^2 Obedience	10

Regarding the structure of the Apodosis of the Scope of Return, the A
sections mark two stages in the return from exile, while the B sections mark
the blessings—associating the state of the people at the return from exile
with Abraham's family (e.g. Gen 12:3). A^1 details the geographical return
from exile, while A^2 expounds the spiritual return from exile employing

---

[16] The relationship of 30:1–10 to 30:11–14 cannot be given adequate attention here
and is treated in my article in *SBJT* cited in note 9. There are two options: (1) Verses
11–14 return the reader to the present and teach that the Torah is not too difficult to
keep. (2) Verses 11–14 continue the eschatological force of verses 1–10, and therefore
the ease of keeping the Torah comes after the heart circumcision event.

circumcision of the heart to explain the internal transformation that will devote the people to a loyal love of Yahweh. The return in Deuteronomy has two distinct stages. Later, Isaiah delineates two returns from exile: the geographical return to be accomplished by the servant Cyrus and the spiritual return to be accomplished by the Suffering Servant.[17] Therefore, Deuteronomy 30:1–10 is at the headwaters of a major theme to be developed by the prophets. The people will return from exile, but they will not undergo spiritual return from exile until sometime later.

Synthesis of 10:16 and 30:6

Heart circumcision appears twice in Deuteronomy, and a comparison and contrast of the two texts and their contexts is illuminating. First, these texts and contexts share a number of parallels. Jason Meyer has noted linguistic parallels between the two contexts:[18]

to love him (10:12)	to love Yahweh (30:6)
with all your heart and all your soul (10:12)	with all your heart and all your soul (30:2, 6)
to keep Yahweh's commands and his statutes (10:13)	to keep his commands and his statutes (30:10)
which I am commanding you today (10:13)	which I am commanding you today (30:2)
for good (10:13)	for good (30:9)
your fathers (10:15, 22)	your fathers (30:5, 9)
circumcise the foreskin of your heart (10:16)	Yahweh will circumcise your heart (30:6)

Beyond these lexical similarities, both heart circumcision texts appear in similar contexts, namely, these texts are solutions to the plights caused by failure in covenant (cf. 9:1–10:11; 29:3 [EV 29:4]).

Although the passages contain many similarities, they have one major *difference*. In 10:16 Moses commands the people to circumcise their own

---

[17] Cf. Gentry and Wellum, *Kingdom Through Covenant*, 437–39 (for Isaiah), 538–41 (for Daniel).

[18] Meyer, *The End of the Law*, 247–48. The list has been slightly revised and adapted.

hearts and to cease being rebellious. In contrast, Deuteronomy 30:6 predicts that the return from exile will include the circumcision of the heart. Part of the second stage in the return from exile includes Yahweh's circumcising the hearts of the people and their descendants. This circumcision will devote the people to him.

Conclusions

Circumcision of the foreskin marked one out for devoted service to Yahweh, and this is consonant with Israel's being called a kingdom of priests and a holy nation (Exod 19:6). Abraham's family bore the sign that marked them as a holy priesthood and devoted them to the service of Yahweh. But Israel's history contradicts the sign they bore. Rather than being a royal priesthood, they were stubborn and rebellious. A people bearing the sign of circumcision of the flesh was a type, a picture of a people devoted to Yahweh and his kingdom within a covenant relationship. Nevertheless, redemptive history reveals that the type underwent development from as early as Deuteronomy 10:16, and the OT was already anticipating the reality to which the type pointed: internal circumcision of the heart. Deuteronomy 30:1–10 and the rest of the OT witness reveal that this heart circumcision was to take place at the second stage of the return from exile, the stage when Yahweh would finally act to bring Babylon out of the hearts of the people.

The Deuteronomic Vision for Heart Devotion in the Major Prophets

This survey will focus on the ways the Deuteronomic vision is developed, specifically in terms of heart circumcision and heart change in Jeremiah and Ezekiel.

Jeremiah's Circumcised and Torah-Inscribed Heart

Of all the prophets Jeremiah alludes to the Deuteronomic vision of the (un)circumcised heart or ear and the extension to the changed heart more than any other (4:4; 6:10[19]; 9:24–25; 31:31–34; 32:37–41).

Jeremiah 4:1–4. This text alludes to the Deuteronomic call to repentance (תָּשׁוּב, "if you return," cf. Deut 30:1–3). Peter Gentry constructs the discourse of 4:1–2 as follows: If you return to Yahweh, if you remove detestable things from Yahweh's presence, *then* you will swear, and the nations shall declare themselves blessed in him (i.e., Yahweh). Gentry says, "The idea expressed in Jeremiah 4:2, that when Israel is faithful in her relationship to Yahweh, blessing will flow to the nations, is based squarely on the Israelite covenant as an outworking of the promises to Abraham."[20] Jeremiah 4:3–4 further explains (כִּי, "for") what "faithfulness in her relationship to Yahweh" means. Verse 3 contains an implied comparison between some part of the covenant relationship and agriculture. The comparison is encrypted, and Werner Lemke has suggested correctly that Jeremiah has derived the imagery "break up your fallow ground" (נִירוּ לָכֶם נִיר) from Hosea 10:12—the only other text to use the exact language.[21] Hosea 10:12 says, "Sow for yourselves

---

[19] This text contains a reference to "uncircumcised" but with respect to the ear not the heart. This condition leaves them unprepared to listen. The OT also has important references to "uncircumcised lips" (Exod 6:12, 30) and "uncircumcised fruit trees" (Lev 19:23). Perhaps these three uses of "uncircumcised" imply that the foreskin is an impediment or obstacle to hearing, speaking, and producing good fruit. Therefore, circumcision has a negative aspect—the one who is uncircumcised will be cut off from his people (Gen 17:14)—and a positive aspect of signifying that one is devoted to God. Stephen Dempster drew my attention to the other two "uncircumcised" texts and suggested that the foreskin blocks the flow of life and therefore the uncircumcised one will die or be cut off. For more on the negative aspects of circumcision, see Gentry and Wellum, *Kingdom Through Covenant*, 274–75. For the view that the foreskin was seen as a barrier to fruitfulness, see also Craig G. Bartholomew and Michael W. Goheen, *The Drama of Scripture: Finding Our Place in the Biblical Story* (Grand Rapids: Baker, 2004), 218–19n26.

[20] Gentry and Wellum, *Kingdom Through Covenant*, 487.

[21] Werner Lemke, "Circumcision of the Heart," in Brent A. Strawn and Nancy R. Bowen, eds., *A God So Near: Essays on Old Testament Theology in Honor of Patrick D. Miller* (Winona Lake, IN: Eisenbrauns, 2003), 303.

righteousness; reap steadfast love; break up your fallow ground, for it is the time to seek the LORD, that he may come and rain righteousness upon you" (ESV). Thus Jeremiah employs the same imagery commanding the people not to sow to thorns (4:3b), which are probably to be understood as covenantal infidelity since the opposite is in Hosea, who instructs the people to sow to righteousness (i.e., do covenant faithfulness) in order that they might reap loyal love (חֶסֶד). Therefore, when heart circumcision is used in verse 4, it is supporting Jeremiah's overall call to covenant loyalty by now calling to the people to circumcise or devote their hearts to Yahweh. The themes of Deuteronomy 10:12–22, then, are in the background. Jeremiah was a prophet of the Deuteronomic vision. His preaching was completely in line with Moses in that they both desired the people to be faithful to Yahweh from an internally devoted heart.

In *Kingdom Through Covenant*, Gentry concluded that Jeremiah 4:2 contained not only an allusion to the Abrahamic covenant but a development or variant to it. The nations will declare themselves blessed in him, that is, Yahweh. In Genesis 22:18, etc., the reference is usually to the nations declaring themselves blessed in Abraham or his descendants. In Jeremiah 4:3–4, he calls the people to go beyond the circumcision of the flesh (Genesis 17) and circumcise their hearts. Thus, Jeremiah 4:1–4 supports a developing typology of the circumcision of the Abrahamic covenant. External circumcision under the Abrahamic covenant was a type that already anticipated an antitype—heart circumcision. This association was already made in Deuteronomy 30:4–7, and Jeremiah now forges the relationship between the Abrahamic covenant and heart circumcision as part of the means by which the nations will declare themselves blessed in Yahweh. This conclusion would be confirmed if Jeremiah denounced confidence in external circumcision and explained that Israel will be judged due to uncircumcised hearts. He takes this step in 9:24–25.

Jeremiah 9:24–25 (25–26 EV). This text describes future days ("Behold days are coming") when Yahweh will visit punishment on *all circumcised with the foreskin*.[22] In verse 25, Jeremiah then lists Egypt, Judah, Edom,

---

[22] This reading is superior to the ESV's "circumcised merely in the flesh" since it incorporates the background of the practice of incomplete circumcision (see discussion

sons of Ammon, Moab, and all who cut the corners of their hair, who dwell in the wilderness, as ones who perform incomplete circumcision. The punishment will come on all of these nations because all of them are partially circumcised, including Judah. Steiner comments:

> It has been plausibly suggested that Jeremiah's aim in this prophecy is the same as his goal in the Temple Sermon (chap. 7): to demolish the illusory psychological refuges of his countrymen. The people of Judah prided themselves on bearing the sign of the Lord's covenant with Abraham, and they relied on it to protect them from the destruction to be visited on the uncircumcised nations. Nations like Egypt and Edom could not boast of possessing this special status, because their circumcision was incomplete. . . . Jeremiah's point is that the difference is imaginary: the circumcision of the Jews is also incomplete.[23]

Steiner's analysis and conclusions are sound. Jeremiah's temple sermon and this judgment oracle are in keeping with Deuteronomy 7:9–10: "Know therefore that the LORD your God is God, the faithful God who keeps covenant and steadfast love with those who love him and keep his commandments, to a thousand generations, and repays to their face those who hate him, by destroying them. He will not be slack with one who hates him. He will repay him to his face" (ESV). From the beginning, Deuteronomy 7 outlined covenant relationship on the basis of election *and* covenant faithfulness— not merely biology or genealogy. Yahweh keeps covenant and steadfast love with those who love him and keep his commandments. Neither this passage nor Jeremiah 9:24–25 offers any assurance of covenant membership to the wayward descendant of Abraham merely due to external circumcision administered in accordance with genealogy. Punishment is coming upon Judah and Israel because the whole house of Israel is uncircumcised of heart. They have abdicated their responsibility of covenant fidelity to Yahweh from a devoted heart.

---

of Egyptian circumcision above) and the grammar of the phrase (מוּל בְּעׇרְלָה, "circumcised *with* a foreskin"). Cf. Steiner, "Incomplete Circumcision," 497–505, for details.

[23] Ibid., 504–5.

Jeremiah employed heart circumcision in similar ways to Deuteronomy itself (esp. Deut 10:12–22). He also extended it to heart change in a way similar to Deuteronomy 30:1–10. The famous passage predicting the new covenant (Jer 31:31–34) explains that the new order will include new hearts with the Torah inscribed on them resulting in a newly created community who all know Yahweh from the least to the greatest.[24] Although the word *circumcision* is not found anywhere in Jeremiah's Book of Consolation, the thematic elements between Deuteronomy 30:1–10 and Jeremiah 30–33 are clear. Both texts refer to restoration of the people after a return from exile (Deut 30:1–3; cp. Jer 30:3). Likewise, both texts envision geographical and internally transformative elements upon the return from exile. The return from exile results in a newly prepared and consecrated people of God who will be devoted to him from a circumcised heart.

Ezekiel's Heart Transplant

Ezekiel employs one reference to heart circumcision (44:6–9) and the extension to heart change on three occasions (11:16–21; 18:30–32; and 36:22–36).[25] In the context of Ezekiel's third temple vision (chaps. 40–48), Ezekiel 44:4–31 treats the matter of regulations regarding temple service.[26] In verses 6–8 Ezekiel reviews past violations of sacred space, focusing on leading the "sons of a foreigner" into the temple. These foreigners (בְּנֵי נֵכָר) are further described as "uncircumcised of heart" and "uncircumcised of flesh." The second descriptor refers to Genesis 17:11. That foreigners who were uncircumcised in the flesh were not to enter sacred space was

---

[24] Cf. the extended discussion of the new covenant in Jeremiah 30–33 in Gentry and Wellum, *Kingdom Through Covenant*, 491–529.

[25] These passages and others within Ezekiel were ably interpreted by Peter Gentry. See Gentry and Wellum, *Kingdom Through Covenant*, 470–81.

[26] For a discussion of the meaning of this vision, see G. K. Beale, *The Temple and the Church's Mission: A Biblical Theology of the Dwelling Place of God*, NSBT 17 (Downers Grove, IL: InterVarsity, 2004), 335–64. Also, see Daniel I. Block, *The Book of Ezekiel 25–48*, NICOT (Grand Rapids: Eerdmans, 1998), 494–506, 616–48. Both scholars read the vision in symbolic or "ideational" terms, to borrow the term from Block, and reject that this temple was ever to be built.

mandated in Exodus 12:48. Given what we have said about heart circumcision, these foreigners were also not devoted to Yahweh and the cult. They were no different from the people of Israel Jeremiah described in 9:25 as "uncircumcised of heart." No specific historical occasion is in view.[27] Rather the vision presents the reader with a sweeping negative review of Israel's history. The people were circumcised in flesh but not in heart (Ezek 36:22–36 has yet to take place); and, therefore, they became negligent when guarding sacred space, and they outsourced the job to foreigners, uncircumcised of heart and flesh.

In verse 9 the messenger formula ("Thus said Adonai Yahweh") introduces Yahweh's immediate response to this abomination: he refuses the foreigner, uncircumcised in heart and flesh, access into sacred space. Those who are not members of the covenant community will not have access to God's presence. The vision symbolically uses familiar categories of covenant membership (i.e., circumcision) in order to instruct the community about access to the temple. Ezekiel's burden is to show that those who are not part of the covenant community will not be permitted into the temple, the dwelling place of God. In his day an ideal member of the covenant community was a circumcised-in-heart-and-flesh Israelite;[28] and, therefore, that person would be admitted into the temple. But Ezekiel himself places the accent on the transformed heart (cf. 11:16–21; 18:30–32; 36:22–36). All those who have undergone the heart transplant (heart of flesh for a heart of stone) will be admitted into God's presence, the new Zion. Therefore, in an indirect way Ezekiel's final vision supports the developing typology that only those circumcised of heart will be true members of the new Zion.

Conclusions

Before moving to the NT and theological application, a summary of the argument is in order. First, the sign of circumcision with Abraham in Genesis 17 and later with Israel is best understood against the background

---

[27] See the options in Block, *Ezekiel*, 622–23.
[28] Cf. Jer 9:25 for the statement about the whole house of Israel as uncircumcised in heart. Therefore, no contemporary Israelite met Ezekiel's idealism in this passage.

of Egyptian circumcision of royal and priestly classes. The ritual of Egyptian circumcision signified devoted service to the deity. This meaning was transferred to Abraham and later Israel with two important differences: every male Israelite underwent the ritual and was eight days old. Thus Israel bore an appropriate sign that would remind them they are a kingdom of priests and a holy nation (Exod 19:6). Second, Deuteronomy 10:12–22 and 30:1–10 contain references to heart circumcision, where the one who has received heart circumcision will become loyal to Yahweh from a devoted heart (cf. Deut 6:4–5). Third, Jeremiah and Ezekiel employ heart circumcision and heart change in ways that extend and develop heart circumcision in Deuteronomy. The prophets emphasize divine initiative and the resultant covenant faithfulness of the people who have undergone heart circumcision and heart change after the return from exile.

While tracing the theme of circumcision through the canon, several important observations were noted: (1) External circumcision as a sign of devotion to Yahweh was immediately riddled with tension since Ishmael, Esau, and the rebellious offspring of Abraham had the sign but were not devoted to Yahweh as the sign indicated. The sign was at odds with the thing signified. (2) Circumcision as the sign of the Abrahamic covenant underwent development from an early time. The reference to heart circumcision in Deuteronomy 10:16 made clear that internal circumcision would manifest itself in covenantally faithful relationships. Henceforth, circumcision of the heart would be the sign of the true covenant member. Deuteronomy 30:4–7 and Jeremiah 4:1–4 collocate other Abrahamic covenantal terms with heart circumcision. This move generated a significant development in the life of the sign of circumcision and the Abrahamic covenant in general, for now the blessings of the Abrahamic covenant will come only to those who have circumcised hearts. (3) Jeremiah 9:24–25 predicts a day when Israel will no longer be shielded from the punishment due the nations because their circumcision was external only. In the final analysis Judah is no better off than the rest of the nations. (4) Deuteronomy 30:1–10 instructs that heart circumcision cannot be attained by human initiative, but Yahweh will perform the ritual on the heart at the second stage of the return from exile, that is, the freedom from sin and death itself.

The OT itself witnesses to a development of the heart circumcision theme before one reaches the NT. The apostle Paul appears to be dependent on this development as he interprets the OT in view of the Christ event.

Heart Circumcision and Change in the New Testament

In the majority of usages of περιτομή "circumcised" (36x) and ἀκροβυστία "uncircumcised" (20x), the NT authors employ the terms to distinguish Jews (including proselytes) and Gentiles (cf. 1 Cor 7:19; Gal 2:7; etc.). On three occasions, however, Paul uses circumcision to indicate fulfillment of the promises in the OT (Rom 2:29; Phil 3:3; Col 2:11).[29]

Romans 2:29

Perhaps the clearest example of NT circumcision of the heart is Romans 2:29, for it is the only NT text to use the phrase "circumcision of the heart" (περιτομὴ καρδίας).[30] Paul's overall argument in the larger unit is to demonstrate that the Jews are accountable to God for sin (2:1–3:8). The relevant section from Romans 2:25–29 is part of a unit (2:17–29) in which Paul argues that there are limitations of the covenant. First, he points out the limitation of the law (2:17–24). Jews dishonor God by boasting in the law and transgressing the same law (2:23). Moo suggests that when Paul took away the benefit of possessing the law, the interlocutor claimed that circumcision, that sign which identified Jews as God's people and heirs of the Abrahamic promises, would keep them from being treated the same as Gentiles (even to the point of experiencing God's wrath, cf. 2:5).[31] In Romans 2:25–29, Paul now seeks to show that external or outward circumcision

---

[29] Ephesians 2:11 contains another instance. Paul does not further elaborate on this use of the metaphor so it will be excluded from close analysis.

[30] Here I depend on the commentary by Douglas J. Moo, *The Epistle to the Romans*, NICNT (Grand Rapids: Eerdmans, 1996), 166–77 (cf. the outline on p. 33).

[31] Ibid., 167.

is only of benefit if one keeps the law. Otherwise, circumcision becomes uncircumcision in the sense that it is of no benefit "to rescue the Jew from the tyranny of sin and the judgment of God" (2:25).[32] The external ritual is not what saves; rather, obedience to the law will determine whether one is righteous at the judgment. Therefore, the one in an uncircumcised state could be reckoned as circumcised if one kept the requirements of the law (2:26). Verse 27 then indicates that the uncircumcised one who completes the law will condemn the one who, although that one has the law and circumcision, is a transgressor of the law.

Verses 28–29 explain ("for," γάρ) how circumcision cannot save the Jew from the power of sin and the judgment of God. In these verses Paul redefines who the Jew is. The clauses may be analyzed episodically:[33]

A. For it is not the Jew who is one visibly who is the Jew,

B. nor is it the visible circumcision, in the flesh, that is circumcision

A. but the Jew who in secret who is the Jew,

B. and circumcision of the heart, in the Spirit, not in letter, is circumcision

The A sections define who is not a Jew and who is a Jew, while the B sections define what is not circumcision and what is circumcision. The points of contrast in both cases are between "what is visible" (φανερός) and "what is secret" (κρυπτός). Given the passages in Leviticus, Deuteronomy, Jeremiah, and Ezekiel, the Jews would have been in complete agreement with Paul's definition of the Jew and circumcision.[34] Nevertheless, the reference to "not in the letter" would probably have unsettled them. Moo comments, "Paul's

---

[32] Ibid., 168.

[33] Ibid., 173–4. For the terminology of "episodic," see Byron Wheaton, "Focus and Structure in the Abrahamic Narratives," *TrinJ* 27 (2006): 143–62.

[34] See also the passage in *Jubilees* 1:23 in the context of restoration of the people in James H. Charlesworth, *The Old Testament Pseudepigrapha*, vol. 2 (New York: Doubleday, 1985), 54. Cf. also the Odes of Solomon (probably a later Christian work) in Charlesworth, *The Old Testament Pseudepigrapha*, 744.

'letter'/'Spirit' contrast is a salvation-historical one, 'letter' describing the past era in which God's law through Moses played a central role and 'Spirit' summing up the new era in which God's Spirit is poured out in eschatological fullness and power. It is only the circumcision 'in the Spirit' that ultimately counts."[35] Therefore, Paul has interpreted salvation history through Christ, signaling that the heart circumcision in the Spirit has come. The internal/secret antitype has arrived, and therefore the external/visible circumcision can no longer distinguish Jew from non-Jew.

Philippians 3:3

In Philippians 3:3 Paul says, "We are the circumcision, who serve [ESV: worship] by the Spirit of God and who boast in Christ Jesus and who do not place confidence in the flesh" (my translation). In 3:2 Paul instructs the church to beware of "those who mutilate the flesh" (ESV; τὴν κατατομήν), that is, the false circumcision of the Judaizers. Paul's own testimony in 3:5 interprets "circumcised on the eighth day" as confidence in the flesh (3:4). In 3:3, however, Paul claims "*we* are the circumcision (ἡ περιτομή)," suggesting Paul is thinking of a specific circumcision. He further describes this circumcision as "those who serve in/with/by the Spirit of God." Paul uses the verb "to serve" (λατρεύω) in 3:3. With this Greek verb, the Septuagint rendered עבד "to serve" 24 times[36] out of 35[37] in Deuteronomy. Significantly, λατρεύω appears in 10:12, 20 where Moses describes covenant loyalty to the people (cf. discussion of 10:16 above). Paul further describes "serving" with "in/with/by the Spirit of God" (πνεύματι θεοῦ). Paul uses the phrase πνεύματι θεοῦ four times in his letters (Rom 8:14; 1 Cor 12:3; 2 Cor 3:3; Phil 3:3). Perhaps 2 Corinthians 3:3 is the most significant analogue, for Paul asserts

---

[35] Moo, *Romans*, 175.

[36] Deuteronomy 4:19, 28; 5:9; 6:13; 7:4, 16; 8:19; 10:12, 20; 11:13, 16, 28; 12:2; 13:3, 7, 14; 17:3; 28:14, 36, 47f; 29:17, 25; 30:17; 31:20. Even at 11:28, where עבד is not present in the Hebrew, the translator renders אַחַר "after" with λατρεύω "to serve."

[37] Deuteronomy 4:19, 28; 5:9, 13; 6:13; 7:4, 16; 8:19; 10:12, 20; 11:13, 16; 12:2, 30; 13:3, 5, 7, 14; 15:12, 18f; 17:3; 20:11; 21:3f; 28:14, 36, 39, 47f, 64; 29:17, 25; 30:17; 31:20.

that the church at Corinth is "the epistle of Christ . . . having been written not with ink but with the Spirit of the living God, not on stone tablets but on tablets of fleshly hearts" (my translation). Paul describes the church at Corinth as the new covenant community (2 Cor 3:6), an epistle written with the Spirit of God. In Philippians 3:3 "the circumcision" serve by the Spirit of God. They boast in Christ and put no confidence in the flesh.

Although the phrase "new covenant" never appears in Philippians, Paul describes them as a new covenant community on four occasions by exhorting them "to think the same," (φρονεῖν τὸ αὐτό; 2:2; 4:2), "to think the one thing," (φρονεῖν τὸ ἕν; 2:2) and "to stand in one spirit, with one soul/ mind contending together" (στήκειν ἐν ἑνὶ πνεύματι, μιᾷ ψυχῇ συναθλοῦντες; 1:27).[38] In this context "the circumcision" who serve by the Spirit of God could only refer to members of the new covenant. The type, circumcision of the flesh, has outlasted its purpose since the antitype, internal circumcision of the heart, has arrived in Christ. Now only those who serve by the Spirit of God can rightfully be called "the circumcision" and be identified as members of the new covenant.

Colossians 2:11–12

No discussion of internal circumcision is complete without discussion of Colossians 2:11–12.[39] The exegesis of the particulars of verse 11 by Martin Salter should be followed.[40] Given the trajectory of visible circumcision to

---

[38] Gentry and Wellum have correctly located the background for these NT references and others like them in the new covenant passages in Jer 32:39, "one heart and one way"; Ezek 11:19, "one heart and a new spirit"; and Ezek 36:26, "new heart and new spirit" (see Gentry and Wellum, *Kingdom Through Covenant*, 474). I also add the reference from the ethical section of Romans 12 (12:16), "thinking the same for one another" (τὸ αὐτὸ εἰς ἀλλήλους φρονοῦντες).

[39] This passage and its implications for the baptism debate became the topic of a spirited exchange between Martin Salter and David Gibson in two articles published in *Themelios*: Salter, "Does Baptism," 15–29. Gibson, "Sacramental Supersessionism," 191–208.

[40] David Gibson acknowledges that the problem with Salter's exegesis is not his analysis of the particulars of exegesis but the overall biblical theological framework in or from which Salter interprets the details. Cf. Gibson, "Sacramental Supersessionism,"

hidden heart circumcision, the "circumcision performed without hands" in verse 11 is a reference to the eschatological circumcision that God would perform on his people at the second stage of the return from exile (cf. discussion of Deut 30:6 above). This should not be described as "spiritual circumcision," but the antitype or fulfillment of the OT type, which resolves a tension from following redemptive history in which the old covenant people could bear the sign of devotion to God in their flesh but not actually have devoted hearts. The prepositional phrase "by circumcision belonging to and performed by Christ" explains how the people have become circumcised with such a circumcision.[41] The Christ event has become the lens Paul uses to interpret the old sign of circumcision. The "tradition of men" and the "elementals of the world" are not according to Christ (2:8). Rather, in him the fullness of deity dwells bodily, and in him the church is filled (2:9–10). Therefore, the circumcision performed by Christ prepares or devotes the church to Christ.[42]

At verse 12, particularly in how the participle συνταφέντες "having been buried" relates to the main verb περιετμήθητε "you were circumcised" (2:11), my analysis differs from Salter's. Rather than attempting to match up textual elements from Colossians 2:11–12 and Romans 6:3–4, we must analyze the grammar of Colossians 2:11–12 more closely.[43] Based on

---

191. It seems to me that at least part of what impeded this discussion was the unfortunate use of the words "physical" and "spiritual" with respect to circumcision and baptism. The biblical categories in which circumcision moves are "sign," "visible," "shadow," "type," "antitype," "hidden," and "substance." This will be unpacked below.

[41] For this interpretation of the complicated genitive phrase "by the circumcision of Christ" (ἐν τῇ περιτομῇ τοῦ Χριστοῦ), see Salter, "Does Baptism," 24.

[42] The phrase "in the removal of the body of flesh" is best understood with Salter as the removal of the old man, that is, the removal of the church from its "in Adam" relationship. Circumcision performed by Christ removes one from being under Adam. Thus "circumcision" devotes the church to God, while the removed body of flesh draws attention to that which the people were previously devoted.

[43] To be fair, Salter did appeal to a study by Charles Anderson. See Salter, "Does Baptism," 25–26. But if the participle is contemporaneous with the main verb, then how does Salter eventually prioritize circumcision under baptism? Romans 6:3–4 becomes the interpretive key, but one could easily object to this comparison because Romans 6 nowhere mentions circumcision.

discourse grammar (which argues that language is full of linguistic choices and authors choose one option over others because each choice is meaningful), Colossians 2:11–12 has one main finite verb "you were circumcised" (2:11), and verse 12 begins with a participle "having been buried." The following choices are available to the author: (1) He could have used a verb plus verb syntax to communicate that the two ideas had equal prominence. The choice to use a participle instead of another verb highlights that the finite verb deserves primary attention.[44] (2) He could have used a participle plus verb syntax rather than a verb plus participle syntax. The first option sets the stage for the main action that follows, but it also "backgrounds" the action of the participle making it less prominent than the action of the main verb.[45] The second option shares the "backgrounded action" of the first, but instead of providing a "circumstantial frame," participles following the main verb emphasize the action of the main verb even less prominently.[46]

Colossians 2:11–12 employs a verb plus participle syntax. According to discourse grammar, then, the main verb "you were circumcised" (ESV) is receiving primary prominence while the participle "having been buried" (ESV) is playing an elaborative role to the action of the main verb. The grammar supports the overall thesis of this paper: circumcision is the primary theme that runs across the biblical canon, and here Paul is concerned to show how in Christ Christians have undergone the antitypical circumcision of the heart. The phrase "having been buried with him in baptism" and the following relative clause "in which you were also raised with him through faith" (ESV) elaborates on the main action of circumcision performed without hands. Therefore, heart circumcision is the overarching biblical category in which baptism is subsumed. Invisible circumcision is the antitype of the type, visible circumcision. Paul does not refer to the type or shadow in this text.

---

[44] Steven E. Runge, *Discourse Grammar of the Greek New Testament: A Practical Introduction for Teaching and Exegesis* (Peabody, MA: Hendrickson, 2010), 248.

[45] Ibid., 250.

[46] Ibid., 262–63.

The use of the participle in verse 12 creates some ambiguity over the exact relationship between heart circumcision and baptism in this text. Nevertheless, we may advance three observations from the grammar: (1) For baptism (v. 12) to replace or fulfill circumcision (v. 11) in this text, one would expect two finite verbs sharing equal prominence, but Paul does not present the ideas in this way. Rather, baptism elaborates heart circumcision in some way. (2) For baptism to be the circumstantial means by which heart circumcision occurs, one would expect the participle to precede the main verb.[47] (3) Most important, Paul does not tie heart circumcision to faith in verse 11 as he ties baptism to faith in verse 12, where faith is presented as the means for being raised ("through faith," διὰ τῆς πίστεως). Thus baptism through faith elaborates or works out the inner circumcision of the heart. This observation is the key to further theologizing about the relationship of heart circumcision to baptism (see below).

Conclusions

This survey of the NT evidence for heart circumcision shows that Paul believed heart circumcision is a reality tied to the eschatological age of the Spirit and the circumcision of Christ (Rom 2:29; Phil 3:3; Col 2:11). In this Paul is in complete continuity with the OT development of circumcision that Yahweh would circumcise the hearts of the people upon the return from the second stage of the exile (Deut 30:6), when he would write the law on their hearts (Jer 31:31–34) and replace their stony hearts with fleshly hearts (Ezek 36:22–36), resulting in a people of God who would be loyal to him and obey him. In Romans 2:29 and Philippians 3:3, Paul has announced that the time of antitypical circumcision has come; and, therefore, it is also time to redefine who the Jew is—both in light of OT anticipation and the inauguration of the new covenant in Christ. The Jew is now one who bears heart circumcision and boasts in Christ not in external circumcision. The true Jew is the one who serves by the Spirit of God.

---

[47] Contra Collins, "What Does Baptism . . . Part I," 19.

Theological Synthesis

This study has direct implications for the topic of ecclesiology, particularly baptism.[48] First, I will clarify the relationship of circumcision in the flesh to heart circumcision. Second, I will explain how baptism relates to the biblical typology of circumcision.

From the beginning, the Abrahamic covenant's sign, circumcision of the flesh, would have indicated that he and his family were devoted or consecrated to the priestly service of Yahweh (Gen 17:11). This is not a purely "physical" act. As a new Adam, Abraham and his family bore the sign which consecrated him and his family for the mission of establishing God's kingdom within the covenant God made with him—kingdom through covenant. As one traverses the canon, however, witnessing the circumcision of Ishmael, Esau, and later rebellious Israel, the sign of circumcision of the flesh did not indicate the thing signified—devotion to Yahweh as king-priests. This tension is realized early, for before one departs from the Pentateuch, one encounters the Deuteronomic call to circumcise the heart (10:16) and the Deuteronomic promise that Yahweh will do it himself upon return from exile (30:6). Therefore, the sign of circumcision in the flesh is best described as a *type*, whose typology is both prospective and escalating. Circumcision of the flesh pointed forward to a greater circumcision since the removal of the foreskin became no guarantee that the sign indicated the thing signified. Only the greater circumcision of the heart would bring about the thing signified—true devoted service to Yahweh.

The antitype, heart circumcision, is better described as "internal" or "hidden" not "spiritual," since there was "spiritual" significance to circumcision as a sign in Genesis 17, but there are clear points of discontinuity between the two circumcisions. The terms *physical* and *spiritual* do not help describe the certain discontinuity involved. Rather, the biblical categories, developed along the axis of redemptive history, suggest a type-antitype

---

[48] For the secondary literature on this vast topic, the reader is directed to Thomas R. Schreiner and Shawn D. Wright, eds., *Believer's Baptism: Sign of the New Covenant in Christ* (Nashville, TN: B&H Academic, 2006), esp., Stephen Wellum, "Baptism and the Relationship Between the Covenants," 97–161.

relationship between the visible sign of circumcision and hidden circumcision introduced at the second stage of the return from exile (i.e., at Christ's first advent). They are similar to each other in that both circumcisions symbolized devotion to God and are tied to covenant initiation. But the differences are also significant. The sign of circumcision in the flesh under the Abrahamic and old covenants did not and could not bring about the reality signified—a truly devoted covenant member.[49]

As redemptive history progressed, the ever-increasing need for God to circumcise the human heart became increasingly apparent. God would perform this act as part of the return from exile, not the geographical return but the new exodus out of sin and death. The new covenant people of God have experienced this heart circumcision, which is tied to Christ's work and ensuing metaphors in the NT, which describe the new creation of the people of God: regeneration (Titus 3:5; cf. born again/from above/from God in John 3:3; 1 Pet 1:3; 1 John 5:1; etc.), Spirit baptism (1 Cor 12:13; etc.), the Spirit poured out (Joel 2:28; Acts 10:45; etc.), and the indwelling of the Spirit (John 14:16–17; cf. John 7:39).[50] The one whose heart is circumcised by God will manifest the inward reality of a devoted heart in service and obedience, and this heart change is promised for all of the members of the new covenant from the least to the greatest (Jer 31:28–34).

Since heart circumcision is the antitype of circumcision in the flesh, does baptism fulfill or replace circumcision in the flesh in any sense, and who are the proper recipients of baptism? In order to establish baptism as a replacement or fulfillment of circumcision, one would need to demonstrate that from its inception through the development of the biblical covenants visible circumcision was to reach its terminus in NT baptism. One should

---

[49] Some may object as to whether the sign should do this or not. Deuteronomy and the prophetic injunctions to keep and maintain the covenant indicated that moral and actual change were expected out of those who bore the covenant sign for devotion. In other words, circumcision did not simply devote; it devoted one to service/worship of God. Isaiah and Jesus expected true worship from the heart when they said the people honored God with their lips but their hearts were far from him (Isa 29:13; Matt 15:8).

[50] The background to these texts is the heart change passages in the OT tied to the anticipated new covenant (Jer 31:31–34; 32:37–41; Ezek 11:16–21; 18:30–32; 36:22–36).

not simply search for and find analogies or parallels between circumcision and baptism and then claim a typological relationship.

The article by C. John Collins will help illustrate the point.[51] In order to establish baptism as a parallel to circumcision, Collins appeals to the following lines of evidence: (1) Colossians 2:11–12; (2) the parallel between household baptism passages (e.g., Acts 16:15) that "echo" the "household circumcision" passage (Gen 17:27); (3) baptism as incorporating one into the covenant community (Rom 6:3–5), just as circumcision did; and (4) an alleged connection between circumcision and cleanness and the subsequent transfer from circumcision to baptism as a washing, which now marks entry into the clean and holy people of God. Of these four lines of evidence, only point one brings baptism and circumcision into the same context (cf. the discussion of this text above). Reason two relies on an "echo," and it is interesting to note that the Lord had already opened Lydia's heart, and then she was baptized.[52] Reason four relies on a comparison between OT washings and circumcision. Although there are parallels between these two rites,[53] washings in the OT are not used for covenant initiation as circumcision was used. Rather, the circumcised undertake the ceremonial washings as members of the covenant. Given this point, one wonders whether OT ceremonial washings are the proper background for

---

[51] Collins, "What Does Baptism . . . Part I,"18–21. He does not claim a typological relationship, but he does claim this is a redemptive historical shift. David Gibson attempts a more sophisticated form of the same argument. Rather than arguing from textual parallels, as Collins, Gibson argues for a replacement of the physical sign of circumcision with the physical sign of baptism based on the premise that both signs point to spiritual circumcision as the thing signified; that is, both signs share an overall parallel significance in their relation to the thing signified. Gibson, "Sacramental Supersessionism," 204.

[52] See also Acts 18:8 for another clear example of Crispus and his family believing the preached gospel and then being baptized.

[53] Collins, "What Does Baptism . . . Part I," 13–14. He lists: (1) the threat of being "cut off from the people" (Gen 17:14; cp. Num 19:13, 20), (2) both are required to eat safely from the various peace offerings (Exod 12:44; cp. Lev 7:20), (3) OT references to the uncircumcised and unclean (Isa 52:1; Ezek 44:7), and (4) sign/signified distinction (Deut 10:16; Prov 30:12).

baptism; and, in fact, this is the argument Collins is making. Why introduce circumcision? Collins introduces circumcision because it is conventional in Christian (Reformed?) theology to do so.[54] Of the four reasons his third point is the strongest. Nevertheless, Romans 6:3–5 makes no distinction between Spirit and water baptism. Rather, baptism into Christ is "part and parcel of the complex of saving events that took place at conversion."[55] Paul is describing conversion by describing their baptism into Christ. There are no distinctions between heart circumcision, baptism, and faith (or repentance) in this text as was observed in Colossians 2:11–12.

None of these alleged parallels establish a proper biblical typology of circumcision to baptism across the epochs of redemptive history, and one needs to trace this precise development to make the case. Rather, what we have shown is that external circumcision performed by hands is a type that undergoes typological development across the canon until it reaches its fulfillment and terminus in the heart circumcision performed by Christ. Therefore, external circumcision does not relate to baptism in any way, when examined from the vantage point of the canon. It pointed forward to a new and better internal circumcision. The next question is, how does baptism relate to heart circumcision?

We have argued that the OT anticipated heart circumcision would be performed on God's people at the second stage of the return from exile. Therefore, it has a clear place in the unfolding of redemptive history. We have also argued heart circumcision is expanded and developed in the prophets (Jeremiah and Ezekiel, who foretell a day when Yahweh will change the hearts of people in order that they might obey him from a devoted heart). The NT associates heart circumcision with the new operations of the Spirit, that is, in terms of Spirit baptism, the pouring out of the Spirit, and the indwelling Spirit. In addition to the imparting of the Spirit, the NT also includes faith, repentance, confession, and baptism in

---

[54] Ibid., 13.

[55] Thomas R. Schreiner, "Baptism in the Epistles: An Initiation Rite for Believers," in *Believers Baptism*, 74–75.

the complex of saving events pertaining to conversion.[56] Regarding the relationship between the Spirit and baptism, we conclude with Stein,

> The intimate tie between the reception of the Spirit and baptism
> in Acts is due to both their close temporal relation and that both
> were essential components, along with faith, repentance, and
> confession, in becoming a Christian. Similarly, Paul received his
> commissioning (9:15–16; see 22:14–15), his filling with the Spirit,
> and his sight (9:17–18a) before he was baptized (9:18b).[57]

This pattern (Spirit → faith—repentance—confession—baptism) is also in continuity with Colossians 2:11–12. The prominence belongs to God's act in performing circumcision, while baptism with its means of faith ("through faith") elaborates on the one who has undergone heart circumcision—a baptized believer. Although baptism is closely grouped together with the other elements of conversion, it is the only part of the conversion complex that has a clear external nature, and it often comes after belief in Christ in Acts.[58] Therefore, baptism's relationship to heart circumcision witnesses and attests to the work of the Spirit in one's life.[59]

The germane implication of this study relates to the subject of baptism. Because the type of circumcision of the flesh has found its fulfillment and terminus in heart circumcision and baptism is a witness to the presence of the latter, the subject of baptism should have experienced the work of the Spirit.

Conclusion

We have argued that circumcision of the flesh marked one out for service to God but that in the OT this sign did not truly equal the thing signified in

---

[56] For the details see, Robert H. Stein, "Baptism in Luke-Acts," in *Believers Baptism*, 35–66.

[57] Ibid., 55.

[58] Acts 2:41; 8:12; 16:31–34; 18:8.

[59] See Diagram 1 on page 158.

the life of the old covenant people of God.[60] This sign of circumcision was also a type, foreshadowing a greater and better heart circumcision, which would bring about the devotion to God signified by the sign. As such, heart circumcision has become the sign for all members of the new covenant who are true Jews in God's kingdom. Baptism, therefore, is not a fulfillment or replacement of circumcision in the flesh, but rather it is an external sign or testimony to the heart circumcision of the member (male and female!) of the new covenant. As a result, it should not be applied to anyone who has not undergone the circumcision of the heart and who has not repented of sin and believed and confessed that Jesus Christ is Lord.

---

[60] Does this entail that no OT saint was regenerate? Two comments concerning this question are in order. First, moving from OT promise to NT fulfillment, one discerns that the Scriptures teach that the scope and operations of the Spirit change in relation to God's people. The new covenant widened the scope of the work of the Spirit, for now not only will Israel's leaders have the Spirit but also the whole community. Furthermore, Jesus' words in John 14:16–17 indicate that the Spirit will be in his disciples as a result of his glorification (cf. John 7:39). John presents this "giving" of the Spirit as a redemptive historical shift obtained uniquely by the historical work of Christ. Second, we must avoid reducing the biblical-theological sense (BT) of "heart circumcision" to systematic theology's (ST) "regeneration." The former points to a larger reality than the latter, which mainly explains why a person believes in the promises of God under either the old or new covenants. "Heart circumcision" with its result of Torah obedience and loyalty to Yahweh is tied firmly to the new covenant era. Therefore, even though BT does not use the term *regeneration* of an OT believer, one could still describe him as "regenerate" in the ST sense as long as one also affirms that OT "regeneration" will undergo development in the new covenant era once heart circumcision has been performed on God's people. In this way one can affirm that God's Spirit stirred up faith in the old covenant people, but this same people longed for a greater and better work of the Spirit to come.

Diagram 1

Abrahamic/Old Covenant	New Covenant
Gen 17; Deut 10:16; 30:6; Jer 4:4; 9:24–25; Ezek 44:6–9	Rom 2:29; Phil 3:3; Col 2:11–12

Circumcision in the Flesh (signifies devoted to God; sign ≠ thing signified)	Heart Circumcision (signifies devoted to God; sign = thing signified)
1. Type	1. Antitype
2. Shadow	2. Reality
3. Visible	3. Hidden
4. External	4. Internal
5. Performed by hands	5. Performed by Christ
6. Created tension in the narrative of redemptive history between sign and thing signified	6. Resolved tension in the narrative of redemptive history between sign and thing signified
7. Underwent development and reinterpretation in the OT toward heart circumcision	7. Fulfillment of the sign and OT anticipation of the devoted heart performed by the Spirit

Typological relationship of circumcision across the covenants, canon, and redemptive history

The solid line indicates a temporal, historical, and typological development from external circumcision to internal circumcision of the heart. The dotted line represents baptism's relationship to internal circumcision as an external witness or testimony to Christ's circumcision of the heart administered upon recognition of heart circumcision. In no way does baptism replace or fulfill physical circumcision. They do not share the same typological relationship, and this is demonstrated by the fact that they perform two different functions. Circumcision devoted one to God. Baptism confirms that one is devoted to God.

Baptism
Testimony or witness to heart circumcision.
Retrospectively performed on the one who believes (pattern in Acts: believed . . . was baptized).
Connected to complex of conversion (i.e. faith and repentance) and therefore comes after heart circumcision/regeneration even if in the NT the complex of events occurred in temporal proximity.

CHAPTER 6

Good-bye and Hello: The Sabbath Command for New Covenant Believers

Thomas R. Schreiner

Introduction

New covenant believers say good-bye to the Sabbath, for it belongs to the old covenant, and we do not live under that administration. But we also say hello to the Sabbath, for the Sabbath is fulfilled in Jesus Christ and points to our future heavenly rest. Entire books have been written on whether the Sabbath command is mandatory for believers in Christ.[1] In a short essay the complex issues on this matter cannot be handled in detail. Instead I will

---

[1] E.g., W. Rordorf, *The History of the Day of Rest and Worship in the Earliest Centuries of the Christian Church* (London: SCM, 1968); R. T. Beckwith and W. Stott, *This Is the Day: The Biblical Doctrine of the Christian Sunday in Its Jewish and Early Christian Setting* (London: Marshall, Morgan, and Scott, 1978); Paul K. Jewett, *The Lord's Day: A Theological Guide to the Christian Day of Worship* (Grand Rapids: Eerdmans, 1971); Samuel Bacchiocchi, *From Sabbath to Sunday: A Historical Investigation of the Rise of Sunday Observance in Earliest Christianity* (Rome: Pontifical Gregorian University, 1977); D. A. Carson, ed., *From Sabbath to Lord's Day: A Biblical, Historical, and Theological Investigation* (Grand Rapids: Zondervan, 1982); C. H. Donato, ed., *Perspectives on the Sabbath: Four Views* (Nashville, TN: B&H Academic, 2011). In this last book MacCarty represents the Seventh Day Adventist view, Pipa a Reformed view, Arand a Lutheran perspective, and Blomberg argues from a Baptist standpoint. My view is very close to

present the broad outlines and major arguments on the question. Believers may differ on the Sabbath (cf. Rom 14:5–6), so I hope my disagreement with some will be taken in a friendly spirit. We may disagree on the Sabbath and concur on the central truths of the gospel.

I will argue in this essay that the Sabbath command is not required for new covenant believers. For Israel the Sabbath command was the sign of the Sinai covenant. Believers in Jesus Christ, however, are not under the old covenant since the new covenant has arrived. The OT Sabbath points forward to the eschatological Sabbath rest, which is now here and which believers will fully enjoy in the heavenly city. Hence, NT writers did not expect or require believers in Jesus Christ to keep the Sabbath.

The essay is divided into five major parts: (1) Sabbath in the OT, (2) Sabbath in Jesus' ministry, (3) Sabbath in Paul's letters, (4) Sabbath in Hebrews, and (5) a short discussion of the Lord's Day. I will argue my case through the various sections and respond to objections.

Sabbath in the OT

Some are surprised to learn that the Sabbath is not mentioned in the creation narrative (Gen 1:1–2:3),[2] but silence regarding the Sabbath in Genesis 2:1–3 explains why nothing is said about the patriarchs (Abraham, Isaac, and Jacob) keeping Sabbath. Nor is there any evidence that Israel kept the Sabbath before they were liberated from Egypt. Genesis 2:1–3 does say that God "completed his work" by "the seventh day," and that he "rested (וַיִּשְׁבֹּת) on the seventh day from all His work that He had done" (2:2).[3] The significance of the seventh day is featured, for God "blessed" it and "declared it holy" since he "rested" (שָׁבַת) from his creation work. God did not rest because he was weary; he rested because his work in creating the

---

Blomberg's, and readers should consult his essay and his responses to the other views for a fuller discussion.

[2] Rightly H. P. Dressler, "The Sabbath in the Old Testament," in *From Sabbath to Lord's Day: A Biblical, Historical, and Theological Investigation*, ed. D. A. Carson (Grand Rapids: Zondervan, 1982), 28.

[3] All references are to the HCSB unless noted otherwise.

world was finished. Hence, God's rest should not be interpreted to mean that he is inactive, for Jesus affirms that the Father is working (John 5:17).

Interestingly, in contrast to the previous six days of creation, we are not told that the seventh day ended. There is no formula about evening and morning as there is with the previous six days, suggesting that the seventh day bears a symbolic significance. Perhaps it signifies the covenantal fellowship God enjoyed with Adam and Eve, a fellowship that was disrupted by the fall. Genesis 3:15 articulates God's plan to restore fellowship and rest. The entrance into the land under Joshua is one stage typologically in the rest, but it is realized more fully and finally in the eschatological rest as Hebrews 4 teaches. The seventh day of creation, then, is not necessarily tied to any particular day of the week: it points to, as Hebrews teaches (4:1–11), and especially in light of the fall, the eschatological rest that believers now enjoy in Christ and will enjoy in fullness in the new creation.[4] The eschatological significance indicates that the seventh day does not necessarily require the observance of one day in distinction from others.[5]

Greg Beale, on the other hand, supports Sabbath keeping from the creation narrative by observing that the blessing of the seventh day and making it holy is for the sake of human beings.[6] Even if this is the case, it does not follow that the seventh day applies to new covenant believers in the same way it applied to Israel, for the text does not speak of the Sabbath but the seventh day, which likely points to the eschatological rest we will enjoy in Jesus Christ (Hebrews 4). Israel, after the exodus, was commanded to keep the Sabbath, but for new covenant believers the seventh day points to the end time, new creation rest.

In his erudite and fascinating defense of sabbatarianism, Beale maintains that the fourth commandment (Exod 20:8–11) unpacks the creation

---

[4] See especially here, Jason S. DeRouchie, "Making the Ten Count: Reflections on the Lasting Message of the Decalogue," in *For Our Good Always: Studies on the Message and Influence of Deuteronomy in Honor of Daniel I. Block*, ed. Jason S. DeRouchie, Jason Gile, and Kenneth J. Turner (Winona Lake, IN: Eisenbrauns, 2013), 428–32.

[5] Against G. K. Beale, *A New Testament Biblical Theology: The Unfolding of the Old Testament in the New* (Grand Rapids: Baker, 2011), 777–81.

[6] Cf. ibid., 778–80.

mandate for Adam.[7] But this is an argument from silence, for nothing is said about Adam or any of the other patriarchs observing the Sabbath. Indeed, the Scriptures emphasize that the law, the Sinai covenant, and the Sabbath began with Moses (e.g., Rom 5:13–14; Gal 3:15–18), suggesting that the Sabbath command was not a creation ordinance.

What is clear is that the command to rest on the Sabbath was first given to Israel under the Mosaic covenant (Exod 20:8–11; 31:12–17; Lev 23:3; Deut 5:12–15). God prohibited Israel from working on the Sabbath, which is equivalent to our Saturday. The ban from work was all encompassing, including children, slaves, and animals. The OT specifies what qualifies as work: gathering manna (Exod 16:22–30), plowing and harvesting (Exod 34:21), lighting a fire (Exod 35:3), gathering wood (Num 15:32), and buying and selling merchandise (Neh 10:31; 13:16–22; Jer 17:21–27). Perhaps military campaigns functioned as exceptions (Josh 6:15; 1 Kgs 20:29; 2 Kgs 3:9; cf. 1 Macc 2:32–41). Cult-related activities were regularly permitted on the Sabbath: dedication feasts (1 Kgs 8:65; 2 Chr 7:8), changing temple guards (2 Kgs 11:5–9), putting showbread out (Lev 24:8; 1 Chr 9:32), offering sacrifices (Num 28:9–10; 1 Chr 23:31; 2 Chr 8:13–14; Ezek 45:17; 46:12; Neh 10:33), the duties of priests and Levites (2 Kgs 11:5–9; 2 Chr 23:4, 8), opening the east gate (Ezek 46:1–3), and circumcision (John 7:22–23).

Israel kept the Sabbath by resting from its labors and by refraining from work. Though certain cultic duties were performed, the OT does not clearly instruct Israelites to gather together and worship the Lord on the Sabbath. Obviously, such assemblies *could* take place on the Sabbath; they are not forbidden, but there are no positive commands or directives about worshipping on the Sabbath.

Beale, like many others, appeals to the creation narrative to support the normativity of Sabbath for Christians, which is the best argument for the ongoing validity of the Sabbath, which I will consider in due course.[8] First, we should consider what it means to observe the Sabbath according

---

[7] Ibid., 777, 782.

[8] Ibid., 789, 923. The argument from creation is standard and appears in almost every defense of Sabbath observance. See e.g., Joseph A. Pipa, "The Christian Sabbath,"

to Beale. One would think he would maintain that believers should refrain from working since, as we just saw, the Sabbath command in the OT is about refraining from work. Beale argues instead that believers observe the Sabbath by worshipping on Sunday. He claims that the Sabbath as creation ordinance remains, the Sabbath has been transferred to Sunday, and the specific features that tie the Sabbath to Israel no longer apply (hence the prohibition from work is no longer in effect) since such features have passed away with the inauguration of the eschaton. Therefore, what continues today is the requirement to worship on Sunday.[9] Those who dispense with Sabbath observance, according to Beale, fall prey to overrealized eschatology, for the creational sign should be observed until the consummation.[10]

Beale's application of the Sabbath command is remarkable, for the command, according to him, requires worship but permits work.[11] What the fourth commandment actually instructs people to do (refrain from work) is no longer required according to Beale. How can the Sabbath apply today when the specifics of the commandment are stripped away? Beale says some of the elements of the Sabbath that pertain to Israel do not apply to believers, and thus the application for us is that we should worship on Sunday. But the OT does not require public worship assemblies of believers on the Sabbath (nor does the NT for that matter). As Blomberg says, "If all we had were the Hebrew Scriptures we might never guess that a day of rest eventually also became a day of worship."[12]

In one footnote Beale points to some texts where Sabbath was linked with worship in the temple,[13] but such cultic activities in the temple do not indicate that Israel assembled for worship on the Sabbath. Perhaps

---

in *Perspectives on the Sabbath: Four Views*, ed. C. H. Donato (Nashville, TN: B&H Academic, 2011), 119–23.

[9] Beale, *A New Testament Biblical Theology*, 775–801.

[10] Ibid., 790–91.

[11] Pipa represents another Reformed view, which seems to be more consistent, for he disallows work on Sunday, which he views as a Christian Sabbath. See Pipa, "The Christian Sabbath," 119–71, esp. 130–34, 142–44, 165–70.

[12] Craig L. Blomberg, "The Sabbath as Fulfilled in Christ," in *Perspectives on the Sabbath*, 307.

[13] Beale, *A New Testament Biblical Theology*, 794n43.

Leviticus 23:3 indicates that Israel worshipped on the Sabbath, but as Blomberg says, "If worship took place, we have no hints here as what it specifically involved."[14] And he quotes D. W. Baker on this text: "The exact nature of these Sabbath gatherings is unclear, since they are not mentioned elsewhere."[15] Beale's Christian Sabbath view takes away what the OT clearly requires for the Sabbath (refraining from work) and substitutes what is not clear in the OT (a requirement to worship on the Sabbath).[16]

Also the Sabbath was never intended to be a permanent ordinance because it functioned as a sign of Yahweh's covenant with Israel.[17] Exodus 31:13 demonstrates that the Sabbath was the covenant sign for the Sinai covenant: "You must observe My Sabbaths, for it is a sign (אוֹת) between Me and you throughout your generations." Just as the sign of the Noahic covenant was the rainbow, so the Sabbath is the sign that the Lord has made a "perpetual covenant" (בְּרִית עוֹלָם) with Israel (31:16). We might think the Sinai covenant never ends since we are told that "it is a sign forever" (אוֹת הוּא לְעֹלָם) of the Lord's covenant with Israel (Exod 31:17),[18] but it is clear from the NT that the Sinai covenant is no longer in force. Dressler says, "The Sabbath is not viewed as a universal ordinance for all mankind but as a specific institution for Israel. As a sign of the covenant it was to last as long as that covenant."[19]

There is still another indication that the Sabbath was restricted to the Sinai covenant so that it no longer functions as such for NT believers. Deuteronomy 5:12–15 recapitulates the injunction from the Decalogue to keep the Sabbath (Exod 20:8–11) but adds something not found in Exodus. The Lord declares, "Remember that you were a slave in the land of Egypt,

---

[14] Blomberg, "Final Remarks," in *Perspectives on the Sabbath*, 397.

[15] Ibid., 397n41.

[16] The title for Psalm 92 indicates that it is a song for the Sabbath. I am not saying Israel refrained from worshipping on the Sabbath; however, such worship was not clearly commanded or mandated. What was demanded was cessation from work.

[17] See here Dressler, "The Sabbath in the Old Testament," 30–31.

[18] Ezekiel reiterates the notion that the Sabbath is a "sign" between Yahweh and Israel (Ezek 20:12, 20), conceiving of the Sabbath as a covenant sign (Ezek 20:12), for he appeals to the covenant formula between Yahweh and Israel.

[19] Dressler, "The Sabbath in the Old Testament," 34.

and the LORD your God brought you out of there with a strong hand and an outstretched arm. That is why the LORD your God has commanded you to keep the Sabbath day" (Deut 5:15). The observance of the Sabbath is linked to liberation from Egypt, to the redemption of Israel, functioning as a sign that the Lord has freed Israel from their slavery to the Egyptians. Hence, the Sabbath points back to the rest lost in creation and forward to the rest that will ultimately be enjoyed in Jesus Christ. Believers should not revert back to the type of the Sabbath any more than they should revert to the type of OT sacrifices.

Why is the link between the Sabbath and the exodus significant as to whether the Sabbath is mandatory today? Because NT believers have not been freed from Egyptian bondage as Israel was. The Lord freed the people of Israel (not the whole world) from Egypt. It does not follow, of course, that the exodus from Egypt is irrelevant to believers. The exodus points forward to another covenant, a better covenant, a new covenant where believers are ransomed from their sins by the blood of Jesus Christ (Luke 22:20; cf. Heb 8:1–10:18). Still, the historical event of the exodus was confined to Israel, and observance of the Sabbath was linked to God's freeing his people from Egypt.

The provisional character of the Sabbath is also suggested by the penalties assessed for nonobservance.[20] Those who do not observe the Sabbath must be cut off from the people of God (Exod 31:4). The penalty in Exodus 35:2 is clear: those who violate the Sabbath are to be put to death. The story in Numbers 15:32–36 illustrates this principle. A man went out and gathered wood on the Sabbath day. Moses consulted the Lord as to what should be done to him, and the Lord instructed Israel to stone him to death, and the penalty was duly carried out. Almost all Sabbatarians maintain such punishments should not be carried out today, for they do not believe we are under the civil provisions of the Mosaic covenant. But the traditional notion that the OT law can be neatly split into moral, ceremonial, and civil

---

[20] Beale actually agrees with the substance of what is being said here, even though he thinks the Sabbath is normative today for other reasons (*A New Testament Biblical Theology*, 796).

laws is not convincing. It is better to say the penalties of the covenant are abrogated because the Sinai covenant as a whole is obsolete.

It is instructive to compare the penalty for the Sabbath breaker after the Sinai covenant was ratified to the penalty assessed before the covenant was established. After the Sinai covenant was authorized, the punishment was death (Num 15:32–36). Before the covenant was official, however, the people were rebuked for violating the Sabbath, but their lives were spared (Exod 16:23–30). As before mentioned, the account in Exodus does not indicate that the Sabbath harkened back to the patriarchs. Quite the contrary. The regulation in Exodus 16 is a new one, and the covenant had not been ratified. Hence the people were admonished instead of being executed for their disobedience. Once the covenant is official, however, the sanctions pertaining to the covenant were inflicted on Sabbath breakers. Why is this important? The Sabbath command and its penalties were officially established when the Sinai covenant was confirmed. The Sabbath was a new command, unknown before Exodus 16, and hence the penalties at the outset were not as strict. The newness of the Sabbath ordinance in Exodus 16 constitutes another piece of evidence supporting the notion that the Sabbath was not given at creation and that it is not intended to last forever.

Many Sabbatarians contend that we are no longer under the civil dimension of the Mosaic covenant, but the Sabbath still stands because it is part of the moral law.[21] The issues raised are complex and disputed and cannot be handled in detail here. Still, NT writers do not make the distinctions between the moral, ceremonial, and civil law that have become common in systematic theology.[22] Instead they argue that believers are no longer under the Sinai covenant as a whole, for that covenant belonged to a previous era of redemptive history that has passed away. A new covenant has dawned with the death and resurrection of Christ (1 Cor 11:25; 2 Cor 3:6; Heb 8:8, 13; 9:15; 12:24), and this new covenant is specifically contrasted with

---

[21] See e.g., Pipa, "A Christian Sabbath," 123–28, 136.

[22] So Blomberg, "The Sabbath as Fulfilled in Christ," 319–22; D. A. Carson, "Jesus and the Sabbath in the Four Gospels," in *From Sabbath to Lord's Day: A Biblical, Historical, and Theological Investigation*, ed. D. A. Carson (Grand Rapids: Zondervan, 1982), 68.

the old covenant (2 Cor 3:14; Heb 8:13) or the first covenant (Heb 8:7; 9:1, 15, 18). The terms "old covenant" and "first covenant" signify that the Sinai covenant is no longer applicable. Now there is a new covenant and a "better" covenant (Heb 7:22; 8:6), an "everlasting covenant" (Heb 13:20), which has been established through the blood of Jesus. The argument is not merely that certain features of the old covenant have been cancelled. The Sinai covenant as a whole has passed away. If the covenant has ended, then the sign of the covenant, the Sabbath, has been terminated along with the covenant.

The evidence for the temporary status of the Sinai covenant is compelling. Paul argues that believers are no longer "under the law" (Rom 6:14–15; 1 Cor 9:21; Gal 3:23; 4:21; 5:18). In other words, a new era of redemptive history has arrived and replaced the former time when the Mosaic law was required. Incidentally, it does not follow from this that believers are free from all and any commands. Believers are not under the law of Moses, but they do abide by the law of Christ (1 Cor 9:21; Gal 6:2).[23] Yes, the law of Christ includes some commands from the Sinai covenant and from the Decalogue. But these commands are not mandated because they are part of the Sinai law. They are required because they reflect the character of God, and we know they are moral norms that apply today for a variety of reasons, including their repetition in the NT.

Paul clearly teaches that the Sinai covenant was an interim covenant established 430 years after the covenant with Abraham (Gal 3:15–18). As a provisional covenant it cannot nullify the promises made with Abraham, and it only continued until the coming of the promised offspring (Gal 3:19). Now that the offspring has come (Jesus Christ), the interim covenant has passed away. The law was a "guardian" (παιδαγωγὸς), functioning like a babysitter until the coming of Christ (Gal 3:23–25). Now that Christ has come, believers are "no longer under a guardian" (Gal 3:25), which is another way of saying they are no longer under the law.

I could point to other texts (e.g., Rom 7:4–6), but what we have seen above is clear. The Sinai covenant has passed away for believers in Jesus

---

[23] See also Blomberg, "The Sabbath as Fulfilled in Christ," 326–28.

Christ. We live under the new covenant instead of the old. It follows, then, that the covenant sign attached to the Sinai covenant is not required for Christians.

The two most significant arguments supporting Sabbath observance are that the Sabbath is a creation ordinance and it is also part of the Decalogue. Probably the strongest argument for continuing Sabbath observance is the argument from creation. In Exodus 20:8–10 Israel is commanded to keep the Sabbath day holy and to refrain from work. Verse 11 provides the reason for the admonition. "For the LORD made the heavens and the earth, the sea, and everything in them in six days; then He rested on the seventh day. Therefore the LORD blessed the Sabbath day and declared it holy." God's rest on the seventh day functions as a pattern for Israel, and since that rest reaches back to creation, Sabbatarians claim we have a transcendent word.

The case for Sabbath observance seems strong, for when NT writers appeal to creation, then the command still applies today. For instance, Jesus argues from creation for the notion that marriage must be between one man and one woman and should last till death do us part (Matt 19:3–12). Similarly, Paul argues from creation that same-sex unions are contrary to God's will (Rom 1:26–27). He also appeals to creation in claiming that women should not serve as pastors; they should not teach and exercise authority over men (1 Tim 2:12–13). Permission to marry and to eat all foods is also rooted in creation (e.g., 1 Cor 10:25–26; 1 Tim 4:1–5), countering ascetics who thought it was more pleasing to God to refrain from marriage and the eating of certain foods. The argument is clear and cogent. Commands rooted in creation still apply today. The Sabbath command appeals to creation; and, therefore, it must be obeyed today.

We can understand, given the argument from creation, why sincere believers in Christ think the Sabbath is binding. Perhaps this explains why Paul himself is not dogmatic on the Sabbath but says, "Each one must be fully convinced in his own mind" (Rom 14:5). Nevertheless, the argument from creation with respect to the Sabbath is not convincing for four reasons.

First, if the Sabbath were truly a creation ordinance, it should have been required for the patriarchs, but we have already seen that it was not mandated. Instead, the Sabbath was instituted when Israel was constituted as a nation, and it was not authorized for Israel until after the exodus (Exodus 16).

Second, everything found in creation is not mandatory for believers today. We are not required, for instance, to cultivate the land and work as farmers; and contrary to Adam and Eve before the fall, we must wear clothes (Gen 2:25).

Third, since everything in creation is not mandatory, how do we determine if we have in the creation accounts a command that applies to today? In some instances this is a difficult question that is not easy to resolve. Ultimately we consider the entire canonical witness found in the Scriptures. In doing so, we have to pay attention to the progress of revelation and to the covenantal shifts that have taken place along the way. It is instructive that when it comes to marriage and divorce, homosexuality, the role of men and women in the church, and the eating of certain foods, the appeals to creation come from the NT, while in the case of the Sabbath, the reference to creation is found in the OT. We have good reason for thinking that grounding in creation indicates a transcultural word in the former instances since the message contained in the NT represents God's last word to human beings until the coming of Christ (Heb 1:2; Jude 3). Of course, the appeal to creation in the case of the Sabbath *could indicate* that the command still applies today. Against this view, however, the entirety of the canonical witness relative to the Sabbath demonstrates that the Sabbath command is no longer in force. Also, we have seen that the Sabbath points back to creation rest and forward to our end-time rest in Christ.

An example might help. Nothing in the canon indicates that the prohibition against homosexuality no longer applies. Same-sex unions are universally condemned, and Paul tells us they do not accord with God's created intention (Rom 1:26–27). But the Sabbath is different. It is enforced during Israel's history; but in the NT, as we shall see, we have significant evidence that the Sabbath command no longer applies. The creation grounding in the case of the Sabbath is not decisive given the entire fabric of biblical revelation, for the NT teaches that the Sabbath is not mandatory for believers.

Fourth, I conclude, then, that the appeal to creation in Exodus 20:8–11 functions as an analogy.[24] The writer sees an analogy between God's resting on the seventh day and Israel's rest every Sabbath. Seeing the reference to creation as analogous fits with the fact that the NT never appeals to creation relative to the Sabbath. The Sabbath rest points back to creation rest and is consummated in our rest in Christ.

This leads to the second objection, which can be handled more quickly. How can it be that one of the Ten Commandments is not normative? The Decalogue, so it is said by some, represents God's will for all people for all time.[25] In reply, several things can be said briefly. First, the Decalogue represents the covenant stipulations for Israel, and the Sabbath is the sign of the Sinai covenant. Believers are not under the Sinai covenant or its stipulations since the new covenant has arrived. Second, some of the covenant stipulations (actually nine of the Ten Commandments) still apply today; but they are required today because they are part of the law of Christ, not because they are part of the Decalogue. Third, we see the same phenomenon elsewhere in the OT law. We all know the command to love our neighbors as ourselves still applies today (Lev 19:18), for the NT regularly cites it as authoritative (Matt 22:39; Mark 12:31; Luke 10:27; Rom 13:9; Gal 5:14; Jas 2:8). The next verse, however, says that animals must not be crossbred and fields should not be sowed with two different kinds of seed (Lev 19:19). Virtually no one thinks the latter commands are binding today. It is not surprising to find, then, two commands right next to each other where one continues to apply and another does not. Whether particular commands continue to be normative today must be established from the entirety of the biblical witness.

Sabbath in Jesus' Ministry

My purpose is to investigate what the disputes surrounding the Sabbath controversies that emerged during Jesus' ministry have to say about whether

---

[24] See here Dressler, "The Sabbath in the Old Testament," 25.
[25] For this view, see, e.g., Pipa, "The Christian Sabbath," 124–26.

the Sabbath is normative today. The ministry of Jesus does not decisively settle the matter either way, though there are hints that the Sabbath's significance is lessened now that Christ has come. Not surprisingly, the Gospels do not provide a conclusive word on this matter, for Jesus lived under the law, and the new covenant was not ratified until his death and resurrection. Similarly, the Gospels say nothing about whether circumcision is required for believers in Christ. The full implications of Jesus' coming are worked out after his resurrection and ascension.

No significance should be assigned, therefore, to women resting on the Sabbath before Jesus' resurrection (Mark 16:1; Luke 23:56) since Jesus and his disciples also observed the law during his earthly ministry. We do not believe we should offer sacrifices today, even though Jesus gave instructions about a right attitude when offering such (Matt 5:23–24). In speaking of sacrifices, Jesus addressed those living under the old covenant. Nor does the admonition to pray that one's flight should not be on the Sabbath signal the normativity of the Sabbath (Matt 24:40). Jesus addresses Jews and recognizes that flight would be difficult where the Sabbath was observed. He does not teach or imply that the Sabbath was required for all generations. Naturally, many Jewish Christians, especially those living in Israel, continued to keep the Sabbath, even after Jesus' death and resurrection. Observance of the Sabbath was not forbidden, and it is natural that Jewish Christians often continued to keep it. Such practices, however, do not indicate that the Sabbath was binding on all believers.

Since the new covenant was instituted and inaugurated after Jesus' death and resurrection, it is imperative to understand that Jesus ministered when the Sinai covenant was still in force. Indeed, Jesus' earthly ministry particularly focused on Israel (Matt 10:6; 15:24). Nevertheless, the Gospels hint that the Mosaic law (and specifically the Sabbath) does not apply in the same way since the Messiah has come (see e.g., Matt 5:17–48; 17:24–27; Mark 7:1–23; John 1:17).[26]

---

[26] Because of space, I cannot pursue these themes in detail here. For a helpful analysis, see Douglas J. Moo, "Jesus and the Authority of the Mosaic Law," *JSNT* 20 (1984): 30–49.

Jesus' first Sabbath controversy, according to Mark (Mark 2:23–28; cf. Matt 12:1–8; Luke 6:1–5), occurred when his disciples plucked heads of grain as they were walking through fields. The Pharisees complained to Jesus that their actions were contrary to the law (Mark 3:2). Presumably, Jesus could have cited Deuteronomy 23:25 saying that the disciples' actions were permitted according to the OT law and did not constitute work. Instead, he appealed to David's taking the showbread when he fled from Saul, even though the bread was reserved for priests (1 Sam 21:1–6; Mark 2:25–26).[27]

What is the fundamental point of the account? It does not seem to be legal, where Jesus appeals to the OT to demonstrate that he and the disciples are innocent. Instead, the main truth of the story is Christological. Jesus is the new and final David, the King promised according to the covenant with David.[28] Hence, those who belong to him have a right to eat on the Sabbath.

The Matthean addition points in the same direction. Sabbath regulations are subordinate to temple requirements, but Jesus is greater than the temple (Matt 12:5–6). If Sabbath regulations take second place to temple requirements, then they also are subservient to Jesus, the greater temple. All three accounts conclude on this note, affirming that Jesus as the Son of Man is Lord of the Sabbath (Matt 12:8; Mark 2:28; Luke 6:5). Certainly Jesus does not abolish the Sabbath command here, but the narrative indicates that the Sabbath stands under the authority of Jesus as the Son of Man. We have a hint that the Sabbath (like the temple!) must be reinterpreted now that the Son of Man has arrived.

The story of the man with the withered hand (Matt 12:9–14; Mark 3:1–6; Luke 6:6–11) should be interpreted along the same lines. In every Gospel the story follows the ringing declaration that Jesus is the Lord of the Sabbath; and hence it must be interpreted in terms of Jesus' authority. In Matthew, Jesus provides a legal argument maintaining that if a sheep is rescued from the pit on the Sabbath, then it is right and good to heal human beings on the Sabbath as well since humans are worth far more

---

[27] Matthew adds that the priests on the Sabbath infringe Sabbath regulations but are innocent of wrongdoing (Matt 12:5).

[28] See here Moo, "Jesus and the Authority," 8, 16–17.

(Matt 12:11–12). Common to every account is the notion that it is fitting to do good on the Sabbath.

Significantly, Jesus regularly chose the Sabbath to heal and free people from disease. Jesus' healings on the Sabbath irked the religious leaders of his day. In Luke 13 the leader of the synagogue complained that Jesus could heal on the other six days of the week and should refrain from doing so on the Sabbath (13:14–15). Jesus criticized the leaders for their hypocrisy (cf. also 14:1–6), arguing that the Sabbath is a most fitting day to heal (13:16). Jesus exercised his sovereignty over the Sabbath by choosing it as the day when he healed others.[29] This is not to say he refrained from healing on other days, though the Gospel writers call attention to his healing on the Sabbath. Healing on the Sabbath is intriguing, for it points back to the seventh day of creation (Gen 2:1–3) and forward to the new creation where the world is free of death and disease. Jesus' healings on the Sabbath signal the inauguration of the kingdom, anticipating a world where there is no disease and death.

John's Gospel is similar to the Synoptics. On one occasion Jesus defends his healing on the Sabbath legally (John 7:22–23). John gives special attention to the healing on the Sabbath of a man who had been ill for thirty-eight years. Interestingly, Jesus instructed him to pick up his mat and walk (John 5:1–9). Jesus did not have to heal on the Sabbath, and he could have omitted the command to pick up the mat, especially since the Jewish leaders believed this constituted work (5:10–12). Such actions precipitated fierce opposition (5:16). Jesus, however, responded in a shocking way, claiming he was working just as the Father was working (5:17). It is hard to imagine him saying anything more provocative. The controversy moves from the Sabbath to Christology, for Jesus claimed equality with God, which the Jews considered to be blasphemous (5:17–18). Jesus responded with a long discourse where he defended his divine sonship (5:19–47). Once again, Sabbath and Christology are closely wedded, indicating that the Sabbath must be interpreted in light of the coming of the Son and suggesting that a new era has arrived with his coming.

---

[29] As Blomberg says, he "intentionally" heals on the Sabbath ("The Sabbath as Fulfilled in Christ," 333).

In a similar incident with the blind man, Jesus provoked the Jewish leaders by healing on the Sabbath (John 9). The provocation goes deeper since Jesus made mud and applied it to the man's eyes (9:14–16). Presumably, Jesus could have avoided both the day and the means he used to carry out the healing. Apparently, he intentionally healed on the Sabbath since, as noted above, both the Sabbath and the healings point to a new creation. At the same time we have another suggestion that the Sabbath's status may be changing.

The Gospels do not clearly teach that the Sabbath command is abolished. On the other hand, they do not commend it as an everlasting commandment. Jesus' healings were often performed on the Sabbath, which vexed the Jewish leaders. Jesus believed Sabbath healings were fitting, probably because both the Sabbath and the healings forecast the new creation that was coming. At the same time, healing on the Sabbath features Jesus' sovereignty and lordship, and his radical actions on the Sabbath hint that Sabbath observance will not continue since such Sabbath healings anticipate the new creation.[30]

Sabbath in Paul's Letters

The Sabbath is not a major issue for Paul; the term *Sabbath* is actually only mentioned in his letters once. That fact alone is worthy of comment. After all, it was central to the Jewish way of life since they kept it every week. If it was important to Paul, the apostle to the Gentiles, seemingly he would have emphasized that Gentiles should keep it.

The almost complete omission of the Sabbath in Paul stands out when we consider another feature that characterized Jew-Gentile relations. Social barriers that separated Jews from Gentiles centered on purity laws (food regulations), circumcision, and Sabbath. When Gentiles thought about the

---

[30] Cf. Carson, "Jesus and the Sabbath in the Four Gospels," 66. As Blomberg says, "It is hard not to see the foundations being laid for a more sweeping challenge to and change in the law that would begin after His death and resurrection among his followers, even if it would only gradually dawn on them just how sweeping the ramifications were" ("The Sabbath as Fulfilled in Christ," 333).

Jews, they were not struck by the fact that the Jews believed murder, adultery, stealing, and lying were wrong. Neither were they astonished that the Torah prohibited coveting and called on God's people to honor their parents. What stood out was the Jewish devotion to only one God, as did the prohibition of images. But we also know from a number of secular writers that Gentiles were puzzled and often dismissive of the Jewish adherence to food laws, circumcision, and Sabbath. Such boundary markers separated Jews from Gentiles in the Greco-Roman world.[31]

Paul regularly teaches that believers are no longer under the Sinai covenant. The stipulations of that covenant belonged to Israel and are not incumbent upon believers in Jesus Christ. In accord with this insight, Paul often emphasizes that believers in Jesus Christ are free from the command to be circumcised (cf. Rom 2:25–29; 3:30; 4:9–12; 1 Cor 7:18–19; Gal 2:3–5; 5:2–6; 6:12–16; Eph 2:11; Phil 3:2–3; Col 2:11–12). Circumcision was mandated for Israelite covenant membership (Gen 17:9–14; 21:4; Exod 4:24–26; 12:44, 48; Lev 12:3; Josh 5:1–9), but now that a new covenant has come, what matters is the circumcision of the heart accomplished by the Holy Spirit and the cross-work of Jesus Christ (Rom 2:28–29; Phil 3:3; Col 2:11–12).

Along the same lines, certain foods were banned for OT believers (Lev 11:1–47; Deut 14:1–21), but such prohibitions are abolished for believers in Jesus Christ (Rom 14:1–23, esp. 14:14, 20; 1 Cor 8:8; 10:23–26; Gal 2:11–14; Col 2:16–23; 1 Tim 4:3–4).[32]

What is the significance of the abolition of food laws and circumcision? Such practices separated Israel from the Gentiles socially in the ancient world.[33] As long as these commands were binding, Gentiles had to join the

---

[31] See J. D. G. Dunn, "Works of the Law and the Curse of the Law (Galatians 3:10–14)," *NTS* 31 (1985): 524–27.

[32] The temporary nature of the food laws is also supported in the teaching of Jesus (Mark 7:1–23), for Mark adds the comment that Jesus "made all foods clean" (Mark 7:19). Peter's experience with Cornelius confirms as well that food laws are not obligatory (Acts 10:1–11:18). God impresses upon Cornelius that all foods are clean (10:13–16), and this truth is important enough to warrant repeating (11:7–10).

[33] See here J. D. G. Dunn, "The New Perspective on Paul," *BJRL* 65 (1983): 95–122; idem, "Works of Law," 523–42.

Jewish people to belong to the people of God. Ephesians 2:11–12 demonstrates that uncircumcised Gentiles were cut off from God as long as they were separated from Israel. But Jesus ended the days of division between Jews and Gentiles. Both groups are now reconciled to God through the blood of Christ Jesus (Eph 2:13), removing the hostility between them and providing peace with God and one another (Eph 2:14–16). The peace between Jews and Gentiles in Christ also involves the abolition of the law and the Mosaic covenant (Eph 2:15).[34] Paul does not limit himself to the ceremonial law here but refers to the whole law. The law that separated Jews from Gentiles is no longer in force. Jews and Gentiles form one people of God under the charter of a new covenant.

To return where I started: the termination of food laws and circumcision indicates that a new covenant has arisen, one that ends the stipulations of the Sinai covenant. God's people are no longer a nationalistic or ethnic entity: a new day has arisen in which the people of God include those from every tribe, tongue, people, and nation.

The application to the Sabbath should be clear, for the Sabbath (like food laws and circumcision) separated Jews from Gentiles. It was the covenant sign for the Sinai covenant; it was the sign that one belonged to the theocratic nation of Israel. Now that Jesus Christ has come, the era in which Jews and Gentiles were segregated by virtue of circumcision, food laws, and Sabbath has ceased.

The discerning reader might object that I have not shown that Sabbath is akin to circumcision and food laws. I have observed that Gentiles put circumcision, food laws, and Sabbath together, but did Paul put them in the same category? I will argue that he did from three texts: Galatians 4:10; Romans 14:5–6; and Colossians 2:16–17.

I begin with Galatians 4:10. Paul reproaches the Galatians: "You observe special days, months, seasons, and years." A few commentators have argued that a pagan calendar is in mind here, but that is very unlikely, for the opponents in Galatia were almost certainly Jewish. They required circumcision for salvation (Gal 2:3–5; 5:2–6, 11–12; 6:12–13), which was the admission

---

[34] In support of this interpretation of Eph 2:15, see Peter T. O'Brien, *The Letter to the Ephesians*, PNTC (Grand Rapids: Eerdmans, 1999), 196–99.

rite to the Sinai covenant (Gen 17:9–14; Exod 12:44, 48; Lev 12:3). We also see that a dispute arose over whether Gentiles must observe Jewish food laws in Galatians 2:11–14. Hence, we can be quite certain that the reference in Galatians 4:10 is to the Jewish calendar and Jewish feasts. It follows, then, that the reference to days includes the Sabbath.[35] Other days apart from the Sabbath may be in mind as well; but it is quite improbable that the Sabbath is excluded, for Jews observed it weekly, and the OT law is quite emphatic about the Sabbath observance.

Furthermore, three of the specific issues mentioned in Galatians are circumcision, food laws, and the observance of days (which almost certainly included the Sabbath). The requirement to keep the Sabbath marked out and separated Jews from the Gentiles. Hence, we have good grounds to think that the Sabbath has passed away along with circumcision and food laws. We can add to this Paul's insistence in Galatians that believers are no longer under the Sinai covenant (Gal 3:15–4:7, 21; 5:18). The covenant and the covenant stipulations have been terminated with Christ's coming.

The issue of days also emerges in Romans 14:5–6. It is likely in Romans 14 that the weak adhered to Jewish food laws and the observance of days on the Jewish calendar, and the strong felt free to eat anything.[36] The dispute over particular days surfaces in Romans 14:5: "One person considers one day to be above another day. Someone else considers every day to be the same." That the weak exalted one day over another, whereas the strong believed that every day was the same, shows there was no warrant for prizing one day over another.

It is almost certain that the weak specially esteemed the Sabbath, for the weekly Sabbath observance was particularly practiced in Jewish circles.[37] Certainly other days may have been included, but the Sabbath would have had pride of place. The strong, on the other hand, rejected the notion that the Sabbath or any other day should be specially observed.

---

[35] See James D. G. Dunn, *The Epistle to the Galatians*, BNTC (Peabody, MA: Hendrickson, 1993), 227.

[36] For a fuller discussion of the weak and strong in Romans 14–15, see Thomas R. Schreiner, *Romans*, BECNT (Grand Rapids: Baker, 1998), 703–10.

[37] In support of this, see ibid., 715.

The debate is not of great importance to Paul. Both the weak and the strong should follow their conscience, and "each one must be fully convinced in his own mind" (Rom 14:5). In other words, those who wish to observe the Sabbath may do so. They are free to follow the dictates of their own consciences. If they observe the day to "honor" the Lord (Rom 14:6), then their Sabbath observance is pleasing to God. Paul is not "against" keeping the Sabbath.

We must also see, however, that Paul did not think Sabbath observance was required. The strong who believe every day is the same are commended. They are pleasing to God if they honor him with their lives and exercise faith. Indeed, Paul's words about the matter reveal that he fundamentally agreed with the strong. The weak, after all, thought it was important to observe the Sabbath and other days. Apparently, they did not insist on such observance for salvation, for in that case Paul would have rejected their view as a false gospel. Then they would have fallen into the same error as the Galatian opponents, who demanded that believers be circumcised and keep the law in order to be saved. Still, the weak were probably convinced that those who kept the Sabbath were more mature and godly.

Paul is tolerant on the matter, permitting the weak to hold their view. And yet it is clear that he sides with the strong theologically. We know this because if Paul agreed with the weak, he would recommend that the strong keep the Sabbath. But that is precisely what he does not say. According to Paul, the matter of observing certain days is entirely a matter of conscience. If Paul believed the Sabbath command was binding, he would not say people could make up their own mind. Like the strong, Paul does not believe the Sabbath command is incumbent on believers today.

Why does he not think the Sabbath is required? There is no need to rehearse here what was said above. Believers are free from the Sabbath because they are no longer under the Sinai covenant.

One final point should be made from Romans. We have seen in Romans 14:5–6 that the Sabbath command is not obligatory for believers. Paul also argues in Romans that believers are free from the requirement of circumcision (Rom 2:25–29; 4:9–12) and that the food laws are no longer binding upon them. Paul affirms that all foods are clean, and nothing is defiled for those who belong to Jesus Christ (Rom 14:14, 20). We see the same constellation of issues we observed in Galatians: circumcision, food laws, and Sabbath divide Jews from Gentiles. Now that Jesus Christ has come, believers are not bound to observe the stipulations that were distinctive to the Sinai covenant.

The last Pauline text to consider is Colossians 2:16–17. Paul says, "Therefore let no one pass judgment on you in questions of food and drink, or with regard to a festival or a new moon or a Sabbath. These are a shadow of the things to come, but the substance belongs to Christ" (ESV). There is no doubt that the Sabbath is in view here since Paul specifically uses the word "Sabbath." Some have attempted to say the reference is to sabbatical years instead of the Sabbath day, but that is surely special pleading.[38] Sabbatical years may be part of what Paul has in mind, but the Sabbath day is particularly in view.

What stands out, of course, is that the Sabbath is not required for believers in Jesus Christ. We cannot imagine Paul saying the same about adultery or murder. But the Sabbath is described as a "shadow" ($\sigma\varkappa\iota\acute{\alpha}$), and the "substance" ($\sigma\tilde{\omega}\mu\alpha$) "belongs to Christ" (Col 2:17 ESV). Paul is not using Platonic language here but writes about eschatological realities. The Sabbath, as part of the old covenant, is a shadow that points forward to the substance, which is Jesus Christ. As a shadow, it was never meant to be a permanent ordinance; once the fullness arrived in Jesus Christ, the shadow falls away.

Interestingly, the same word "shadow" ($\sigma\varkappa\iota\acute{\alpha}$) is used in Hebrews. The law and its sacrifices are "only a shadow of the good things to come, and not the actual form ($\varepsilon\grave{\iota}\varkappa\acute{o}\nu\alpha$) of those realities" (Heb 10:1). The author of Hebrews refers here to OT sacrifices, identifying them as a "shadow" in contrast to the actual reality, which is the sacrifice of Christ. Now that Christ has come, the OT sacrifices are no longer

---

[38] For further discussion of this matter, see Douglas J. Moo, *The Letters to the Colossians and to Philemon*, PNTC (Grand Rapids: Eerdmans, 2008), 220–22; James D. G. Dunn, *The Epistles to the Colossians and to Philemon*, NIGTC (Grand Rapids: Eerdmans, 1996), 172–77.

needed. Such sacrifices point forward to and are fulfilled in Christ's sacrifice, but with Christ's coming they are no longer practiced. The same principle applies to the Sabbath as we see in Paul's argument in Colossians, and hence it does not need to be kept since the end-time reality has arrived in Jesus Christ.

I return to my earlier observation. The Sabbath is not a creation ordinance that applies to every generation; for otherwise NT writers would not identify it as a shadow, nor would they say it does not matter if people observe it. We learn from the entire biblical witness what place the Sabbath should occupy in the life of the people of God.

Colossians joins together the Sabbath as a shadow with the notion that regulations regarding food and drink are also a shadow (Col 2:16–17, 21–22). The reference to the Sabbath and new moons indicates that Jewish regulations are in view, and thus the foods here are almost certainly those from the OT. Such rules are part of the old covenant, which has passed away with the coming of Jesus Christ and the inauguration of the new covenant.

We must notice that the Sabbath is put on the same plane as OT food regulations. If the latter are not mandated, neither is the former. The Sabbath is not separated from the food regulations as if it is a continuing moral norm. It is lumped together with them and identified as a shadow of the things to come.

Some have suggested that the Sabbath should still be observed since the new covenant is inaugurated but not consummated,[39] but Paul gives no hint that such is the case. Instead, he links the Sabbath, as he did in Galatians and Romans, with food laws and circumcision (Col 2:11). Like them the Sabbath has passed away with the coming of Jesus Christ and the ratification of the new covenant. Naturally one can observe the Sabbath if one wishes to do so, just as one can be circumcised or keep the food laws if one wishes to do so. But such rules are not to be imposed on others; they are not moral norms binding on all Christians, and they are certainly not required for salvation.

---

[39] This is the view of Beale (who is discussed on pp. 161–65) and Gaffin (who is discussed on pp. 182–86).

Sabbath in Hebrews

The word *Sabbath* does not occur in Hebrews, but the word *rest* is prominent in 3:7–4:11, and in 4:9 the author uses the term "Sabbath rest" (σαββατισμὸς), which is the only time the word occurs in either the OT or the NT.
Furthermore, the author specifically recalls in his argument that God rested
from his works on the seventh day, forging a connection between entering
the eschatological rest and the seventh-day rest of God (4:3–4, 9–10).

What does this text teach us about Sabbath observance today? We
should back up and set the context briefly, recognizing that we cannot provide a full exegesis of this passage in the space allotted here. The author
of Hebrews begins by citing Psalm 95:7–11, where the psalmist warns his
readers not to harden their hearts as the wilderness generation did. Because
the wilderness generation did not trust in or obey the Lord, they did not
enter the promised land, which is designated as a place of rest.

In 3:12–4:13 the writer applies the OT text to his readers. They must
be on guard lest they fall into the same sin as the wilderness generation
(3:12–13). A wicked heart of unbelief leads to apostasy, and only those who
persevere until the end will be saved (3:14). The fundamental reason the wilderness generation did not enter the land was unbelief and disobedience, and
the readers will not enter God's rest if they follow their example (3:18–4:2).

The author pulls in God's creation rest in 4:3–4, indicating that the
rest promised to believers transcends residence in the land. The Sabbath
points back to the rest of creation which was lost in the fall and is ultimately
fulfilled in the new creation, as Hebrew argues. God rested on the seventh
day of creation; and he rested, as the author makes plain, because his work
was finished. The rest offered to the wilderness generation, then, is not the
ultimate and final rest for the people of God. The generation under Joshua
found rest (Josh 1:13, 15; 21:44; 22:4; 23:1), just as God promised, but
the rest under Joshua cannot be the final rest since the Lord promised in
Psalm 95 a rest for those who lived in David's day. We see here how the
writer reads the OT temporally and historically, finding significance in the
epoch in which people lived. He concludes from the later word about rest
in Psalm 110 that the rest is still available to his readers; they are promised
a Sabbath celebration if they persevere in faith and obedience. The word

used here (σαββατισμὸς) does not so much designate Sabbath rest as a fes-
tive and joyous Sabbath celebration.[40]

Believers enter into this rest eschatologically when they cease from
their works as God rests from his (Heb 4:10). In the OT the rest was experienced on the Sabbath pointing back to God's creation rest, at the entrance
into the land, and presumably during the reigns of David and Solomon. Still
this rest points forward to a greater rest realized in Jesus Christ (cf. Matt
11:28–30). The author of Hebrews is not talking about works righteousness
here; the one who enters rest ceases from his works, just as God did from
his. Obviously, God, in ceasing from his works, did not forsake works righteousness. God rested because he was finished with his work, and so too
human beings rest eschatologically when their works, their labors on earth,
are finished. The thought is similar to Revelation 14:13, "Then I heard a
voice from heaven saying, 'Write: The dead who die in the Lord from now
on are blessed.' 'Yes,' says the Spirit, 'let them rest from their labors, for their
works follow them!'"

According to Hebrews, then, God's creation rest points to the eschatological rest, to the final reward which is promised to the people of God.
Hebrews emphasizes that believers are not under the old covenant but the
new, for Jesus has offered the final and definitive sacrifice for sins (8:1–
10:18). The Sabbath points backward to the rest of creation lost in the
fall and forward to the heavenly rest which belongs to those who believe
in Christ. What should be noticed is that there is no reference to keeping
a weekly Sabbath in Hebrews 3–4. The rest is the eschatological refreshment promised to believers. Now that the fulfillment has come the type has
passed away.

Alternatively, Richard Gaffin argues from Hebrews that believers should
continue to keep the Sabbath as a sign and marker of the eschatological rest

---

[40] Peter T. O'Brien, *The Letter to the Hebrews*, PNTC (Grand Rapids: Eerdmans,
2010), 170–71; Jon Laansma, *'I Will Give You Rest': The Rest Motif in the New Testament
with Special Reference to Mt 11 and Heb 3–4*, WUNT 2/98 (Tübingen: Mohr Siebeck,
1997), 276–77.

to come.[41] The church is presently in the wilderness, traveling as exiles and sojourners to obtain the promised rest. While Christians live as exiles in the wilderness, they must continue to observe the Sabbath. In Gaffin's view the rest is entirely future; for, as exiles, believers cannot be enjoying rest, for if they do, then they are not in the wilderness. The experience of believers is analogous, says Gaffin, to Acts 14:22 where believers are told they will experience many afflictions before entering the kingdom of God. Since the rest is wholly future, the sign of end-time rest (i.e., the Sabbath) cannot cease before the end-time reality arrives. Those who dispense with the weekly Sabbath fall prey to an overrealized eschatology, according to Gaffin, since the rest is entirely future.

Gaffin makes a most stimulating case for keeping the Sabbath today. He bases his argument on the rest being wholly future, rejecting the notion that believers experience the inaugurated rest during this present evil age. What can we say about Gaffin's proposal? First, I will argue that his notion that the rest is entirely future is unpersuasive. Second, even if he is right and the rest is entirely future, his notion that we should observe the Sabbath still fails to convince.

First, the rest is not entirely future, though the emphasis is certainly on the future rest, on the consummation of the rest.[42] There are hints that an already-but-not-yet dimension of the rest is also present.[43] Most importantly, those who think the rest is only future sever what the author says about the

---

[41] Richard B. Gaffin Jr., "A Sabbath Rest Still Awaits the People of God," in *Pressing Toward the Mark: Essays Commemorating Fifty Years of the Orthodox Presbyterian Church*, ed. C. G. Dennison and R. C. Gamble (Philadelphia: The Committee for the Historian of the Orthodox Presbyterian Church, 1986), 49–68.

[42] For the notion that the rest is only future, see also Laansma, *I Will Give You Rest*, 305–10; Gaffin, "A Sabbath Rest Still Awaits the People of God," 41–46; Beale, *A New Testament Biblical Theology*, 782–87.

[43] Cf. A. T. Lincoln, "Sabbath, Rest, and Eschatology in the New Testament," in *From Sabbath to Lord's Day: A Biblical, Historical, and Theological Investigation*, ed. D. A. Carson (Grand Rapids: Zondervan, 1982), 210–13; Richard Ounsworth, *Joshua Typology in the New Testament*, WUNT 2/328 (Tübingen: Mohr Siebeck, 2012), 62; Kenneth L. Schenk, *Cosmology and Eschatology in Hebrews: The Settings of the Sacrifice*, SNTSMS 143 (Cambridge: Cambridge University Press, 2007), 60–63.

rest from his teaching about the heavenly city.[44] The heavenly Jerusalem is an end-time reality, and believers wait for its coming (Heb 11:10, 13–16; 13:14). At the same time the author says (12:22) that the readers have "come (προσεληλύθατε) to the city of the living God (the heavenly Jerusalem)."[45] Obviously, believers on earth are not in the heavenly Jerusalem, the city to come, for that is their final reward. And yet the author also says believers have already arrived and are currently members of this city. They experience the suffering that constitutes life in "the city of man"; they are still in the wilderness! But it is also true that they are now members of the heavenly city.

It seems that the same is true of the rest, for the rest and the heavenly city describe the same referent, the eschatological hope that awaits believers. The rest is fundamentally eschatological, and yet the eschaton has penetrated the present. Those who believe enter God's rest now (Heb 4:3). The present tense of the verb "enter" (Εἰσερχόμεθα) does not necessarily indicate that believers now enjoy rest, but the correlation of the rest with the heavenly city suggests the present tense in this instance denotes

---

[44] O'Brien thinks the rest is future for a variety of reasons (*Hebrews*, 165–66): (1) the promise to enter the rest remains; (2) the promise is not yet obtained (Heb 10:32–39); (3) the present tense does not necessarily designate present time; (4) the context of chapters 3–4 clarifies that one must persevere to obtain the final reward; (5) there is a corporate entering of the rest which is only fulfilled eschatologically; (6) entering the rest is dependent on striving to do so; and (7) believers do not rest from their works now. These excellent arguments may indeed demonstrate the rest is only future. Nevertheless, most of the arguments made by O'Brien still stand if the rest has an already-not-yet character. This is seen most clearly when we compare the rest to the heavenly city. Believers are already members of the city (12:22), and yet they seek the city to come and must strive to enter the city. If they fall away, they will not be members of the city. Believers are even now part of the corporate eschatological gathering (12:22–23), and yet there is an eschatological fulfillment still to come for such a gathering. It seems as if the same tension could be true of the rest, particularly since the rest describes from a different angle the final reward for believers. O'Brien's best argument is that believers do not rest from their labors until the eschaton. I concur. Still it seems that in this verse the author focuses on the consummation of rest. When we speak of the already-not-yet character of rest, it is not necessary to argue that every aspect of the rest has a present fulfillment. In the same way, believers are now members of the heavenly Zion, but they do not fully enjoy the benefits of their citizenship.

[45] See here O'Brien, *Hebrews*, 482n200. It is surprising that O'Brien thinks the rest is entirely future since he thinks believers are now members of the heavenly city.

a present reality. Hence, believers already enjoy a rest that will be consummated on the last day.

Believers enter God's rest, which has been accessible since the day of creation, but they have not entered it fully, for they must continue to believe and to obey until the end to obtain it. Such a reading fits with the already-but-not-yet eschatology that is pervasive in the NT.[46] It is somewhat surprising that Gaffin appeals to Acts 14:22, which speaks of entering the kingdom of God after experiencing afflictions, to support the notion that the rest is entirely future. Certainly the kingdom of God is a future reality, but the NT clearly teaches as well that the kingdom is an already-but-not-yet reality. Such an eschatological tension fits with the entirety of the NT witness.

Against Gaffin, then, observing the Sabbath is not required since believers even now enjoy God's end-time rest. The same reality is present with respect to sacrifices. The new covenant has been ratified through the death and resurrection of Jesus Christ, and yet the full realities of the new covenant are not yet. Even though the complete new covenant blessings are not consummated, believers do not continue to offer sacrifices; and in the same way they are not obligated to observe the Sabbath, for now that the fulfillment has come, the type has ceased.

But even if Gaffin is correct and the rest is entirely future, why does that necessarily lead to the conclusion that the Sabbath should be observed in the present age? Hebrews says nothing about observing the Sabbath, and when the author refers to regularly gathering together, he noticeably leaves the Sabbath out (Heb 10:25). Indeed, Gaffin's argument works only if the weekly Sabbath fits with new covenant realities, for even Gaffin does not think we should observe circumcision, food laws, or sacrifices, recognizing these are all old covenant regulations. The same principle applies to the Sabbath, and hence there is no warrant for observing it today.

Interestingly, Laansma agrees with Gaffin that the rest is wholly future, and yet he concludes that Hebrews 3–4 does not refer to the weekly Sabbath and that there is no basis for Sabbath keeping from this text. He

---

[46] The notion that the kingdom has an already-but-not-yet dimension is a standard feature of NT theology and does not need to be defended here. See Thomas R. Schreiner, *New Testament Theology* (Grand Rapids: Baker, 2008), 41–79.

says, if anything, "One might as well read there the idea that the weekly Sabbath has come to fulfillment in Christ's salvation and is of no binding significance for the Christian. . . . [A]long with temple worship generally it is obsolete and fading."[47] So, even if Gaffin is right about the rest being wholly future, the move he makes from future rest to Sabbath observance is not grounded in the text, for the letter to the Hebrews clearly teaches that believers are not under the old covenant, that the new covenant has arrived and the old is obsolete.

To sum up, the letter to the Hebrews teaches that God's seventh-day rest points to the eschatological rest believers will enjoy in the heavenly city—a rest provided at creation, lost in the fall, and restored in Jesus Christ. It says nothing about observing the Sabbath until that final day comes, even when it speaks of gathering together regularly as believers (Heb 10:25). Instead the letter emphasizes that the new covenant has come and that the old covenant has ended. Believers are no longer under the former covenant and its stipulations. The old covenant pointed forward to and anticipated the new, and believers in Jesus Christ even now enjoy membership in the heavenly city that is to come.

The Lord's Day

My comments on the Lord's Day must be exceedingly brief.[48] All of the Gospel writers call our attention to the fact that Jesus rose from the dead on the first day of the week (Matt 28:1; Mark 16:2; Luke 24:1; John 20:1, 19). The day of the resurrection signifies the inauguration of the new creation. Even by stating that it was the first day of the week, the authors assign a special significance to that day. We also see hints elsewhere in the NT that the church gathered for worship on the Lord's Day, the first day of the week (Acts 20:7; 1 Cor 16:2; cf. Rev 1:10). Such a practice is most naturally linked to Sunday being the day on which the Lord rose from the dead, though no

---

[47] Laansma, *I Will Give You Rest*, 316–17.
[48] It is evident that this paragraph is dependent on the work of Richard Bauckham. On the Lord's Day, see R. J. Bauckham, "The Lord's Day," in *From Sabbath to Lord's Day*, 221–50.

explicit link is made between the two. In any case, worship on Sunday must have come from the earliest days of the Palestinian church, for there was no debate about worshipping on Sunday. The lack of debate is striking when we compare it to the dispute over circumcision in the early church.[49]

Nor was there any move toward saying the Lord's Day was the Sabbath either in the NT or the second-century church.[50] It was understood that the Sabbath was on Saturday and the Lord's Day was on Sunday, and hence Ignatius contrasts the two (*Magn.* 9:1). In the same way, the Ebionite church practiced the Lord's Day and the Sabbath, showing that the former did not displace the latter for them.[51] Along the same lines, most of the early church fathers claimed the Sabbath did not apply literally to believers; they interpreted it eschatologically and spiritually. It is evident, then, that the Lord's Day was not equated with the Sabbath but distinguished from it. Neither was the Lord's Day understood as a day of rest (the early Christians had to work on Sundays!) but a day of worship, and even such worship was not conceived of as a fulfillment of the Sabbath command. Bauckham argues that the notion that the Lord's Day replaced the Sabbath is a medieval development.[52] The Puritans continued this vein of thought by understanding the Lord's Day in sabbatarian terms.[53]

Conclusion

Believers in Jesus Christ are under no obligation to keep the Sabbath. Christians may observe the Sabbath if they wish to, but they must not impose it as a requirement on other believers. The Sabbath was the sign

---

[49] See here ibid., 231, 236–38.

[50] See the outstanding detailed discussion in R. J. Bauckham, "Sabbath and Sunday in the Post-Apostolic Church," in *From Sabbath to Lord's Day*, 251–98. Bauckham says the first clear evidence that Sunday should be understood as the Sabbath hails from Eusebius of Caesarea in AD 330 (282).

[51] Ibid., 270.

[52] See R. J. Bauckham, "Sabbath and Sunday in the Medieval Church in the West," in *From Sabbath to Lord's Day*, 299–309.

[53] See R. J. Bauckham, "Sabbath and Sunday in the Protestant Tradition," in *From Sabbath to Lord's Day*, 311–41.

of God's covenant with Israel, just as the rainbow was God's covenant sign with Noah. In other words, the Sabbath is the sign of the old covenant not the new. The Sabbath was given particularly to Israel as a sign and seal of God's covenant with them.

When we consider the entirety of the scriptural witness, it is clear that the Sabbath is not a creation ordinance that applies to believers today. The NT teaches us that the new covenant has arrived with the death and resurrection of Jesus Christ. The old covenant pointed forward to and is fulfilled in Jesus Christ; but now that the new covenant has come, the old is no longer in force. Hence, Christians are not under the stipulations of the old covenant, which includes the commands to be circumcised, to observe food laws, and to keep the Sabbath. Such laws functioned as a social barrier separating Jews from Gentiles. Jesus Christ has removed such barriers, abolishing the law with its commandments, and has reconciled Jews and Gentiles through his suffering on the cross. Now Jewish and Gentile believers are equally members of the people of God as citizens of the new covenant.

The Sabbath as a shadow pointed forward to the reality, to the fulfillment, which has come in Jesus Christ. We see in Hebrews that God's creation rest and the Sabbath rest point forward to the end-time rest believers will enjoy in the heavenly city. The author of Hebrews says nothing about keeping a weekly Sabbath. Instead, he argues that the old covenant and its sacrifices are no longer needed. Such sacrifices were also a shadow (like the Sabbath) that pointed to the atoning work of Jesus Christ. The temple, sacrifices, food laws, circumcision, and the Sabbath are no longer binding now that the fulfillment in Christ has arrived.

Christians, of course, are still required to be wise. Rest, refreshment, and recreation are needed in order to sustain our lives, but there is no requirement that such rest is taken on a particular day. Here we can follow the practice of the early church. We are not required to keep the Sabbath, but we do gather together with other Christians and worship our God through Jesus Christ on the Lord's Day.

CHAPTER 7

The Warning Passages of Hebrews and the New Covenant Community

CHRISTOPHER W. COWAN

The warning passages of Hebrews are perennial troubled waters.[1] Because of these texts, some in the early church resisted accepting the letter into the canon,[2] a few scholars have reversed their position on Christian apostasy,[3] and a great deal of ink has been spilled attempting to interpret them.[4] The interpretation of several covenant theologians, however, has received little attention in Hebrews commentaries or works addressing the warnings. Their view deserves interaction. Despite significant variations

---

[1] Though scholars differ over where exactly each warning begins and ends, they generally agree in identifying some portion of these five passages as warnings: Heb 2:1–4; 3:12–4:13; 6:4–8; 10:26–31; 12:12–29.

[2] See Craig R. Koester, *Hebrews*, AB (New York: Doubleday, 2001), 23, 25.

[3] See, e.g., Clark H. Pinnock, "From Augustine to Arminius: A Pilgrimage in Theology," in *The Grace of God and the Will of Man*, ed. Clark H. Pinnock (Minneapolis: Bethany, 1989), 17; Scot McKnight, "Why I Kissed Calvinism Goodbye," accessed May 8, 2014, http://www.patheos.com/blogs/jesuscreed/2006/08/29/why-i-kissed-calvinism-good-bye.

[4] For examples of scholarly works devoted to the warnings, see those cited in Christopher W. Cowan, "'Confident of Better Things': Assurance of Salvation in the Letter to the Hebrews" (PhD diss., The Southern Baptist Theological Seminary, 2012), 1–2n4.

among these interpreters, they share an important premise: the warnings
of Hebrews imply there are *nonelect members of the new covenant* who will
commit apostasy.

I will summarize the arguments of these interpreters and offer a brief
critique. Then I will suggest an alternative (and, I believe, better) paradigm
for understanding the warning passages and respond to some objections to
this view.

The Warnings Passages of Hebrews According to Covenant Theologians

Few of the following covenant theologians engage in detailed exegesis of the
warning passages. In many cases they are discussing the new covenant and
its membership, but the role played by the warning passages in Hebrews is
prominent in their arguments. These authors argue that the warnings are
evidence for the "mixed" nature of the new covenant community. But, to do
this, they assume a particular reading of the warnings that is already consistent with covenant theology.

The Views of Covenant Theologians Summarized

Jeffrey Niell discusses the use of Jeremiah 31:31–34 in Hebrews 8:8–12 to
answer how the new covenant is both new and not new. When Hebrews
quotes Jeremiah's promise that "they will all know Me, from the least to the
greatest of them" (8:11 HCSB), Niell insists this "cannot mean that every
single member of the new covenant knows the Lord savingly." For, similar
to old covenant members, new covenant members are warned not to rebel
against the covenant. As evidence, Niell cites the five warning passages
in Hebrews (as well as other New Testament [NT] warnings). Thus, he
concludes, "We must avoid equating covenant membership with election."[5]

---

[5] Jeffrey D. Niell, "The Newness of the New Covenant," in *The Case for Covenantal
Infant Baptism*, ed. Gregg Strawbridge (Phillipsburg, NJ: P&R, 2003), 132–33.

Also speaking to the issue of new covenant membership, Gregg Strawbridge argues:

> If it can be proved that there are people under new covenant obligations (i.e., "in the covenant") who become apostates, then the claim that only regenerate people are in the new covenant will be shown to be false. . . . Several passages teach that there are people *set apart* in the new covenant (without the full blessings of salvation) who indeed fall away. Thus, there are unregenerate members of the new covenant.[6]

Strawbridge quotes the warnings in Hebrews 6:4–6 and 10:29–31 for support. When Hebrews says the apostate has regarded as unclean "the blood of the covenant by which he was sanctified" (10:29 HCSB), Strawbridge claims the term translated "sanctified" (*hagiazō*) "often refers to the consecration of the visible people of God (Ex. 19:10, 14 LXX; cf. Heb. 9:13–20)," and Hebrews 10:29 draws "directly from this ceremonial typology." These apostates "did not lose their salvation, but they did become covenant *breakers*."[7]

Richard Pratt discusses Jeremiah 31:31–34 and its use in Hebrews 8:8–12. He responds to opponents of infant baptism who claim, in light of Jeremiah's promises, that (1) the new covenant cannot be broken, (2) the new covenant is fully internalized, and (3) all participants in the new covenant are redeemed.[8] Pratt argues these things *will be* true but are not so yet. Christ inaugurated the new covenant at his first coming, but it will "reach complete fulfillment only when Christ returns." So Jeremiah's prophecy is only partially fulfilled.[9] Returning to the three arguments above, Pratt demonstrates how each of these aspects of the new covenant is only partially fulfilled—and Hebrews 10:28–31 is a key piece of his evidence. This text shows: (1) it is possible for someone to break the covenant until

---

[6] Gregg Strawbridge, "The Polemics of Anabaptism from the Reformation Onward," in *The Case for Covenantal Infant Baptism*, 280–81 (emphasis in original).

[7] Ibid., 281 (emphasis in original).

[8] Richard L. Pratt Jr., "Infant Baptism in the New Covenant," in *The Case for Covenantal Infant Baptism*, 158–61.

[9] Ibid., 169.

Christ returns; (2) one can be "sanctified" in an external sense only; and (3) the new covenant community will include unbelievers before the final judgment.[10]

Douglas Wilson highlights the different assumptions about covenant membership between Baptists and paedo-baptists. For Baptists the old covenant included some regenerate members and some who were not, but the new covenant has only regenerate members. For paedo-baptists both covenants contain regenerate and unregenerate members.[11] According to paedo-baptists then, "the *elect* and the *covenant members* are not identical sets of people."[12] How does one decide which view is biblical? Wilson concludes that the covenants are *alike* regarding membership because, like the Jews under the old covenant, Christians are repeatedly warned against unbelief in the NT—particularly in Hebrews.[13]

Sinclair Ferguson defends paedo-baptism in a similar way. He quotes Hebrews 10:26–29 to demonstrate that Hebrews "underlines that the dynamic enshrined in the old covenant continues to function in the new"— that is, if the covenant is "spurned in disobedience, the curse inevitably follows."[14] Thus, even in the context of explaining the fulfillment of Jeremiah's new covenant promise, the author of Hebrews highlights that "the new covenant also knows of an apostasy from it."[15]

Michael Horton, in a book debating "eternal security," acknowledges a dilemma: some NT texts seem to promote "eternal security" while others warn against apostasy. Theological perspectives that affirm one or the other set of texts cannot properly account for both, but "a covenantal interpretation appears to offer a third alternative that does greater justice to the text."[16]

---

[10] Ibid., 169–73.

[11] Douglas Wilson, *To a Thousand Generations* (Moscow, ID: Canon, 1996), 34–35.

[12] Ibid., 34 (emphasis in original).

[13] Ibid., 35. Wilson cites Heb 3:19–4:1, 11; 10:28–29 and then also points to warnings passages in Paul (pp. 35–37).

[14] Sinclair B. Ferguson, "Infant Baptism View," in *Baptism: Three Views*, ed. David F. Wright (Downers Grove, IL: InterVarsity, 2009), 99.

[15] Ibid., n41.

[16] Michael S. Horton, "A Classical Calvinist View," in *Four Views on Eternal Security*, ed. J. Matthew Pinson (Grand Rapids: Zondervan, 2002), 36.

"Covenant theology can integrate both sets of proof texts precisely because it recognizes a third category besides 'saved' and 'unsaved': the person who belongs to the covenant community and experiences thereby the work of the Spirit through the means of grace, and yet is not regenerate." Such an individual appears in Hebrews 6:4–5, which Horton interprets as describing "the recipient of the Spirit's sealing in baptism and of the promise of forgiveness in the Supper ('tasting the heavenly gift')." In a real sense this person shares in the Holy Spirit "through word and sacrament."[17] But apostates benefit from the ministry of the Spirit through these means of grace "as merely formal or external members of the covenant community."[18] Horton claims, in light of the warnings, "Not everyone who belongs to the covenant community will persevere to the end."[19]

Another covenantal view appears in two writings by Rich Lusk on Hebrews 6:4–8. Similar to other covenant theologians, Lusk contends, "'Covenant membership' = 'elected to final salvation' is a false equation. Not all who are in the covenant persevere to the end. Some break covenant. That's the whole point of the warnings in Hebrews and elsewhere."[20] However, Lusk disagrees with the view that Hebrews 6:4–8 is describing something less than full saving grace or regeneration.[21] They are not "secretly unregenerate Christians" or "merely external Christians."[22] Instead, "Hebrews 6:4–8 describes the real blessings that every covenant member receives."[23] It addresses those who "have been genuinely converted."[24] The problem for reprobates is they do not persevere to the end. They "may temporarily

---

[17] Ibid., 37.

[18] Michael Horton, *The Christian Faith: A Systematic Theology for Pilgrims on the Way* (Grand Rapids: Zondervan, 2011), 683. See also 778.

[19] Michael Horton, *God of Promise: Introducing Covenant Theology* (Grand Rapids: Baker, 2006), 185.

[20] Rich Lusk, "Staying Saved: Hebrews 6:4–8 Revisited," 16 (cited May 20, 2014), accessed May 8, 2014, http://trinity-pres.net/essays/Staying_Saved.pdf.

[21] See Rich Lusk, "New Life and Apostasy: Hebrews 6:4–8 as Test Case," in *The Federal Vision*, ed. Steve Wilkins and Duane Garner (Monroe, LA: Athanasius, 2004), 271–73.

[22] Lusk, "Staying Saved," 24.

[23] Lusk, "New Life and Apostasy," 277.

[24] Lusk, "Staying Saved," 20.

experience a quasi-salvation,"[25] but "[t]heir need is *not* for true conversion, but for patient endurance."[26]

> God mysteriously has chosen to draw many into the covenant community who are not elect in the ultimate sense and who are not destined for final salvation. These non-elect covenant members are actually brought to Christ, united to Him and the Church in baptism, receive various gracious operations of the Holy Spirit, and may even be said to be loved by God for a time. They become members of Christ's kingdom, stones in God's living house, and children in God's family. . . . In some sense they were really joined to the elect people, really sanctified by Christ's blood, and really recipients of new life given by the Holy Spirit. . . . But God withholds from them perseverance and all is lost.[27]

For Hebrews 6:4–8, Lusk relies in part on the work of Martin Emmrich, who argues that the wilderness generations' experience serves as the typological background to the warning in Hebrews 6:4–6.[28] Like Israel of old, "the members of the congregation qualify as *believers* because (or so long as) they are *pilgrims*. No further distinction is intended until they decide to separate themselves from the wandering people of God."[29] Yet this does not deny election because the author approaches his audience from a pastoral perspective not a divine perspective and does not know their "ultimate spiritual condition." Hebrews 6:4–6 describes the "*realized* blessings of the

---

[25] Lusk, "New Life and Apostasy," 286.

[26] Lusk, "Staying Saved," 15 (emphasis in original).

[27] Lusk, "New Life and Apostasy," 287–88. Douglas Wilson seems to articulate a similar view in his *"Reformed" Is Not Enough: Recovering the Objectivity of the Covenant* (Moscow, ID: Canon, 2002), 132.

[28] Martin Emmrich, "Hebrews 6:4–6—Again! (A Pneumatological Inquiry)," *WTJ* (2003): 83–87. Other interpreters before Emmrich have argued similarly about the Old Testament background to the warnings in Hebrews, though their interpretation of those described in Heb 6:4–8 differs from his. See, e.g., G. H. Lang, *The Epistle to the Hebrews* (London: Paternoster, 1951), 98–103; Noel Weeks, "Admonition and Error in Hebrews," *WTJ* 39 (1976): 72–80; Dave Mathewson, "Reading Heb 6:4–6 in Light of the Old Testament," *WTJ* 61 (1999): 209–25.

[29] Emmrich, "Hebrews 6:4–6—Again!," 89 (emphasis in original).

eschaton already enjoyed by the community."[30] But these blessings are "provisional" since salvation is "yet to be gained."[31] Every blessing in Hebrews 6:4–6, "including the gift of the Spirit—can be forfeited. . . . Consequently if a (former) member of the community has apostatized . . . there is no more ground for any continuing salvific work of the Spirit."[32] Emmrich points to intertestamental Jewish literature to demonstrate that their "retributive pneumatology" viewed possession of the Spirit as "contingent on obedience," and he claims this idea is "firmly embedded in the Hebrew Scriptures."[33] "If they refuse to stay the course," Emmrich says of the recipients of Hebrews, "the gift of the Spirit will be irrevocably lost."[34]

A Brief Response to the Covenantal View

Before offering an alternative model for interpreting the warnings, I want to respond to some of the above comments. Space limitations prevent an exhaustive interaction, yet several brief observations and rebuttals are necessary regarding how to understand the new covenant blessings and the warnings in the context of Hebrews.

First, "sanctified" (from *hagiazō*) in Hebrews 10:29 should not be understood as speaking of mere external sanctification or ceremonial consecration. Hebrews 9:13, which speaks of the external cleansing afforded by the old covenant animal sacrifices, is the sole use of the verb in Hebrews with this meaning. The other five instances in Hebrews besides 10:29 (2:11 [x2]; 10:10, 14; 13:12) all refer to the definitive sanctification that comes through the new covenant sacrifice of Christ.[35] The sanctification in 10:29

---

[30] Ibid. (emphasis in original).

[31] Ibid., 89n27.

[32] Ibid., 90.

[33] Ibid. For his discussion, see 90–94.

[34] Ibid., 94.

[35] David Peterson: "The verb *hagiazein* . . . is consistently employed in Hebrews to describe the consecration of believers through the death of Christ. We have been decisively and definitively cleansed and sanctified" (*Possessed by God: A New Testament Theology of Sanctification and Holiness* [Downers Grove, IL: InterVarsity, 1995], 74).

is clearly a result of Christ's sacrifice, so a mere "ceremonial" sanctification is entirely inconsistent.

Second, the most straightforward reading of the warnings (esp. 6:4–6 and 10:29) is that they describe genuine Christian conversion—not pseudo-believers. Nevertheless, affirming a "false-believer" view does not require one to accept that the warnings describe "non-elect covenant members" as covenant theologians contend. Rather, according to such a "false-believer" view, these persons are not genuine covenant members. Though they have affiliated themselves with the church, they have not experienced true conversion and the blessings of the new covenant.[36]

Third, Pratt's view that Jeremiah's new covenant promises are "partially fulfilled" is an example of how covenant theologians assume their reading of the warnings. Pratt argues that, since some of those in the covenant community ultimately prove to be unbelievers, the new covenant blessings are only partially realized. Yet this interpretation is not necessary. Only by assuming such persons are *covenant members* can Pratt conclude the new covenant is partially fulfilled. But nothing makes such an individual a covenant member other than his affiliation with the covenant community. Jeremiah, though, distinguishes features that make one a new covenant member: they will have God's law written on their hearts, God will acknowledge that they are his people, all of them will know the Lord, and their sins will be forgiven (Heb 8:8–12). While one might argue for an inaugurated fulfillment of these promises in the lives of *believers*, none of these blessings is true of *unbelievers*, not even in a *partial* sense.

Fourth, Hebrews 8:9 is a significant and often overlooked text for this discussion. The quotation of Jeremiah in Hebrews 8:8–12 includes the Lord's *reason* for making a new covenant. It will not be like the old covenant he made with those he led out of Egypt, "because [ὅτι] they did not

---

[36] Wayne Grudem is one such Baptist interpreter who argues for this view in "Perseverance of the Saints: A Case Study from Hebrews 6:4–6 and the Other Warning Passages in Hebrews," in *The Grace of God, the Bondage of the Will: Historical and Theological Perspectives on Calvinism*, ed. T. R. Schreiner and B. A. Ware (Grand Rapids: Baker, 1995), 133–82. For my critique of Grudem and others who hold to the false-believer view, see Cowan, "Confident of Better Things," 175–99.

continue/remain [ἐνέμειναν] in my covenant" (8:9)—that is, they committed *apostasy*. This reading of their actions as apostasy is consistent with the earlier discussion of the wilderness generation in 3:7–4:13. In light of their faithless disobedience (3:7–11), the author warns his readers to beware of having "an evil, unbelieving heart that falls away [ἀποστῆναι] from the living God" (3:12 NASB).[37] According to Jeremiah, this is exactly the kind of faithless heart the new covenant will rectify: God will write his laws on the hearts of his people (Heb 8:10). *All* his people will know him (8:11). But, if the new covenant is intended to remedy apostate covenant members (8:9), how can it be possible for new covenant members to apostatize—according to covenant theologians? How can the new covenant be "not like" the old (8:9) if new covenant members can fail to "continue" in it?[38]

Fifth, I agree with Lusk that Hebrews 6:4–8 describes those who have been genuinely converted. But his "quasi-salvation" category for reprobates to whom God grants new life but withholds perseverance is unwarranted. His desire to take the warnings at face value and not bend them to fit a grid of systematic theology is commendable.[39] Yet systematic theology on some level is unavoidable and necessary. Lusk's advocacy of a genuinely-converted-but-nonpersevering reprobate—in order to avoid the Arminian position that some believers will lose their salvation—is itself an attempt to maintain his Calvinistic position and adherence to the Westminster Confession of Faith. It is not a question of *whether* we bring together various texts into a coherent theology but *how*. To divide new covenant members—all of whom have received the new covenant

---

[37] On the use of the verb ἀφίστημι for "apostasy" from God in the Septuagint and the NT, see Heinrich Schlier, "ἀφίστημι, et al.," in *TDNT*, 1:512–13; Ulrich Kellermann, "ἀφίστημι," in *EDNT*, 1:183.

[38] I am using the term "apostasy" to refer to the actions of one who, having once been a covenant member (whether under the old or new covenant) departs from it. As will become plain, I do not believe genuine apostasy is possible for new covenant members, given the nature of the new covenant according to the NT authors. Therefore, those who formally affiliate with the new covenant community and subsequently depart from the faith experience *phenomenological* apostasy. They are examples of 1 John 2:19, demonstrating they were never actually new covenant members in whom the promises of Jer 31:31–34 had been fulfilled.

[39] See Lusk, "Staying Saved," 16–18.

blessings—into those elected to persevere and those *not* elected to persevere, based on the warnings of Hebrews, is an extreme exegetical jump. A better understanding of the warning passages will not require an unsubstantiated "quasi-salvation" category.

Sixth, Emmrich's argument that new covenant members can lose the Spirit is unpersuasive. He claims the idea is "firmly embedded in the Hebrew Scriptures," yet he identifies only three example OT texts: God's threatened departure in Exodus 32–33, Samson in Judges 16:20, and Saul in 1 Samuel 16:14. Not only does Emmrich assume the new covenant brings nothing new regarding the reception of the Spirit, but he also omits the prophetic passages that speak of the eschatological gift of the Spirit to God's people (Isa 44:3–5; Ezek 11:19–20; 36:25–27; Joel 2:28–32). According to the promises of the prophets and the testimony of the apostles, reception of the Holy Spirit is a defining feature of God's new covenant people.[40] Paul argues that to belong to Christ is to have the Spirit (Rom 8:9), who seals believers as the down payment of their eternal inheritance (Eph 1:13–14).[41] How, then, can new covenant members lose the Spirit? This is a peculiar argument from one who affirms "sovereign election."[42]

An Alternative View: The Warnings as a Means of Salvation

I will contend for a viable, alternative way to read the warning passages of Hebrews—a reading that does not require one to assume there are nonelect covenant members who apostatize. Thomas Schreiner and Ardel Caneday

---

[40] See D. A. Carson, "Reflections on Christian Assurance," *WTJ* 54 (1992): 11–12.

[41] Thomas R. Schreiner, *Run to Win the Prize: Perseverance in the New Testament* (Nottingham, UK: Apollos, 2009), 93–94.

[42] See Emmrich, "Hebrews 6:4–6—Again!," 89. Emmrich's conclusion notes the disjunction between his interpretation and the testimony of Paul. Emmrich observes that, if his conclusions are correct, the "pneumatological convictions" of the author of Hebrews "differ from those known from the Pauline epistles, where there is no hint of retributive nuances, let alone the irrevocable forfeiture of the Spirit's presence" (ibid., 95).

have offered the most recent and sustained articulation of this interpretation of biblical warnings, which they describe as the "means-of-salvation view."[43]

The Means-of-Salvation View Summarized

This view argues that the warning passages of the NT "are addressed to *believers*, and they are threatened with eternal destruction . . . if they commit apostasy."[44] But genuine believers will not apostatize. Truly, believers must heed the warnings to be saved. But the warnings are themselves a means of preserving grace God uses to ensure the perseverance of his saints.[45] Schreiner and Caneday confess that this view is not original with them; it "has been expressed clearly in prior generations but not recently."[46] Past interpreters who viewed biblical warnings as a divine means of salvation for God's people (whether biblical warnings in general or specific passages) include Herman Bavinck, Richard Baxter, Louis Berkhof, G. C. Berkouwer, James P. Boyce, John Calvin, William Cunnigham, Robert L. Dabney, John Dagg, Jonathan Edwards, Andrew Fuller, Charles Hodge, E. Y. Mullins, John Owen, Charles H. Spurgeon, and A. W. Pink.[47]

According to the broad NT witness, believers in Jesus—both new converts and experienced Christians—are never assured they will inherit the kingdom of God regardless of their actions. Rather apostolic teaching

---

[43] See Thomas R. Schreiner and Ardel B. Caneday, *The Race Set Before Us: A Biblical Theology of Perseverance and Assurance* (Downers Grove, IL: InterVarsity, 2001); Schreiner, *Run to Win the Prize*; idem, "Perseverance and Assurance: A Survey and Proposal" *SBJT* 2 (Spring 1998): 32–63; idem, "Warning and Assurance: Run the Race to the End," in *The Perfect Saviour: Key Themes in Hebrews*, ed. Jonathan Griffiths (Nottingham, UK: InterVarsity, 2012), 89–106.

[44] Schreiner, "Perseverance and Assurance," 52 (emphasis in original).

[45] See ibid., 55.

[46] Schreiner and Caneday, *The Race Set Before Us*, 14.

[47] G. C. Berkouwer advocated this interpretation in *Faith and Perseverance*, trans. Robert D. Knudsen (Grand Rapids: Eerdmans, 1958). For quotations from the writings of the other listed interpreters, see the appendix in Cowan, "Confident of Better Things," 234–42.

regularly includes exhortations to persevere in order to obtain eternal life.[48] This is not a denial that Christians now possess eternal life; instead, it is an acknowledgment that the NT presents salvation with both present and future dimensions. This "already-but-not-yet character of salvation" is a reality because the cross and resurrection of Christ "constitute the invasion of God's end-time work into the present age."[49] While the letter to the Hebrews *primarily* presents salvation as a future reward,[50] the letter also clearly reflects the "inaugurated eschatology" of the rest of the NT.[51] According to the NT, believers presently possess salvation because they have received God's Holy Spirit who is the pledge of their redemption—the future fulfillment of which they yet await. Viewing God's promises and warnings through the already-but-not-yet orientation of the NT is therefore essential.[52] Apostolic authors use a variety of metaphors to describe the one "prize" of eschatological life in the kingdom of God, but all of them have a present and future dimension—that is, each metaphor indicates that salvation has been inaugurated but not yet consummated.[53] How does one obtain the prize of salvation? The redemptive work of Jesus Christ is the *objective* basis of salvation, but the *subjective* means of salvation is the individual exercise of faith in Christ. Christians must persevere in faith to the end; they must "run the race" to finally receive eternal life.[54] As with salvation, the NT also uses a variety of metaphors to describe the complexities

---

[48] Schreiner, *Run to Win the Prize*, 15–23.

[49] Schreiner and Caneday, *The Race Set Before Us*, 47.

[50] Ibid., 199.

[51] On the present and future aspects of eschatology in Hebrews, see, e.g., C. K. Barrett, "The Eschatology of the Epistle to the Hebrews," in *The Background of the New Testament and Its Eschatology*, ed. W. D. Davies (Cambridge: Cambridge University Press, 1956), 363–93; A. T. Lincoln, "Sabbath, Rest, and Eschatology in the New Testament," in *From Sabbath to Lord's Day: A Biblical, Historical, and Theological Investigation*, ed. D. A. Carson (Grand Rapids: Zondervan, 1982), 197–220; Paul Ellingworth, *The Epistle to the Hebrews: A Commentary on the Greek Text*, NIGTC (Grand Rapids: Eerdmans, 1993), 76–77; Koester, *Hebrews*, 100–104.

[52] Schreiner and Caneday, *The Race Set Before Us*, 143–44.

[53] See ibid., 46–86.

[54] Ibid., 89.

of faith. Together these metaphors demonstrate that faith is a gift received from God but also an action one must exert.[55]

To provoke and encourage faith, NT authors employ both conditional promises and warnings. God's promises assure eternal life on the condition that one believes in Jesus. God's warnings threaten eternal judgment on the condition that one falls into unbelief. Divine promises and warnings are not opposed to one another but are complementary, both elaborating on the initial call to believe the gospel. Promises and warnings function together, eliciting a faith in God that perseveres.[56] "[T]he warnings serve the promises, for the warnings urge belief and confidence in God's promises. Biblical warnings and admonitions are the means God uses to save and preserve his people to the end."[57]

While the warnings of Hebrews are recognized as especially intense, such passages are not restricted to Hebrews but are found throughout the NT.[58] The function of warnings is to admonish readers to persevere—not because they *have* fallen away but so they *will not*. "The warnings are *prospective*, not *retrospective*," writes Schreiner. "They are like road signs that caution drivers of dangers ahead on the highway. They are written so that readers will heed the warnings and escape the consequences threatened."[59] The author does not use the warnings as retrospective declarations that certain individuals were never Christians in the first place. Instead, he admonishes the readers to persevere to obtain final salvation, which is not yet consummated.[60]

The purpose of the warnings in the NT in general and Hebrews in particular "is redemptive and salvific."[61] They arouse believers from laziness (Heb 5:11; 6:12) and incite them to a healthy fear of God (Heb 4:1). Heeding them "is the means by which salvation is obtained on the final

---

[55] Ibid., 100–141.

[56] Ibid., 40–43.

[57] Ibid., 40.

[58] See the surveys of New Testament warnings in Schreiner, *Run to Win the Prize*, 27–50; Schreiner and Caneday, *The Race Set Before Us*, 147–204.

[59] Schreiner, *Run to Win the Prize*, 50 (emphasis in original).

[60] For a critique of those who view the warnings as retrospective, see Schreiner and Caneday, *The Race Set Before Us*, 198–99.

[61] Schreiner, *Run to Win the Prize*, 50.

day."[62] The warnings "draw our focus to the not-yet aspect of salvation without doing damage to the fact that believers already have salvation. Biblical admonitions and warnings link the already and the not yet."[63]

Such a model for understanding the warning passages enables one to make sense of the tension between assurance and warning in Hebrews and to integrate the two.[64] The means-of-salvation view recognizes the warnings as genuine admonitions believers must heed to be saved. But they are not intended to call assurance of salvation into question. Nowhere does Hebrews say the readers *have actually fallen away*.[65] He warns them *not to fall away* and urges them to continue in faith. "The warnings do not quench assurance but are one of the means the Lord uses to strengthen it."[66] Therefore, it is not inconsistent for the author of Hebrews to speak of the once-and-for-all sacrifice of Christ and the corresponding realization of the new covenant promises in the "hearts" of his readers (Heb 8:7–12;

---

[62] Schreiner, "Perseverance and Assurance," 53.

[63] Schreiner and Caneday, *The Race Set Before Us*, 16.

[64] For an analysis of texts and themes in Hebrews that promote assurance of salvation, see Cowan, "Confident of Better Things," chaps. 2 and 3.

[65] See Ellingworth, *Hebrews*, 75. B. F. Westcott argues that the conditions of apostasy in Heb 6:4–6 have not actually been fulfilled (*The Epistle to the Hebrews*, 3rd ed. [New York: Macmillan and Co., 1920], 167). Buist M. Fanning claims the readers may be on the verge of danger, but they have not taken the frightening step described in the warnings. The author speaks of the failure as "*potential* rather than *actual*" ("A Classical Reformed View," in *Four Views on the Warning Passages in Hebrews* [Grand Rapids: Kregel, 2007], 206, [emphasis in original]). Though Scot McKnight believes 10:25 suggests some "had already abandoned Christianity" ("The Warning Passages of Hebrews: A Formal Analysis and Theological Conclusions," *TrinJ* 13 NS [1992]: 42), Fanning regards this as "a worrisome precursor—a sign of lethargy [which the author *does* accuse them of in 5:11]—rather than an indication of actual 'falling away'" (ibid., 181n17). William L. Lane calls 10:25 "a *prelude* to apostasy on the part of those who were separating themselves from the assembly" (*Hebrews 9–13*, WBC [Dallas, TX: Word, 1991], 290, [emphasis added]). The γάρ ("for") beginning 10:26 demonstrates its connection to 10:25. The warning against apostasy in v. 26, P. T. O'Brien contends, "implies that people who deliberately and persistently abandon the fellowship of Christian believers are in danger . . . of abandoning the Lord himself!" (*The Letter to the Hebrews*, PNTC [Grand Rapids: Eerdmans, 2010], 371).

[66] Schreiner, *Run to Win the Prize*, 112.

10:10–17, 22),[67] while warning them not to have an evil, unbelieving "heart" that falls away from the living God (Heb 3:12). The heart transformation they have undergone ensures they will heed the warnings the author gives. Even though he admonishes them, he is "confident of better things" for them—things pertaining to salvation (Heb 6:9).[68] Of course, the means-of-salvation view does not argue that biblical warnings prevent believers from falling into *sin*—even grievous sin.[69] The purpose of the warnings is to enable believers to persevere in faith and bear fruit to the end—in spite of repeated failures along the way. Divine warnings prevent believers from *apostatizing* from Christ.

According to the means-of-salvation view, then, the author of Hebrews warns believers (not pseudo-believers) to avoid apostasy and the corresponding punishment of eternal damnation. Yet this view maintains such warnings do not imply believers *can or will* apostatize. Biblical warnings are "the means God uses to save and preserve his people to the end."[70] Genuine believers will heed the warnings and persevere. Those who separate themselves from the covenant community demonstrate they were never true believers whose hearts had been transformed.[71]

---

[67] See Cowan, "Confident of Better Things," chap. 2 ("Perfection and the New Covenant Promises").

[68] For discussion of 6:9–20, see ibid., chap. 3 ("The Author's Confidence, God's Oath, and the Believer's Hope: Hebrews 6:9–20").

[69] Schreiner and Caneday describe Peter's sin in particular as "loathsome" and "aggravated" (*The Race Set Before Us*, 241–42). "Nowhere [in the NT] is sin tolerated or dismissed as trivial. On the other hand, the authors do not conclude from the presence of sin in the churches that the recipients are unbelievers. . . . Naturally, no room or excuse is given for sin in the lives of believers, and yet there is an implicit understanding that believers are not outside the realm of sin and do not conquer sin perfectly" (Schreiner, *Run to Win the Prize*, 58–59).

[70] Schreiner and Caneday, *The Race Set Before Us*, 40.

[71] To answer the question of the identity of those who *do* actually fall away, Schreiner and Caneday look to other NT passages that truly are *retrospective*, such as Matt 7:21–23; 1 Cor 11:19; 2 Tim 2:18; 1 John 2:19 (see *The Race Set Before Us*, 214–44; Schreiner, *Run to Win the Prize*, 108–16). Speaking of 1 John 2:19, Schreiner writes, "Here is the retrospective view that is missing from the warnings. No one who is truly elect will ever fall away, for those who do apostatize reveal that they were never genuinely saved" (Schreiner, *Run to Win the Prize*, 109).

Does This View Make the Warnings Artificial and without Purpose?

The means-of-salvation view contends that the warnings are addressed to believers, but genuine believers cannot and will not fall away. Therefore, some claim this view causes the warnings to lose their force and become artificial.[72] How is one to be alarmed by warnings when perseverance is inevitable?

Though not responding specifically to Schreiner and Caneday, one author objects to the notion that believers would be affected by warnings against apostasy if they cannot actually fall away: "If it is true that the readers are true Christians and that they are therefore eternally secure, it is ludicrous to think that the warnings would have any significant impact."[73] Michael Horton and Rich Lusk offer similar arguments (though they also are not specifically responding to Schreiner and Caneday). Horton argues that, unless one acknowledges his third category, the "eternal security" advocate must explain Hebrews 6:4–6 as a "hypothetical warning." In other words, "it never actually happens that people who enjoy these spiritual benefits fall away and lose them."[74] Insisting that the warnings are *actual* not *hypothetical*, Lusk claims, "If they are saved, and therefore eternally secure, why bother with the warning? The text is eviscerated of its rhetorical force by way of systematic theology. . . . The warning is, at best, a scare tactic."[75]

How are the warnings to have any real significance if genuine believers will always heed them and never fall away? Why the need to admonish someone not to commit apostasy if God's preserving grace will keep him from actually apostatizing anyway? First, we must be clear to distinguish between the means-of-salvation view and the so-called hypothetical view of the warning passages.[76] In the means-of-salvation view, the warnings are

---

[72] See Schreiner, *Run to Win the Prize*, 97.

[73] Joseph C. Dillow, *The Reign of the Servant Kings: A Study of Eternal Security and the Final Significance of Man*, 2nd ed. (Miami Springs, FL: Schoettle, 1992), 224.

[74] Horton, "A Classical Calvinist View," 36.

[75] Lusk, "Staying Saved," 14.

[76] Advocates of the "hypothetical view" include, e.g., Thomas Hewitt, *The Epistle to the Hebrews: An Introduction and Commentary*, TNTC (Grand Rapids: Eerdmans,

genuine admonishments delivered to Christians not to fall away. The author of Hebrews is not offering a hypothetical scenario to correct his readers' thinking. He is warning them of a real danger so they do not apostatize.

Second, we must consider the assumption behind the critique. "The problem with this objection," Schreiner writes, "is that it assumes that the warning plays no role or function in keeping believers from falling away."[77] In other words, the objection seems to conceive of perseverance in terms of an abstract doctrine. But life for the believer is not lived in the abstract. It requires faith, without which it is impossible to please God (Heb 11:6). Perseverance demands a faith that trusts God in spite of unseen realities (11:1–2) and rises to action (11:3–36). Therefore, the doctrine of perseverance is no "*a priori* guarantee" that enables believers "to get along without admonitions and warnings." G. C. Berkouwer explains, "Perseverance is not something that is merely handed down to us, but it is something that comes to realization only *in the path of faith*."[78] Believers are enabled to persevere in faith and hold fast to their confession in Jesus, *for the very reason* that they are admonished to "hold on to the confession of [their] hope without wavering, for He who promised is faithful" (10:23 HCSB).

A NT passage that illustrates this tension is Acts 27, narrating Paul's treacherous voyage and shipwreck.[79] Here a warning must be obeyed in order for the ship's passengers to be saved (Acts 27:30–32), in spite of the fact that a divine promise was given earlier to Paul that everyone's life would be preserved (Acts 27:21–26). The threat was not hypothetical but real: if the sailors fled the ship, the remaining passengers would perish. The author

---

1960), 108; and Homer A. Kent Jr., *The Epistle to the Hebrews* (Grand Rapids: Baker, 1972), 113. For discussion of the distinction between the hypothetical view and the means-of-salvation view, see Cowan, "Confident of Better Things," 217–18.

[77] Schreiner, *Run to Win the Prize*, 97.

[78] Berkouwer, *Faith and Perseverance*, 110–11 (emphasis in original).

[79] See the discussions of Acts 27 in Robert L. Dabney, *Lectures in Systematic Theology* (1878; repr., Grand Rapids: Zondervan, 1971), 697; Louis Berkhof, *Systematic Theology*, 3rd rev. and enlarged ed. (Grand Rapids: Eerdmans, 1946), 107; Herman Bavinck, *Holy Spirit, Church and New Creation*, vol. 4 of *Reformed Dogmatics*, ed. John Bolt, trans. John Vriend (Grand Rapids: Baker, 2008), 267–68; Charles Hodge, *1 Corinthians* (Wheaton, IL: Crossway, 1995), 144; Schreiner and Caneday, *The Race Set Before Us*, 209–12; Schreiner, *Run to Win the Prize*, 97–99.

of Acts apparently saw no discrepancy between the divine guarantee to Paul of safety and Paul's subsequent warning as the necessary means of ensuring that safety.

Though D. A. Carson does not himself advocate the means-of-salvation view of the warning passages, his discussion of the tension between the two biblical perspectives of divine sovereignty and human responsibility is nevertheless instructive.[80] Carson argues that these two perspectives are repeatedly taught in both the OT and the NT.[81] Yet he contends that believers must ensure "that these complementary truths function in our lives in the same ways they function in the lives of believers in Scripture." Biblical "exhortations to believe and obey" never function to present God "as fundamentally dependent on us" or to "reduce God to the absolutely contingent." Instead they function "to increase our responsibility, to emphasize the urgency of the steps we must take." Similarly, the biblical emphasis on divine sovereignty does not function to encourage an "uncaring fatalism" or moral indifference. It functions, instead, as the ground for believing in "God's gracious control" of all things.[82] Carson goes on to discuss several examples in which biblical figures intercede in prayer, pleading that their sovereign God would relent of the disaster he threatens (such as Moses in Exodus 32). He concludes:

> God expects to be pleaded with; he expects godly believers to
> intercede with him. Their intercession is *his own appointed means*

---

[80] See D. A. Carson, *Divine Sovereignty and Human Responsibility: Biblical Perspectives in Tension* (Eugene, OR: Wipf & Stock, 1994). Carson applies this tension to a variety of contexts, including prayer (*A Call to Spiritual Reformation: Priorities from Paul and His Prayers* [Grand Rapids: Baker, 1992], 145–66) and suffering (*How Long O Lord? Reflections on Suffering and Evil*, 2nd ed. [Grand Rapids: Baker, 2006], 177–203).

[81] Carson articulates the two truths in this way: "1. God is absolutely sovereign, but his sovereignty never functions in Scripture to reduce human responsibility. 2. Human beings are responsible creatures—that is, they choose, they believe, they disobey, they respond, and there is moral significance in their choices; but human responsibility never functions in Scripture to diminish God's sovereignty or to make God absolutely contingent" (*A Call to Spiritual Reformation*, 148).

[82] Ibid., 160–61.

for bringing about his relenting, and if they fail in this respect,
then he does not relent and his wrath is poured out. . . . In God's
mercy Moses proved to be *God's own appointed means*, through
intercessory prayer, for bringing about the relenting that was
nothing other than a gracious confirmation of the covenant with
Abraham, Isaac, and Jacob.

The really wonderful truth is that human beings like Moses
and you and me can participate in bringing about God's purposes
through *God's own appointed means*.[83]

Thus, Carson argues, an end assured by God does not negate the divinely
appointed means to that end requiring human response.

The warning texts in Hebrews ought to be viewed similarly. On the
one hand, the author's exposition in Hebrews of the fulfillment of the new
covenant promises in the lives of believers functions to promote assurance
of salvation; it does not function to encourage the readers to apathy. On
the other hand, the warnings of the letter do not function to call into question Christ's once-and-for-all perfecting work in the lives of Christians; they
function to admonish the recipients that if they cease trusting in Christ,
they will perish.

Berkouwer is correct: Scripture nowhere allows one to take the con-
tinual and immutable nature of God's grace for granted or to respond to it
with passivity.[84] Moses did not presume on the security of God's promise of
blessing to Abraham, Isaac, and Jacob. Rather, he petitioned God to relent
of his threat to destroy the people so the promise of blessing would be
remembered and fulfilled (Exod 32:11–14). Paul did not presume on the
security of God's promise to deliver all of the ship's passengers. Rather, he
admonished the soldiers, "Unless these men stay in the ship, you cannot be
saved" (Acts 27:31 HCSB). In the same way, the readers of Hebrews must
not presume on the security Christ's one sacrifice for sins has perfected
them forever. Instead they must take care lest they have an evil, unbelieving

---

[83] Ibid., 164 (emphasis added).
[84] Berkouwer, *Faith and Perseverance*, 97.

heart that leads them to fall away from the living God (Heb 3:12). They will inherit the promised salvation precisely by heeding the warnings. These warnings urge them to embrace faith—that is, to hold fast their confession in Jesus and boldly approach the throne of grace (4:16). The warnings also urge them *not* to commit apostasy—that is, to trample on the Son of God and profane the covenant blood by which they were sanctified (10:29).

One should view the warning passages as analogous to the initial call to believe the gospel. Those who affirm a Reformed soteriology understand salvation as an act of divine election; nevertheless, they do not cast aside the *means* God uses to call sinners to believe in Jesus.[85] Though God decides according to his electing purposes to whom he will show mercy (Rom 9:11–18) and predestines them for adoption through Christ (Eph 1:5), the elect cannot call on and believe in him unless the good news of the gospel is preached to them (Rom 9:14). One might object that the call to believe is meaningless and unnecessary if God's elect will certainly believe. Nevertheless, exhorting sinners to believe in Jesus is exactly what the apostles did. They did not call on their hearers to determine if they were elect but to repent of sin and believe in Christ (e.g., Acts 2:38; 3:19–20; 10:43; 13:38–39; 16:31).[86] God's electing purposes from before creation do not invalidate the requirement that sinners must have faith in Jesus to be saved. Paul contends that God promises to call, justify, and glorify those whom he predestines (Rom 8:30), but the gospel must be preached so people may be saved (1 Cor 9:16–23). "Belief is a *condition* to be saved, but God through his grace has promised to fulfill that condition in the lives of his elect. . . . Those who hear must believe and repent to be saved, and they are summoned to respond with the utmost urgency."[87]

The means-of-salvation view of the warning passages should be understood in the same way. Schreiner explains:

> God has promised that his elect will persevere, just as he
> promised to grant faith to his chosen ones. Such a promise

---

[85] See Schreiner, *Run to Win the Prize*, 106.
[86] Ibid., 105–7.
[87] Ibid., 106.

does not eliminate the need to persevere. Both the summons to persevere and the initial call to believe in the gospel are conditions that must be fulfilled to be saved, but in both instances God grants the grace so that the conditions will certainly be fulfilled in those who belong to him. The certainty that God will grant perseverance does not remove the moral urgency to persevere in faith, just as the certainty that God will grant faith to the elect does not lessen the need to believe.[88]

"To say that the warnings are . . . artificial if no one can commit apostasy is like saying the call to belief is a charade if all the elect will certainly believe."[89] Thus, it does not follow that the warnings are superfluous if believers will certainly heed them anymore than the proclamation of the gospel is superfluous if the elect will certainly be saved. Both the call to faith *and* the call to persevere in faith are the means God uses to save his own.[90]

Consider another analogy—this one with Jesus. According to Hebrews, he was perfected for his role as high priest through suffering (Heb 2:10), which involved experiencing the full range of human temptations (2:18; 4:15). He offered up tears and prayers to the one able to save him from death (5:7). Through his suffering he learned obedience and was perfected, becoming the source of eternal salvation (5:8–9). Though he was tempted to reject God's will, his declaration was, "I have come to do your will, O God" (10:7 ESV). Yet the author assures us that Jesus was without sin (4:15). He was holy, innocent, and undefiled (7:26). So, does his moral perfection render his temptations void? If Jesus suffered and was genuinely tempted to disobey God, does this not necessarily imply that it was *possible* for him to disobey God? Apparently not, according to Hebrews. Herman Bavinck, who also interprets the warnings as a means-of-salvation, insists:

It is . . . completely mistaken to reason from the admonitions of Holy Scripture to the possibility of a total loss of grace. This conclusion is illegitimate as when, in the case of Christ, people

---

[88] Ibid., 106–7.

[89] Schreiner, "Perseverance and Assurance," 55.

[90] Schreiner, *Run to Win the Prize*, 107.

infer from his temptation that he was able to sin. The certainty
of the outcome does not render the means superfluous but is
inseparably connected with them in the decree of God.[91]

It was impossible for Jesus to sin. Yet his temptations were real and purpose-
ful that he might be made a merciful and faithful high priest to make pro-
pitiation for the people (2:17). The objective of warnings and admonitions
is to "appeal to the mind to conceive how actions have consequences."[92]
Therefore, they do not "confront us with an uncertain future. They do
not say that we may perish. Rather they caution us lest we perish. They
warn that we will surely perish if we fail to heed God's call in the gospel."[93]
Though believers are recipients of the new covenant promises and perfected forever (10:14), they are tempted to fall away, and so the author of
Hebrews admonishes them to hold fast. Such warnings do not indicate that
it is possible for them to commit apostasy. Yet these admonitions do serve a
genuine purpose in their lives: to cause them to consider the miserable end
of rejecting Christ's sacrifice and to endure in diligence so they "may not be
apathetic but imitators of those who, through faith and patience, inherit the
promises" (6:12, my translation).

Conclusion

Pointing to the warning passages of Hebrews, covenant theologians argue
that the new covenant includes nonelect covenant members who will commit apostasy. I have argued, however, that their interpretation is not exegetically satisfying. Instead, the means-of-salvation view is a more viable
reading of the warnings. Thus the view that the new covenant community
is by nature a mixed community is not proven by the presence of biblical
warnings.

---

[91] Bavinck, *Holy Spirit, Church and New Creation*, 267–68.
[92] Schreiner and Caneday, *The Race Set Before Us*, 207.
[93] Ibid., 208.

To conclude, I give the final word to several past theologians (paedo-baptist and Baptist) regarding the role of biblical warnings as a means of salvation in the lives of believers:[94]

Herman Bavinck: All of the above-mentioned admonitions and threats that Scripture addresses to believers, therefore, do not prove a thing against the doctrine of perseverance. They are rather the way in which God himself confirms his promise and gift through believers. They are the means by which perseverance in life is realized.[95]

Louis Berkhof: [Warnings] do not prove that any of the addressed will apostatize, but simply that the use of means is necessary to prevent them from committing this sin.[96]

James P. Boyce: The warnings of God's word are also means to the same end [of salvation]. They imply the importance of Christian exertion, and the value of effort as well as the possibility of danger. . . . The doctrine we are considering does not regard the believer as preserved and as persevering only through himself. He is thus kept by God; not by his own power. One of the means by which this is done, is that he is warned of the danger . . . that he may co-operate with God, so as not only to be preserved, but also to persevere in the divine life.[97]

Robert L. Dabney: The certainty that he will not [apostatize] arises, not from the strength of a regenerated heart, but from God's secret, unchangeable purpose concerning the believer; which purpose He executes towards and in him by moral means consistent with the creature's free agency. Among these

---

[94] For the extended versions of these quotations, as well as quotations from others, see the appendix in Cowan, "Confident of Better Things," 234–42.

[95] Bavinck, *Holy Spirit, Church and New Creation*, 267–68.

[96] Berkhof, *Systematic Theology*, 548.

[97] James P. Boyce, *Abstract of Systematic Theology* (Cape Coral, FL: Founders, 2006), 433.

appropriate motives are these very warnings of dangers and wholesome fears about apostasy.[98]

Charles Hodge: God's telling the elect that if they apostatize they will perish prevents their apostasy.[99]

John Owen: If we are in Christ, God hath given us the lives of our souls, and hath taken upon himself in His covenant the preservation of them; but yet we may say, with reference unto the means that he hath appointed, when storms and trials arise, unless we use our diligent endeavors, "we cannot be saved." Hence are the many cautions that are given us . . . that we should take heed of apostasy and falling away.[100]

Arthur W. Pink: To say that real Christians need no such warning because they cannot possibly commit that sin, is, we repeat, to lose sight of the connection which God Himself has established between His predestined ends and the means whereby they are reached. The end to which God has predestined His people is their eternal bliss in Heaven, and one of the means by which that end is reached, is through their taking heed to the solemn warning He has given against that which would prevent their reaching Heaven.[101]

Charles H. Spurgeon: God preserves his children from falling away; but he keeps them by the use of means; and one of these is, the terrors of the law, showing them what would happen if they were to fall away. There is a deep precipice: what is the best way to keep any one from going down there? Why, to tell him that if he did he would inevitably be dashed to pieces. . . . So God says,

---

[98] Dabney, *Lectures in Systematic Theology*, 697.

[99] Hodge, *1 Corinthians*, 144.

[100] John Owen, *An Exposition of the Epistle to the Hebrews with Preliminary Exercitations*, ed. William H. Goold (Carlisle, PA: The Banner of Truth Trust, 1991), 4:157–58.

[101] Arthur W. Pink, *An Exposition of the Sermon on the Mount* (Grand Rapids: Baker, 1953), 616.

"My child, if you fall over this precipice you will be dashed to pieces." What does the child do? He says, "Father, keep me; hold thou me up, and I shall be safe." It leads the believer to greater dependence on God, to a holy fear and caution, because he knows that if he were to fall away he could not be renewed, and he stands far away from that great gulf, because he knows that if he were to fall into it there would be no salvation for him.[102]

---

[102] Charles Spurgeon, "Final Perseverance" in *The New Park Street Pulpit*, accessed August 12, 2012, http://www.spurgeon.org/sermons/0075.htm.

CHAPTER 8

Progressive Covenantalism and the Doing of Ethics

STEPHEN J. WELLUM

H ow should Christians apply the whole Bible as our ethical standard?
Today this question is important for at least two reasons: First, in
a growing secular and pluralistic age, we need to articulate God's moral
standards as necessary, good, and objectively true. Second, in response to
various unbelieving critics, we need to demonstrate that Scripture's ethical teaching is consistent across the canon because it is grounded in God's
unchanging nature and will.

Covenant theology has sought to do ethics and establish the basis for
moral law by following the venerable tradition of dividing the Mosaic law into
three parts: moral, civil, and ceremonial.[1] With the coming of Christ, the law's
civil and ceremonial parts are now fulfilled and abrogated, yet God's eternal
moral law as revealed in the Decalogue remains unchanged.[2] A direct equation

---

[1] For example, see Greg L. Bahnsen, "The Theonomic Reformed Approach to Law
and Gospel," in *The Law, the Gospel, and the Modern Christian: Five Views*, ed. Wayne
G. Strickland (Grand Rapids: Zondervan, 1993), 93–173; John M. Frame, *The Doctrine
of the Christian Life* (Phillipsburg, NJ: P&R, 2008), 203–36; Philip S. Ross, *From the
Finger of God: The Biblical and Theological Basis for the Threefold Division of the Law*
(Fearn, Ross-shire, Scotland: Christian Focus, 2010). On this point see Jason Meyer's
chapter in this volume.

[2] Within covenant theology there is debate over the application of civil law to
the state as represented by theonomy. Additionally, in regard to the application of the

is made between the Decalogue and eternal moral law[3] and a general hermeneutical rule is followed: unless the NT explicitly modifies or abrogates the Mosaic law (as in the ceremonial and civil parts), it is still in force today. This rule becomes *the* principle by which moral law is established across the canon.

There is much to commend about this approach, and it is important not to exaggerate the differences between progressive covenantalism and covenant theology in doing ethics. In the end, both views arrive at similar conclusions regarding God's moral demands today. However, the difference lies in *how* we arrive at our conclusions given progressive covenantalism's rejection of the tripartite distinction of the law as *the* principle by which moral law is biblically established. This difference is also illustrated in the ongoing debate over the present-day application of the Sabbath command—a debate that functions as a crucial test case for *how* the biblical covenants are "put together" and moral law is established.[4]

In this chapter I will outline in five steps how progressive covenantalism seeks to determine what the moral law is and thus establish the biblical norm for doing ethics. Given our rejection of the tripartite distinction, what is our alternative approach? How do we escape the charge of being antinomian? How do we establish God's moral norms, especially in our secular and pluralistic age, as those who now live under the new covenant?

1. All Scripture Is Authoritative and Thus Provides the Norm for Christian Ethics

What is our standard for ethics? How do we establish moral norms? The simple answer: *all* of Scripture is our standard, and it alone establishes moral norms. In this regard, 2 Timothy 3:15–17 is a crucial text. Paul describes

---

moral law, a distinction is made between general moral precepts as represented by the Decalogue and specific applications of those precepts, i.e., case laws. Today Christians are to apply the former to our lives and not necessarily the latter.

[3] For a discussion of how the Mosaic law is equated with moral law, see Douglas J. Moo, "The Law of Christ as the Fulfillment of the Law of Moses: A Modified Lutheran View," in *The Law, the Gospel, and the Modern Christian*, 170–71, who makes this point.

[4] On this point, see Tom Schreiner's chapter in this volume.

Scripture, specifically the OT, as God's breathed-out word and thus fully authoritative for Christians. In other words, the *entire* OT, including the law covenant, functions for us as the basis for our doctrine *and* ethics. Although Christians are not "under the law" *as a covenant*, it still functions *as Scripture* and demands our complete obedience.[5]

At the beginning of our discussion, we want to establish that *all* Christians ought to confess that God's nature and will are the objective standard of morality, and as creatures we know this standard by revelation. Christian ethics is not antinomian. Although Scripture is not an exhaustive revelation, it is a true and objective revelation of God's moral will. Our triune God has not left us to ourselves; Scripture is our sufficient and authoritative moral standard.

Nevertheless, although *all* Scripture is our standard, its moral instruction requires careful application depending on our covenantal location. Some specific commands under the old covenant such as circumcision, food laws, gleaning laws, and so on, which are all moral laws, no longer apply to us today in exactly the same way (Gen 17:9–14; Leviticus 11; 19:9–10; cf. Mark 7:1–23; Hebrews 5–10). This is why it is crucial to distinguish between biblical morality and Christian ethics.[6] As Michael Hill explains, "Biblical morality has to do with the morality found in the Bible."[7] It describes God's moral demands in specific places in redemptive history, but "Christian ethics is locating what is normative for Christians in this present age."[8] As Hill grants, "Some unreflective Christians believe that the revelation of God is exactly the same in any part of the Bible."[9] Thus the *doing* of ethics is simply taking "a moral rule, principle or virtue from any part of the Bible and without further interpretation apply it directly as moral

---

[5] On this point, see Brian S. Rosner, *Paul and the Law: Keeping the Commandments of God*, NSBT 31 (Downers Grove, IL: InterVarsity, 2013).

[6] See Michael Hill, *The How and Why of Love: An Introduction to Evangelical Ethics* (Kingsford, Australia: Matthias Media, 2002), 43–54; and John S. Feinberg and Paul D. Feinberg, *Ethics for a Brave New World*, 2nd ed. (Wheaton, IL: Crossway, 2010), 40–49.

[7] Hill, *How and Why of Love*, 43.

[8] Ibid.

[9] Ibid., 44.

guidance for Christians today."[10] But this ethical use of the Bible fails to do justice to the Bible's own teaching and the progressive unfolding of the biblical covenants.

So *all* Scripture is for our ethical instruction, but *not* all Scripture applies to us in exactly the same way! How, then, do we rightly apply the entire canon to us as our ethical norm?

2. The Tripartite Distinction of the Mosaic Law Is *Not* the Means for Determining What Is Morally Binding for Christians Today

As already noted, covenant theology determines what is morally binding upon Christians by appealing to the tripartite distinction of the Mosaic law. Although this approach is noteworthy, we reject it for the following three reasons.

First, Scripture views the old covenant as a unit or package, and it does not appeal to the tripartite distinction as *the* means by which the continuity and discontinuity of moral law is established for Christians today. This is not to say that within the law covenant distinctions can be made (e.g., certain principles are more important [Matt 5:24; 9:13], weightier matters of the law [Matt 23:23], laws regarding sacrifices [Leviticus 1–7] versus civil matters, or even noting the central place of the Decalogue [Exodus 20; Deuteronomy 5]). Instead, it is to say that Scripture views the law covenant as a unit that serves a specific role in God's plan for the life of Israel, and as an entire covenant it is brought to fulfillment in Christ and the new covenant.[11]

Texts such as Galatians 5:3 and James 2:8–13 point in this direction. Keeping or breaking one part of the law assumes the keeping or breaking of

---

[10] Ibid.

[11] For the detailed defense of this point, see Peter J. Gentry and Stephen J. Wellum, *Kingdom Through Covenant: A Biblical-Theological Understanding of the Covenants* (Wheaton, IL: Crossway, 2012). Also see D. A. Carson, "The Tripartite Division of the Law: A Review of Philip Ross, *The Finger of God*," in *From Creation to New Creation: Essays in Honor of G. K. Beale*, ed. Daniel M. Gurtner and Benjamin L. Gladd (Peabody, MA: Hendrickson, 2013), 226–28; Rosner, *Paul and the Law*, 26–44; Hill, *How and Why of Love*, 74–75; and Moo, "Law of Christ as the Fulfillment of the Law of Moses," 336–37.

the whole law. Or, as the author of Hebrews argues, the law covenant is an integrated whole grounded in the priesthood (Heb 7:11); and with a change in priesthood (Psalm 110; Hebrews 7), there is *necessarily* an entire covenantal change, not merely parts of it (Heb 7:12; 8:7–13). Or think of how Paul views himself as a Christian: before he was under the law covenant as a Jew, but now he no longer is. Instead, he is under God's law by being ἔννομος Χριστοῦ (1 Cor 9:21), i.e., under the new covenant. Paul views the covenants as entire packages, the old having reached its end in Christ.

Second, Scripture teaches that the entire law covenant was temporary in God's plan, serving a number of purposes, but ultimately pointing forward to its fulfillment, *telos*, and terminus in Christ (Rom 10:4; Gal 3:15–4:7; Heb 7:11–12).[12] In order to grasp the role of the law covenant in God's redemptive plan, we must locate it with the progressive unfolding of the covenants. When one does so, Scripture teaches the opposite conclusion of first-century Judaism. Jewish thought believed the old covenant was eternal and unchangeable (e.g., Wis 18:4, *Ag. Ap.* 2.277; *Mos.* 2.14; *Jub* 1:27; 3:31; 6:17); the NT teaches that as important as the law covenant is in God's unfolding plan, it has now come to its end *as an entire covenant.*[13]

For this reason the Mosaic law *as a covenant* is no longer directly binding on the Christian. In fact, the law's supervising God's people and directing their behavior as a παιδαγωγὸς (Gal 3:24) have reached their end with Christ's coming and the new covenant (Gal 4:1–7).[14] Two important implications follow. First, it is difficult to separate the law covenant into three parts and suggest that only its moral parts apply to us today. Second, given that the law covenant has reached its *telos* in Christ, we only apply its ethical instruction to us in and through Christ and the new covenant.

---

[12] On this point, see Moo, "Law of Christ as the Fulfillment of the Law of Moses," 321–24; Thomas R. Schreiner, *40 Questions About Christians and Biblical Law* (Grand Rapids: Kregel, 2010), 67–71.

[13] D. A. Carson, "Mystery and Fulfillment: Toward a More Comprehensive Paradigm of Paul's Understanding of the Old and the New," in *The Paradoxes of Paul*, vol. 2 of *Justification and Variegated Nomism*, ed. D. A. Carson, Peter T. O'Brien, and Mark A. Seifrid (Grand Rapids: Baker, 2004), 412.

[14] On this point, see Moo, "Law of Christ as the Fulfillment of the Law of Moses," 338. Also see idem, *Galatians*, BECNT (Grand Rapids, Baker, 2013), 192–247.

Third, and related to the previous points, the NT teaches that Christians are no longer "under the law" as a covenant, and thus it no longer functions as a "direct authority" for us (e.g., Rom 6:14–15; 1 Cor 9:20–21; Gal 4:4–5; 5:13–18).[15] On this point Paul's argument is thoroughly redemptive-historical: the old covenant served its purpose in God's plan, but now in Christ it has reached its *telos* (end and goal) (Rom 10:4; Gal 3:15–4:7).[16] A common way to avoid this conclusion is to interpret Paul as saying that Christians are no longer "under the law" either by a legalistic misuse of it or in its ceremonial requirements.[17] Both of these interpretations fail, however, since Paul does not equate "law" (νομός) with a "legalistic" misunderstanding of it; instead, "law" refers to the entire law covenant, which Christians are no longer under in Christ.[18]

On this point, 1 Corinthians 9:20–21 is a crucial text. As a Christian, Paul no longer sees himself as "under the law"; *and*, remarkably, he does not equate God's law with the Mosaic law! Instead, Paul views himself as under God's law, but God's law is now defined completely in relation to Christ (ἔννομος Χριστοῦ).[19] This entails, as Moo suggests, "The 'law' under which Christians live is continuous with the Mosaic law in that God's eternal moral norms, which never change, are clearly expressed in both. But there is discontinuity in the fact that Christians live under the 'law of Christ' and *not* under the Mosaic law. Our source for determining God's eternal moral law is Christ and the apostles, not the Mosaic law or even the Ten

---

[15] Douglas J. Moo, "Response to Greg L. Bahnsen," in *The Law, the Gospel, and the Modern Christian*, 166; Rosner, *Paul and the Law*, 45–81; and Schreiner, *40 Questions*, 73–76.

[16] On Rom 10:4, see Douglas J. Moo, *The Epistle to the Romans*, NICNT (Grand Rapids: Eerdmans, 1996), 636–43, and idem, "The Law of Moses or the Law of Christ," in *Continuity and Discontinuity: Perspectives on the Relationship Between the Old and New Testaments*, ed. John S. Feinberg (Wheaton, IL: Crossway, 1988), 206–8.

[17] For example, see Bahnsen, "Theonomic Reformed Approach to the Law and Gospel," 96–108; cf. the discussion in Schreiner, *40 Questions*, 35–64, 73–76.

[18] See Moo, "Law of Christ as the Fulfillment of the Law of Moses," 328–33; Rosner, *Paul and the Law*, 45–81. Cf. Stephen Westerholm, *Perspectives Old and New on Paul: The "Lutheran" Paul and His Critics* (Grand Rapids: Eerdmans, 2004), 297–340.

[19] On this point, see Carson, "The Tripartite Division of the Law," 235.

Commandments."[20] This fact helps make sense of why Christians do not "do" or "keep" the law; instead, in Christ, we "fulfill" the law due to Christ's work and the power of the Spirit.[21]

What do these three points teach us? Scripture does not appeal to a tripartite division in the law as *the* basis for determining the moral law today. The law covenant is viewed as a whole. It has now reached its end in Christ. This is why the law covenant is not *directly* binding on Christians. This is *not* to say that it has no present relevance. In fact, if we ask, what is the purpose of the law? (Gal 3:19), diverse answers may be given.[22]

Central to the law's purpose was to reveal God's character and the nature of human sin by imprisoning Israel under sin, and also to instruct how God would graciously redeem in priesthood and sacrifice (e.g., Rom 3:19–20; 5:20; 7:7–12; 8:2–3; Col 2:14; Heb 7:11; 10:3). The law covenant held out the promise of life (Lev 18:5; Rom 2:13; Gal 3:12), but due to human sin it could not save us despite being "holy, righteous and good" (Rom 7:12 NIV).[23] In fact, ultimately, the law covenant was never intended to save; yet in its typological patterns (e.g., sacrificial system, tabernacle/temple, priesthood, etc.), it pointed forward to how God would save. In the end God's righteousness comes apart from the old covenant (Rom 3:21), and it is only found in the new covenant—that to which the law pointed (Rom 3:21–31; 8:2–4; Gal 3:13–14; 4:4–7). For a time the Mosaic law supervised God's people (Gal 3:24; 4:1–7), but now that Christ has come its supervisory work is done. Yet the law covenant still functions for us as *Scripture*, teaching us about God's glorious plan of redemption, making us wise to salvation in Christ, and instructing us how to live wisely in the world as God's new covenant people.[24]

---

[20] Douglas J. Moo, "Response to Willem A. VanGemeren," in *The Law, the Gospel, and the Modern Christian*, 89.

[21] See the discussion of this point in Rosner, *Paul and the Law*, 83–109.

[22] See Moo, "The Law of Christ as the Fulfillment of the Law of Moses," 324–43; Schreiner, *40 Questions*, 81–84.

[23] See Rosner, *Paul and the Law*, 45–81.

[24] Ibid., 135–205, speaks of the law as *Scripture* still functioning for Christians as *prophecy* (i.e., unfolding God's redemptive plan and pointing forward to Christ [Matt 11:13] and *wisdom* (i.e., giving us instruction on how to live even though the old covenant is not directly binding on Christians *as a covenant*).

3. Viewing All Scripture through the Lens of Christ and the New Covenant Determines What Is Morally Binding upon Christians Today

Although Christians are not "under the law" *as a covenant*, it still functions for us *as Scripture*. As with any biblical text, however, before we directly apply it to our lives, we must first place it in its covenantal location; *and* then second, we must think through how that text points forward, anticipates, and is fulfilled in Christ.[25] Only by doing this can we correctly apply *any* biblical text to our lives as Christians. In fact, apart from following this hermeneutical process, we will incorrectly apply Scripture.

For example, if we ask, does the Levitical sacrificial instruction apply to us today?, the answer is no, if we mean *as* God's covenant instruction to Israel. We, as Christians, live *after* Christ, who by his glorious work has brought the OT sacrifices to their *telos* (Hebrews 5–10). Yet Leviticus *as Scripture* does apply to us in diverse ways—*as* prophecy, instruction, and wisdom—but now only in light of Christ. What is true of Leviticus is also true of the law covenant (e.g., circumcision, food laws, civil laws, and Decalogue). No part of the law is applied to us without first placing it in its covenantal location (immediate and epochal context), and then asking how the entire covenant is fulfilled in Christ (canonical context).

In answering the question, what is the moral law for Christians today?, we must follow the same path. We first gladly confess that the *entirety* of Scripture is our standard. But we must simultaneously add that *all* of Scripture's moral teaching is only binding on us *in light of its fulfillment in Christ*. Both of these points are needed to discern God's moral demands for new covenant believers, and Hill nicely emphasizes these points in his discussion of the Ten Commandments and their application to us today.

On the one hand, Hill notes that "[t]he Law of Moses does not provide a complete and binding guide to Christian morality."[26] Moo rightly asserts

---

[25] For a development of these hermeneutical points, see Gentry and Wellum, *Kingdom Through Covenant*, 81–108.

[26] Hill, *How and Why of Love*, 74.

that "[t]he entire Mosaic law comes to fulfillment in Christ, and this fulfillment means this law is no longer a *direct and immediate* source of, or judge
of, the conduct of God's people. Christian behavior, rather, is now guided
directly by 'the law of Christ.'"[27] For Moo the "law of Christ" reflects all that
God has given to us under the new covenant, especially "the teaching and
example of Jesus and the apostles, the central demand of love, and the guiding influence of the indwelling Holy Spirit."[28]

On the other hand, as Hill insists, the Mosaic law cannot be ignored
either since it is authoritative Scripture. *As a covenant* the law does not
govern us directly, yet *as Scripture*, and applied to us in Christ, it now
takes on a prophetic-wisdom function. Hill comments: in the Mosaic law
"[t]he basic shape of God's rule, and God's just order established at creation, is confirmed and further delineated in the Law. Yet it is delineated
in positive and negative ways"[29]—ways that ultimately point forward to a
better covenant. Hill rightly notes that "[w]hile Christians are not under
the package called the Law (a package designated as the 'Old Covenant'),
the moral elements in the Law are part of a continuum that gives shape to
an ideal."[30] That ideal is first given in creation, distorted in the fall, recov-
ered in the law covenant, but ultimately it is only fully restored in Christ.
In this way the law covenant expresses God's moral demands, but it also
points forward to a greater covenant. In the new covenant the previous
moral instruction is not dismissed; rather it continues *and* is transformed
in light of the ideal that has begun in Christ and that will be consummated
at Christ's return. The new covenant, then, not only replaces the old, but
it also fulfills it.

The NT teaches both the *replacement* and *fulfillment* of the old covenant.[31] On the one hand, in the new covenant the old is *replaced* by the
law of Christ (1 Cor 9:20–21). Instead of reliance upon the law, we rely on

---

[27] Moo, "Law of Christ as the Fulfillment of the Law of Moses," 343; emphasis in
original.

[28] Ibid. Cf. idem., *Galatians*, 376–78.

[29] Hill, *How and Why of Love*, 74.

[30] Ibid.

[31] See Rosner, *Paul and the Law*, 111–34.

Christ (Gal 2:19–20; Phil 3:4–14), and we discern God's will in Christ and apostolic instruction (1 Cor 7:19; 9:21; Gal 6:2). As Rosner contends:

> Christians are not under the Law of Moses, but under the law of Christ, the law of faith and the law of the Spirit. We have died to the law, Christ lives in us and we live by faith in the Son of God. . . . We do not keep the law, but fulfil the law in Christ and through love. We do not seek to walk according to the law, but according to the truth of the gospel, in Christ, in newness of resurrection life, by faith, in the light and in step with the Spirit.[32]

On the other hand, the new covenant *fulfills* the old. A crucial text in this regard is Matthew 5:17–20. Although debate surrounds this text, *fulfillment* is best understood in a redemptive-historical sense (see Matt 1:22; 2:15, 17, 23; 4:14; 8:17; 12:17; 13:35; 21:4; 27:9). Jesus fulfills the Law and the Prophets in that they point forward to him, and Jesus is the one who brings them to their intended end. The Law *and* the Prophets, then, have a *prophetic* function as they foreshadow and predict the coming of Christ.[33] Obviously, the prophetic foreshadowing varies depending on whether it is a typologi-cal pattern (e.g., exodus, sacrifices, priesthood, and temple), or whether it is the law's instruction. Yet, in light of the antitheses in Matthew 5:21–48, Jesus teaches that just as he has "fulfilled OT prophecies by his person and actions, so he fulfilled OT law by his teaching."[34] As Carson notes, "In no case does this 'abolish' the OT as canon, any more than the obsolescence of the Levitical sacrificial system abolishes tabernacle ritual as canon. Instead, the OT's real and abiding authority must be understood through the person and teaching of him to whom it points and who so richly fulfills it."[35]

If this is so, it is important to see that in his *teaching* Jesus *fulfills* the law not simply by extending, annulling, or merely intensifying it but by

---

[32] Ibid., 134.

[33] See Moo, "Law of Christ as the Fulfillment of the Law of Moses," 347–76, Schreiner, *40 Questions*, 161–69; D. A. Carson, "Matthew," in *Expositor's Bible Commentary*, vol. 8 (Grand Rapids: Zondervan, 1984), 142–45.

[34] Carson, "Matthew," 144.

[35] Ibid.

demonstrating "the direction in which it [OT law] points."[36] In so doing, Jesus views himself as "the eschatological goal of the OT, and thereby its sole authoritative interpreter, the one through whom alone the OT finds its valid continuity and significance."[37] From this text Moo draws the following ethical implication: Jesus teaches us that "[t]he OT law is not to be abandoned. Indeed, it must continue to be taught (Matt 5:19)—but interpreted and applied in light of its fulfillment by Christ. In other words, it stands no longer as the *ultimate* standard of conduct for God's people, but must always be viewed through the lenses of Jesus' ministry and teaching."[38]

In order for Christians, then, to determine what God's moral law is, we must apply *all* of Scripture in light of Christ. God's moral law is not discovered, as covenant theology teaches, in an *a priori* manner, that is, by isolating the Decalogue from the law covenant and then applying it directly to us. Instead, "moral law" is determined from the *entire* Bible in an *a posteriori* way, that is, by reading and applying biblical texts to us, first in their covenantal location and then in light of Christ. Carson is right to insist:

> We do not begin with a definition of moral law, civil law, and ceremonial law but observe (for example) what laws change least, across redemptive history, in the nature and details of their demands, and happily apply the category 'moral' to them. This seems to me to reflect better exegesis and allows space to see the teleological, predictive, anticipatory nature of *Tanakh* as it points forward to the new covenant and beyond to the consummation.[39]

What this entails is a careful reading/application of the whole Bible in ethics. The *entire* OT, including the law covenant, is for our moral instruction. Reading Scripture by placing each covenant in its immediate, epochal, and canonical context is the way we determine what God's moral law is. We do not follow either the hermeneutical rule that says unless the NT explicitly modifies or abrogates the Mosaic law (as in the ceremonial and

---

[36] Ibid.
[37] Ibid.
[38] Moo, "Law of Moses or the Law of Christ," 206.
[39] Carson, "The Tripartite Division of the Law," 236.

civil parts), it is still in force today, or even the rule Moo suggests, namely that Christians are only bound "to that which is clearly repeated within New Testament teaching."[40] The former approach wrongly assumes the validity of a tripartite distinction of the law as *the* principle by which moral law is canonically established *and* it fails to grasp the law covenant's place in the progression of the covenants. The latter approach, if not careful, is open to the charge that since certain behaviors are not clearly repeated in the NT—e.g., bestiality (Exod 22:19; cf. Lev 18:23; 20:16) or the cursing of the deaf (Lev 19:14)—then we have no NT warrant to say these actions are immoral.[41] What is needed is a "whole Bible" hermeneutic, unpacking the Bible's own internal categories, placing texts in the Bible's unfolding story line according to their covenantal location, and then thinking through their relation to Christ. Let us develop this approach briefly in the last two points.

4. The *Doing* of Ethics Requires a Careful Unpacking of the Bible's Story Line and Categories

How is ethics done from a whole Bible? I will stress one central point. In using Scripture to do ethics, it is crucial to unpack the Bible's own intrasystematic categories,[42] which involve both the Bible's progressive unfolding of the covenants *and* the larger biblical-theological framework of creation, fall, redemption, and new creation.[43]

Why is this important? Just as it is crucial to begin the Bible's story line and covenantal unfolding in creation in order to grasp God's plan,[44] it is also necessary to ground ethics in the norm of creation. As Hill rightly insists,

---

[40] Moo, "Law of Christ as the Fulfillment of the Law of Moses," 376.

[41] See Bahnsen, "Response to Doug Moo," in *The Law, the Gospel, and the Modern Christian*, 386–87, who levels this charge against Moo.

[42] For this term, see Michael S. Horton, *Covenant and Eschatology: The Divine Drama* (Louisville: Westminster John Knox, 2002), 1–19.

[43] See Hill, *How and Why of Love*, 65–78, 121–35, who unpacks the Bible's larger biblical-theological framework of creation, fall, redemption, and new creation for ethics.

[44] On this point, see Gentry and Wellum, *Kingdom Through Covenant*, 601–52.

the original creation with its revealed goals or purposes "provides us with the basis for determining what is morally good."[45] This point is especially significant in ethical discussions over the nature and dignity of humans, the proper use of our sexuality, marriage, the value of labor, and so on.

For example, take the case of bestiality. Before the law forbids it (Exod 22:19), we know from creation that there is a qualitative distinction between humans and animals and that the only valid expression of our sexuality is in heterosexual marriage (Gen 2:18–25). Given our sin and rebellion, in the law covenant God reminds Israel what is and is not morally acceptable, but this does not entail that we only know bestiality is wrong from the law covenant. Also, even if the new covenant does not explicitly forbid bestiality, this does not entail that the Mosaic law is still in force unless the NT explicitly modifies/abrogates it or that we are only bound to that which is clearly repeated in the NT. Both of these approaches fail to do justice to a "whole Bible" reading, grounded in the Bible's own biblical-theological framework and moving across the covenants from creation to the consummation.

In order to discern God's moral will, we need first to begin in creation, then think through how sin has distorted God's order, walk through the covenants, and discover how God's redemptive promise will restore and transform the created order—a reality that has now been realized in Christ. At every stage in redemptive history, the covenants reflect God's moral demands, thus explaining why we expect *and* find a continuity of moral demand across the canon. But earlier covenants on their own do not provide a complete and binding guide for Christian morality.[46] No doubt, the earlier covenants are crucial parts of God's one redemptive plan; but now, due to Christ's work, *as covenants* they have been fulfilled. *As Scripture* all of the covenants, including the law covenant, are instructive for us, since as Hill observes, "The basic shape of God's rule, and God's just order established at creation, is confirmed and further delineated in the Law."[47] But applying specific ethical instruction to us must be done by a whole Bible reading

---

[45] Hill, *How and Why of Love*, 66.
[46] See ibid., 74.
[47] Ibid.

viewed in Christ—the one in whom "all the elements of the moral ideal are realized and revealed. . . . In [Christ] we see God's just and good order."[48]

5. Consider Some Illustrations of Doing Ethics from a "Whole Bible" and under the New Covenant

Hill summarizes how Christians ought to approach Scripture and draw ethical conclusions. He writes:

> On any particular issue we will need to put together the relevant sections of Scripture so that we can know what is good in particular cases. The basic creation pattern is the starting-point for this exercise. The Law and the Prophets point to the original shape and purpose of God's good order and highlight the fractures and disorder caused by sin. Finally, the revelation in Christ gives us a glimpse of the completed and perfected order. With minds renewed by the Spirit of God through the work of Christ believers can use this information to discern what is right and good. Such discernment is the substance of wisdom.[49]

A few examples may help, but admittedly, the discussion is brief, a kind of priming of the pump.

Sexual Ethics

Let us first think about sexual ethics. Scripture teaches us God's norm for human sexuality is in creation (Gen 1:26–30; 2:15–25). In the creation of male and female, God designed human sexuality to function within the permanent, covenant relationship of heterosexual marriage (Matt 19:4–9). All misuses of our sexuality—fornication, adultery, divorce, homosexuality,

---

[48] Ibid., 75.
[49] Ibid., 78. Also see Rosner, *Paul and the Law*, 207–22.

bestiality, and even polygamy—are distortions viewed against the backdrop of God's creation intent for us. Sadly, in light of the fall, all sexual distortions are introduced. In earlier stages of redemptive history, a less than normative behavior is sometimes allowed (e.g., polygamy); but viewed against God's creation order and in light of the greater Christ-church relationship, polygamy is never viewed as normative.[50] For this reason, with the dawning of the new covenant polygamy is no longer acceptable. God's creation standard is reaffirmed and lived out in the church.

Although the Mosaic law explicitly forbids specific sexual distortions (Lev 18:1–30), all of its prohibitions simply unpack the "one flesh" ideal of creation. In addition, given the prophetic function of the law covenant, as the law anticipates a greater righteousness to come, the ethical demand under the new covenant is greater. Also in the prophets, as they anticipate the dawning of the new creation, they speak of a day when God will so transform the entire community that God's new covenant people will become covenant keepers and not breakers (Jer 31:31–34; Ezek 36:25–27), which is precisely what our Lord addresses in his teaching regarding the kingdom (Matt 5:17–48).[51] In Christ's coming and work, the new order has arrived. By the regenerating work of the Spirit, those who enter God's kingdom are united to Christ and freed from Adam and the old era. In Christ, individuals and the church are the "new creation" (2 Cor 5:17; Eph 2:8–21), hence the reason we begin to live out what it means to be God's new creation, even though we still live between the times. The NT, in calling the church to a proper use of our sexuality, grounds it both in creation and in what we are in Christ. This is why God's moral demand on us today is greater—greater in restoring us to what we were created to be in the first place *and* in calling us to live now as God's new creation people.[52]

---

[50] On this point, see R. C. Ortlund Jr., "Man and Woman" and "Marriage," in *NDBT*, 650–57.

[51] See Carson, "Matthew," 140–61.

[52] See Rosner, *Paul and the Law*, 121–34, 196–205; Hill, *How and Why of Love*, 139–205.

Personal and Social Ethics

Let us now think about various life issues. Given our creation as image bearers, human life is precious (Gen 1:26–28; cf. Gen 9:6). Strife, anger, murder, and our inhumane treatment of others is a result of the fall. In the law covenant these wrong behaviors are explicitly forbidden and punished, but their prohibition is basically the outworking of who we are as created beings. Jesus is clear that God's intent from the beginning was for his image bearers to love God and their neighbors, which is precisely what the entire canon emphasizes (Lev 19:18; Deut 6:5; cf. Matt 22:34–40). Yet in the new age the full intent of how we are to love as God's people is now realized in a greater way. This is why Jesus stresses that it is not merely the absence of the act of murder, adultery, or lying which is forbidden, but also our heart attitude toward one another (Matt 5:21–48). What God demands of his people is love. In the old era the law covenant demanded it, but it also anticipated something more. Now, in Christ, what the old anticipated is now here. This is why Paul can say that love *fulfills* the law (Rom 13:8–10; Gal 5:14)—not an amorphic love but one governed by God's will and our renewal in Christ by the Spirit. As this understanding of humans and love is applied to ethical issues such as abortion, infanticide, and euthanasia, even though each issue involves other matters,[53] a sanctity of life ethic is foundational to a Christian ethic and consistent in all of Scripture.

Applying the Law Covenant as Scripture to Christians Today

Let us now turn to some illustrations of how to apply the law covenant to us today. We do not apply the Mosaic law to us today as if we are still under it *as a covenant*. No doubt, prior to the coming of Christ, that is precisely how

---

[53] The other matters I am thinking of are various exceptions and/or complications. For example, the taking of human life is wrong except in areas of ectopic pregnancy, self-defense, war, etc. Or in the case of euthanasia, we still have to wrestle with caring for the terminally ill with ordinary versus extraordinary means. On these points, see Frame, *The Doctrine of the Christian Life*, 684–745.

it was applied to God's people. Nevertheless, as new covenant believers, the law covenant is no longer directly applicable to us in this way. Thus, in reading the law's various moral demands, we do not directly apply them to our lives until we have first wrestled with how these moral demands have been brought to fulfillment in Christ. For example, in regard to such demands as not sowing two seeds in a field, not eating unclean foods, the need to circumcise our male children, or the treatment of blood disorders, etc., we do not directly obey these commands as covenantal obligation. However, *as Scripture*, the law covenant is for our instruction. As we apply these commands, we must think through whether old covenant commands are tied to creation, whether they are tied solely to the old era, and how they are fulfilled in the NT. By following this procedure, we learn how to apply all of Scripture to us in Christ.

For example, even though the sacrificial system no longer functions for us covenantally, yet as Scripture the entire system instructs us about our sin; it teaches us something about God's holy demand and gracious provision; and most importantly, it reveals our need for someone greater. Or think of the food laws. Even though they no longer apply to us directly, they are instructive for us. In thinking through why God gave them in the OT *and* how they are fulfilled in Christ, we discover that their primary purpose was to separate God's people from the nations and to instruct them about their need for an internal heart transformation (Mark 7:1–23; Acts 10–11). Although these two purposes have ended in Christ, we, as new covenant believers, are still instructed by them. In fact, the Jerusalem Council had to resolve the theological and practical implications of these issues; otherwise the entire gospel was at stake (Acts 10–11; 15; Rom 14:1–15:13; Gal 1:6–10).

Or think about the various capital punishments required in the OT. Given the change from Israel to Christ *and* a church-state distinction in the new covenant, we do not directly apply the civil law of Israel to governments today; yet two points need to be made. First, given the God-ordained role of government and the sanctity of human life, the state's role is to protect life and to punish those who do not protect it (Gen 9:6; Rom 13:1–7); and as such, some forms of capital punishment are consistent throughout time. Yet in other areas there is no NT warrant to practice specific punishments today as they functioned for Israel under the law covenant. Second, the church functions as a theocracy in the new covenant, and the church's exercise of church discipline picks up some of the punishments of the old covenant in a greater way. For example, think of various sexual sins. Under the law covenant sexual sin was punishable by death. Under the new covenant the church does not deal with sexual sin in this way; instead she deals with it through the exercise of church discipline (Matt 18:15–20; 1 Corinthians 5). But if the guilty party does not repent, the verdict of excommunication is far greater than anything in the old since it is viewed as a verdict with eternal consequences (see Heb 2:1–4).

Lastly, let us think more specifically about the application of the Decalogue to us today. It too must be applied in a similar manner, that is, by locating it in its covenantal location and then applying it to us in light of Christ. So, for example, as we read the opening preamble (Exod 20:1–2), we are keenly aware of its covenantal location; yet it is now applied to us in light of God's unfolding plan of redemption culminated in Christ. Unlike Israel we have not been redeemed from our bondage to Egypt, but in a far greater way we have been redeemed from that which the exodus typologically pointed toward (along with the prophets [Isaiah 11; 42; 53]), namely our exodus deliverance from sin in Christ's cross (Luke 9:31). Then, as we apply each commandment in light of our redemption in Christ, we discover that there is a greater incentive, obligation, and demand on us to have no other gods before us (Exod 20:3) and to honor the great name of our triune God (Exod 20:7). In one sense the moral demand has not changed; in another sense it is greater in Christ.

As we approach the Sabbath command (Exod 20:8–12), once again we apply it in the same way. In thinking through the Sabbath's covenantal location—that which looks back to the covenantal rest at creation (Gen 2:1–3), a day to be obeyed by Israel under the law, and a day that typologically pointed forward to a greater rest to come (Psalm 95; cf. Matt 11:28–30; Heb 3:7–5:13)—it is now applied to us in light of its fulfillment, namely Christ who has achieved for us salvation rest. All of the other commandments (Exod 20:12–17) are applied in the same way.

What about the fifth commandment (Exod 20:12)? Surely, given that Paul quotes it directly in Ephesians 6:2, this demonstrates that the Decalogue has direct relevance for us today. But before we draw this conclusion, it is important to observe that even though there is moral continuity in this command, as there is in the other commands, there is also a major transformation. Paul no longer says that honoring our parents will yield long life in the land; instead he expands the promise to the whole earth, thus giving further confirmation that the law covenant is applied to us today in and through Christ and his glorious new covenant work.[54]

Concluding Reflection

How does progressive covenantalism apply the entire Bible as our ethical standard? I have sought to give a brief answer to that question. Most Christians, regardless of their commitment to covenant or dispensational theology, will arrive at similar conclusions. But, as noted above, where the important difference lies is in *how* we get there. In the end our aim is to achieve two results simultaneously: first, to employ a consistent hermeneutic that properly "puts together" the biblical covenants on the Bible's own terms; and, second, to learn anew to obey all that Scripture teaches. My prayer is that this chapter will achieve both results, especially the latter.

---

[54] See Moo, "Law of Christ as the Fulfillment of the Law of Moses," 370; and P. T. O'Brien, *The Letter to the Ephesians*, PNTC (Grand Rapids: Eerdmans, 1999), 442–45.

CHAPTER 9

The Dispensational Appeal to Romans 11 and the Nature of Israel's Future Salvation

RICHARD J. LUCAS

Introduction

Dispensationalists frequently appeal to Romans 11 as proof for their theological system because they understand it to teach a future salvation for ethnic Israel (e.g., "all Israel will be saved" in v. 26 ESV).[1] Yet a mere appeal to this text is not sufficient to prove their distinctive dispensational teachings. Some within covenant theology, including both amillennialists[2] and

---

[1] Michael G. Vanlaningham, "Romans 11:25–27 and the Future of Israel in Paul's Thought," *TMSJ* 3 (1992): 141–74; J. Lanier Burns, "The Future of Ethnic Israel in Romans 11" in *Dispensationalism, Israel and the Church: The Search for Definition*, ed. Craig A. Blaising and Darrell L. Bock (Grand Rapids: Zondervan, 1992), 188–229; S. Lewis Johnson Jr., "Evidence from Romans 9–11" in *A Case for Premillennialism: A New Consensus*, ed. Donald K. Campbell and Jeffrey L. Townsend (Chicago: Moody, 1992), 211–19; and Harold W. Hoehner, "Israel in Romans 9–11" in *Israel, the Land and the People: An Evangelical Affirmation of God's Promises*, ed. H. Wayne House (Grand Rapids: Kregel, 1998), 149–59.

[2] Kim Riddlebarger, *A Case for Amillennialism: Understanding the End Times*, rev. ed. (Grand Rapids: Baker, 2013), 217–21; Michael Horton, *Introducing Covenant Theology* (Grand Rapids: Baker, 2006), 131–32; Cornelis P. Venema, *The Promise of the Future* (Carlisle, PA: Banner of Truth, 2000), 127–39; and Geerhardus Vos, *The*

postmillennialists,[3] also affirm a future salvation for ethnic Israel from this passage. Thoughtful dispensationalists recognize this shared conviction and so argue for not only a future *salvation* but also a future *restoration* of Israel. Michael Vlach elaborates on this distinction:

> The concept of "restoration" certainly includes the idea of salvation, but it goes beyond that. "Restoration" involves the idea of Israel being reinstalled as a nation, in her land, with a specific identity and role of service to the nations. In other words, in a literal, earthly kingdom—a millennium—the nation Israel will serve a functional role of service to the nations. This point is something all dispensationalists affirm while all nondispensationalists deny.[4]

Yet none of these "restoration" features are explicitly mentioned in Romans 11.[5] So, where do dispensationalists find this restoration teaching in this passage? They make several nuanced textual appeals. Dispensationalists find support for a national future restoration of Israel in Romans 11 by several *implications* they draw from their exegesis of the text. The problem is not with drawing implications per se but whether these implications are

---

Pauline Eschatology (Princeton, NJ: Princeton University, 1930; repr., Phillipsburg, NJ: P&R, 1994), 87–88.

[3] Keith A. Mathison, *Postmillennialism: An Eschatology of Hope* (Phillipsburg, NJ: P&R, 1999), 125–29; and Tim Gallant, "Judah's Life from the Dead: The Gospel of Romans 11," in *The Glory of Kings: A Festschrift in Honor of James B. Jordan*, ed. Peter J. Leithart and John Barach (Eugene, OR: Wipf and Stock, 2011), 45.

[4] Michael Vlach, "What Is Dispensationalism?" in *Christ's Prophetic Plans: A Futuristic Premillennial Primer*, ed. John MacArthur and Richard Mayhue (Chicago: Moody, 2012), 33. Most of the material in Vlach's three chapters from this book also appeared earlier in his *Dispensationalism: Essential Beliefs and Common Myths* (Los Angeles: Theological Studies, 2008).

[5] This claim could be expanded beyond just Romans 11. Waltke writes, "*Not one* clear NT passage mentions the restoration of Israel as a political nation or predicts an earthly reign of Christ before his final appearing. *None* depicts the consummate glory of Christ as an earthly king ruling over the restored nation of Israel. The Spirit's silence is deafening." Bruce K. Waltke, "Kingdom Promises as Spiritual" in *Continuity and Discontinuity: Perspectives on the Relationship Between the Old and New Testaments*, ed. John S. Feinberg (Wheaton, IL: Crossway, 1988), 273 (emphasis in original).

justified and congruent with the larger canonical teaching. I will explain each of these textual appeals and then offer a response.

Future New Covenant Physical Blessings for Israel

The first textual appeal dispensationalists make is that the reference to the new covenant in the OT quotation in Romans 11:27 implies that Paul has more in mind than just soteriological benefits but also promised physical blessings to national Israel.

The Dispensational Argument Regarding the Fulfillment of the New Covenant

Dispensationalists seem to agree universally that Romans 11:26 indicates a future salvation for Israel.[6] Nevertheless, in the quotation immediately following the climatic statement of Romans 11:26, dispensationalists make a distinctive textual appeal in support of their system. According to Vlach, while Romans 11:26 teaches a future *salvation* of Israel: "Romans 11:27 links Israel's salvation with the new covenant promises of the OT that predicted Israel's *restoration*. Thus, Rom 11:27 ties Israel's *salvation* with the OT promises of a *restoration* of Israel to its land."[7] There is an assumption

---

[6] The view that Romans 11 teaches a future mass conversion of ethnic Israelites was contained in Peter J. Gentry and Stephen J. Wellum, *Kingdom Through Covenant: A Biblical-Theological Understanding of the Covenants* (Wheaton, IL: Crossway, 2012), 501, and also reaffirmed in idem, "'Kingdom Through Covenant' Authors Respond to Bock, Moo, Horton," The Gospel Coalition, September 20, 2012, accessed August 27, 2014, http://thegospelcoalition.org/article/gentry-and-wellum-respond-to-kingdom-through-covenant-reviews. But one could hold another view (as some of the contributors to this volume do) and still hold to progressive covenantalism.

[7] Michael J. Vlach, *Has the Church Replaced Israel?: A Theological Evaluation* (Nashville, TN: B&H Academic, 2010), 162 (emphasis added). This is a consistent line of argumentation for dispensationalists. John Walvoord in the 1950s argued essentially the same way. In a chapter titled "Will Israel Be Restored as a Nation?," he states in reference to Rom 11:25–27 that "the *nature* of the salvation of Israel indicated here is described by a citation of Old Testament prophecy." So he is relying on the OT

that all the material blessings that accompanied the new covenant promises
to Israel are implied by this OT quotation of Isaiah 59:21 in Romans 11:27.[8]
Fred Zaspel draws out the logic of this assumption by arguing:

> The language [in the quotation from Rom 11:26–27] is
> reminiscent of more passages, particularly from the prophets,
> in which the Davidic, Abrahamic, and new covenants are held
> in view for the people. Significantly, these same passages speak
> to a time when Israel, in her own land, will again enjoy her
> prominence among the nations. . . . Are we to understand Paul as
> *limiting* their fulfillment to a soteric sense only? And if so, why?
> The Prophets certainly did not understand their word to be so
> restricted; they plainly held out a hope of salvation *and* restoration
> to the land *and* Israelite prominence among the nations. The
> hope of forgiveness which they offered the people was inseparably
> linked to and formed the basis of these other hopes, hence their
> equally vigorous heralding of them all. . . . The question then is
> this: what exegetical warrant is there for allowing only a part of
> the covenants' promises (i.e., the forgiveness of sins) and not the
> whole of them?[9]

---

quote to fill in the details about what the nature of this future salvation looks like.
He goes on, "According to the Scripture, Israel will also be delivered in that day from
her persecutors, regathered from all over the earth and brought back to her ancient
land, and there blessed spiritually *and materially.*" He then admits that "all these events
are not mentioned here [in this passage]." Nevertheless, he is assuming spiritual salvation also entails material salvation. See John F. Walvoord, *The Millennial Kingdom*
(Findlay, OH: Dunham, 1959), 190–92 (emphasis added). Cf. also Robert L. Saucy,
*The Case for Progressive Dispensationalism: The Interface Between Dispensational and
Non-Dispensational Theology* (Grand Rapids: Zondervan, 1993), 261–63; and Craig
A. Blaising and Darrell L. Bock, *Progressive Dispensationalism* (Grand Rapids: Baker,
1993), 270.

  [8] Cf. Michael J. Vlach, "Have They Found a Better Way? An Analysis of Gentry and
Wellum's *Kingdom Through Covenant,*" *TMSJ* 24 (2013), 12.

  [9] Fred G. Zaspel, *Jews, Gentiles and the Goal of Redemptive History: An Exegetical
and Theological Analysis of Romans 9–11* (Hatfield, PA: Interdisciplinary Biblical
Research Institute, 1995), 25–26 (emphasis in original). Zaspel is a prominent pro-
ponent of new covenant theology, but at this point his reasoning is consistent with the

Also at work in this argument is a particular understanding of how the new covenant is fulfilled. While dispensationalists are not united in one single approach to the new covenant,[10] the best of progressive dispensational thinking has posited a two-stage fulfillment of the new covenant. There is "already" a partial fulfillment following Christ's first coming; however, the final realization is "not yet" complete until Christ's second coming. Bruce Ware represents this dispensational approach of applying inaugurated-consummated eschatology to the fulfillment of the new covenant. He writes, "Only the spiritual aspects of the new covenant promise are now inaugurated in this age; the territorial and political aspects, though part of God's new covenant promise, await future fulfillment."[11] So in this conception Ware divides the two-stage fulfillment in terms of the initial spiritual aspects from the final territorial and political aspects of the new covenant. He goes on to further define the spiritual aspects as the forgiveness of sins and the indwelling of the Spirit and the material blessings to be bound up with Israel's national restoration to the physical land of Palestine.[12] The dispensational logic would argue that the current initial fulfillment of these spiritual aspects of the new covenant is evidence that final material aspects are likely to come. The only way to make room for this fulfillment in dispensational reasoning is in a literal millennial kingdom with a distinct existence of Israel separate from the church mediating blessings to the nations. Therefore, even though Romans 11 only explicitly speaks of these initial spiritual aspects in reference to the new covenant (vv. 26–27), because of the reasoning just outlined, Romans 11 also implicitly gives evidence for the distinctive dispensational teaching of a future national restoration of Israel as well.

---

dispensational argument from this passage. I do not, however, intend to insinuate that he affirms all the points of dispensationalism that are being critiqued in this chapter.

[10] See e.g., Mike Stallard, ed., *Dispensational Understanding of the New Covenant: 3 Views* (Schaumburg, IL: Regular Baptist Press, 2012). The three views represented in this book all come from traditional (nonprogressive) dispensationalists.

[11] Bruce A. Ware, "The New Covenant and the People(s) of God," in *Dispensationalism, Israel and the Church: The Search for Definition*, ed. Craig A. Blaising and Darrell L. Bock (Grand Rapids: Zondervan, 1992), 94–95.

[12] Ibid., 95. Cf. also Vlach, *Has the Church Replaced Israel?*, 158.

Response to the Dispensational Argument

Dispensationalism is not wrong to argue for the application of inaugurated-consummated eschatology in the fulfillment of the new covenant, but they misconstrue that application. Instead of arguing that only part of the new covenant has been inaugurated (i.e., the spiritual blessings) and the other part is yet to be consummated (i.e., the material blessings), it is better to see the entire new covenant (both spiritual and material blessings) as already inaugurated with the final consummation of these promises not yet realized. It is artificial to divide the new covenant into spiritual and material blessings and explain their fulfillment as though each happen in completely separate stages.

Some dispensationalists readily acknowledge that the spiritual blessings of the new covenant are not summarily fulfilled in Christ's first advent. For example, after discussing the inaugurated blessings of the new covenant (which he too identifies as the forgiveness of sins and the indwelling of the Spirit), Craig Blaising maintains that some "new covenant promises are not yet fully realized."[13] The particular blessings he goes on to describe are the consummation of the *spiritual* blessings that await the new covenant believer. "The new covenant promised to remove the heart of rebellion against God and give us hearts fully compliant to His direction. However, in our present experience, we are not fully free from the experience of resistance to God's will."[14] Even though believers have been forgiven of sin and given the indwelling Spirit, there is an ongoing battle against sin. Blaising concludes, "This is the condition of living under *inaugurated* new covenant blessings. Only in the future will those blessings be granted in full, and the complete transformation promised by the new covenant will be realized."[15]

If dispensationalists admit that the spiritual blessings of the new covenant have both inaugurated and consummated aspects to their fulfillment, why not see the same sort of fulfillment with the so-called material blessings? The reason dispensationalists cast all the physical blessings of the new

---

[13] Blaising and Bock, *Progressive Dispensationalism*, 208.
[14] Ibid., 209.
[15] Ibid. (emphasis in original).

covenant into the future is because they do not allow the land promise to be viewed as typological of the new creation and thus already inaugurated. It is beyond the scope of this chapter to expand on this point,[16] but suffice it to say at least one physical fulfillment of the new covenant promises has already begun. Greg Beale explains, "The *physical* way that these land promises have begun fulfillment is that Christ himself introduced the new creation by his *physical* resurrection."[17] Jesus is the first man of the new creation and as such has inaugurated the fulfillment of the land promises that will be expanded to include the whole new creation when the promises are consummated at his return. Correctly situating the land promises as typological of the new creation allows one to see how the entire new covenant, both the spiritual and the physical aspects, has already been inaugurated.

In answer to Zaspel's penetrating question from the quote above, I am not proposing limiting the fulfillment of the covenants' promise in a soteric sense only. It is quite the opposite. The whole covenant will be fulfilled, both the spiritual and the physical promises, but not in separate stages and not in the manner dispensationalism proposes. The whole new covenant is already established, and the fullness of its blessings will be consummated. Dispensationalism is not wrong to see Israel's salvation linked to the fulfillment of new covenant promises in Romans 11:26–27, but they are presupposing what that fulfillment will look like (i.e., national restoration) and

---

[16] For an elaboration on this point, see Gentry and Wellum, *Kingdom Through Covenant*, 703–16; Oren R. Martin, *Bound for the Promised Land: The Land Promise in God's Redemptive Plan*, NSBT 34 (Downers Grove, IL: InterVarsity, 2015); and his chapter in this volume.

[17] G. K. Beale, *A New Testament Biblical Theology: The Unfolding of the Old Testament in the New* (Grand Rapids: Baker Academic, 2011), 751 (emphasis added). Beale labors for several chapters making a series of interlocking arguments in his work (227–354, 750–72). He argues that resurrection is conceptually equivalent to new creation because the way the redeemed participate in the new creation is through being transformed with newly created bodies. Also, resurrection in Scripture is tied to the eschatological fulfillment of the new creation. When resurrection (which is tied to new creation) happens, the end of the age has dawned. Of course there is an already-not-yet aspect to that fulfillment, but the fact that Christ *now* has that resurrection body, fit for the new creation, means at least in this way that the new creation has dawned, which begins fulfillment of the land promises (again assuming the typological role they serve).

then reading it into the passage. Nothing in these verses proves the anticipation of a future national restoration of Israel as a distinct fulfillment of the new covenant apart from the Gentiles or as a separate stage (subsequent to the church age) of new covenant fulfillment. The implication dispensationalists read into this text is unwarranted.

Future Gentile Blessings Mediated Through Restored Israel

The second textual appeal dispensationalists make is that the salvation sequence delineated in Romans 11:12 and 15 provides the expectation for a future Gentile blessing subsequent to the church age and mediated through a restored national Israel.

The Dispensational Argument Regarding Future Gentile Blessings

Gentile salvation is clearly taught in the OT (e.g., Gen 12:2–3; Isa 19:23–25; Jer 16:19)[18] and is not in dispute among dispensationalists.[19] The OT also describes Israel's salvation as the means of bringing about Gentile salvation (e.g., Isa 49:5–6; 59:20–60:3ff.). The established salvation-historical order is therefore "Israel first, then Gentiles," which is reaffirmed in both the beginning and end of Romans (1:16; 15:8–9). Nevertheless, the sequence of salvation in Romans 11 seems to follow a different order. In Romans 11 Paul is teaching not just *that* Israel will be saved but *how* they will be saved. He is explaining the larger purpose for the hardening that has come upon Israel (Rom 11:7–10). Paul's rhetorical question in Romans 11:11 asks if the divine purpose in the hardening was to leave Israel in desolation. In the negative response an alternate purpose is given, that is "to make [Israel] jealous" through salvation coming to the Gentiles. As is made clear in verse 14,

---

[18] See also Pss 67:2–3; 117:1; Isa 14:1; 42:6; 45:20; 49:6; 66:18–21.
[19] Saucy, *The Case for Progressive Dispensationalism*, 122–25; and Vlach, *Has the Church Replaced Israel?*, 170–71.

Paul is connecting Israel's jealousy with her salvation. God's hardening of Israel was never meant to be permanent but served a purpose in ultimately leading to their eventual salvation. The temporary hardening allowed a time for the Gentiles to come to faith and so save all of God's chosen people, Jew and Gentile (cf. Rom 11:30–32). In this way Israel's hardening was the first in a three-stage process that culminates in Israel's final salvation.[20] Israel was rejected by God, which led to the inclusion of the Gentiles, which in turn will lead to the inclusion of Israel. This "three stage process by which God's blessing oscillates between Israel and Gentiles is at the heart of this entire section."[21] Therefore, in Romans 11 Paul is arguing for a salvation sequence of "Gentiles first, then Israel." How one reconciles this apparent discrepancy goes to the heart of the disagreement with dispensationalists.

Dispensationalists generally recognize this three-step salvation-historical pattern during the church age (hardening of Israel → salvation of the Gentiles → salvation of Israel). However, as Robert Saucy states, "The present salvation of the Gentiles before that of Israel is not in harmony with the basic Old Testament picture."[22] The dispensational solution to this dilemma is to posit a fourth step in the salvation-historical sequence after the church age (during the millennial kingdom), which would leave "time for the Old Testament picture of the blessings of Gentiles *subsequent to* and *mediated through* a restored Israel."[23] Furthermore, they believe Romans 11 gives evidence of this proposal by an implication they find in the text.

---

[20] Moo points out in reference to this three-stage process that "a key issue is whether Paul envisions this sequence as a repeated historical pattern or as a single movement spanning the course of salvation history" (Douglas J. Moo, *Encountering the Book of Romans: A Theological Survey*, EBS [Grand Rapids: Baker Academic, 2002], 167). Those who see a future mass conversion for ethnic Israel in Romans 11 would argue for the latter, while those who see Romans 11 teaching only the salvation of the elect remnant of Israel throughout the church age would argue for the former.

[21] Douglas J. Moo, *The Epistle to the Romans*, NICNT (Grand Rapids: Eerdmans, 1996), 684. For a table displaying this pattern throughout Rom 11:11–32, see Andrew David Naselli, *From Typology to Doxology: Paul's Use of Isaiah and Job in Romans 11:34–35* (Eugene, OR: Pickwick, 2012), 18–19.

[22] Saucy, *The Case for Progressive Dispensationalism*, 259.

[23] Ibid. (emphasis in original).

Paul is arguing from the lesser to the greater. "If [Israel's] trespass means riches for the world [i.e., the Gentiles], and if [Israel's] failure means riches for the Gentiles, how much more will [Israel's] full inclusion mean!" (Rom 11:12 ESV). Israel's trespass and failure refer to the present stage of Jewish hardening, which has led to Gentile inclusion in the church ("riches for the world/Gentiles"). The coming "fullness" of Israel is their future salvation at the end of the current age, which leads to something even greater. Dispensationalists understand this "how much more" that follows Israel's future salvation as continuing the interaction between Israel and the Gentiles. So, if Israel's hardening brought salvation to the Gentiles, Israel's eventual restoration must bring the Gentiles something even greater in the future. In reference to Romans 11:12, Vanlaningham writes that Paul's "words are best accounted for if Israel is present in its own land and the blessings for the world flow from the nation under God's governance in accordance with OT expectations."[24]

Verse 15 reiterates the same *a fortiori* argument but adds more description to the vagueness of the "how much more" of verse 12. If Israel's rejection, by means of the present hardening, leads to Gentile salvation during the church age ("reconciliation of the world"), then Israel's future salvation ("their acceptance") will bring about "life from the dead." The meaning of this last phrase is a source of great debate. Vanlaningham suggests that "it probably refers to spiritual revivification rather than the general resurrection, so that what Paul foresees is a time when the Gentile world erupts with spiritual life following Israel's restoration."[25] Saucy maintains that "even if it means the resurrection, we need not take that to be the final general resurrection that issues immediately into the eternal state. . . . Thus time is provided for the blessing of the world through restored Israel before the eternal state."[26] The key issue for the dispensational argument

---

[24] Michael G. Vanlaningham, "The Jewish People According to the Book of Romans," in *The People, the Land, and the Future of Israel: Israel and the Jewish People in the Plan of God*, ed. Darrell L. Bock and Mitch Glaser (Grand Rapids: Kregel, 2014), 122–23.

[25] Ibid., 122.

[26] Saucy, *The Case for Progressive Dispensationalism*, 260.

from this text is not the specificity of what that future stage will be like but that a future time is implied to fulfill the remaining promises directed to the nations through the restored nation of Israel. Therefore, dispensationalists believe the implications drawn from Romans 11:12 and 15 provide textual evidence for their distinctive theological claims. They attempt to correlate the OT expectation of "Jew first, then Gentiles" by positing a blessing for the Gentiles (that is apparently different from/greater than their present salvation in the church) that is mediated through a restored Israel subsequent to the church age.

Response to the Dispensational Argument

The dispensational solution to correlating the salvation-historical pattern of Romans 11 (Gentiles first, then Jews) with the OT expectation of "Jews first, then Gentiles" is ultimately unsatisfactory. Paul is revealing a previously hidden "mystery" in Romans 11, which is described by three clauses: (1) Israel's partial hardening, (2) the "fullness" of the Gentiles (i.e., their salvation), and (3) the final salvation of Israel (Rom 11:25–26). Independently, each of these components is not new revelation. The combination of each of these components in this particular sequence is what is new.[27] Again Paul is concerned not just with the *fact* of Israel's salvation but with the *manner* of her salvation as it relates specifically to the Gentiles.[28] Israel's hardening will persist *until* the fullness of the Gentiles has come in. The "fullness" of the Gentiles refers to the full number of the elect Gentiles who will come to saving faith.[29] Only after and by means of the inclusion of the Gentiles will all Israel be saved

---

[27] D. A. Carson, "Mystery and Fulfillment: Toward a More Comprehensive Paradigm of Paul's Understanding of the Old and the New," in *The Paradoxes of Paul*, vol. 2 of *Justification and Variegated Nomism*, ed. D. A. Carson, Peter T. O'Brien, and Mark A. Seifrid (Grand Rapids: Baker, 2004), 419–21.

[28] In Rom 11:26 οὕτως is functioning as an adverb of manner. Israel's partial hardening has presently led to the salvation of the full number of the Gentiles, *and in this manner*, namely the Gentiles provoking Israel to jealousy (Rom 10:19; 11:11, 14), all Israel will be saved.

[29] Colin G. Kruse, *Paul's Letter to the Romans*, PNTC (Grand Rapids: Eerdmans, 2012), 443.

(Rom 11:26). Once the salvation of the "fullness" of the Gentiles (Rom 11:25) and the "fullness" of Israel (Rom 11:12) takes place, the end of salvation-history will have been reached. The climax of this age is the resurrection following Christ's return and is, therefore, the likely reference for the phrase "life from the dead" in Romans 11:15.[30] Tom Schreiner is right to conclude, "If the fullness of the Gentiles enters in before Israel is saved, it is inconceivable that there will be a great ingathering among the Gentiles *after* this event."[31]

Dispensationalists downplay what it means for the fullness of the Gentiles to come in during the church age in order to accommodate the demands of their theological system. Saucy writes: "The benefits for the Gentiles that Paul sees resulting from Israel's conversion rules out the 'full number' as the culmination of all gentile salvation in the divine program. There must yet be some time following the coming in of this 'fullness' that permits the even greater blessing of the world to take place."[32] When Saucy speaks of this current age as not exhausting "all gentile salvation," I assume he means a greater experience of salvation for the same Gentiles, not that a greater number will be saved in the future. Even with this interpretive concession, what is the nature of these "greater blessings" for the Gentiles in the next age? Dispensationalists are forced to propose some sort of Gentile blessings beyond the salvation they have already experienced. Vanlaningham refers to a rather nebulous eruption of spiritual life among the Gentile world. Vlach is slightly more descriptive. In reference to Romans 11:12, he writes, "The nations of the world as a whole also appear headed for some form of *restoration*."[33] Vlach does not elaborate on the form of this restoration for the Gentiles, but even this explanation presents problems for dispensationalists. The future "fullness" ($\pi\lambda\acute{\eta}\rho\omega\mu\alpha$) Israel expects to experience according to Romans 11:12 is more than just spiritual salvation in the dispensational

---

[30] C. E. B. Cranfield, *A Critical and Exegetical Commentary on the Epistle to the Romans: Commentary on Romans IX–XVI and Essays*, ICC (London: T&T Clark, 1975), 562–63; Thomas R. Schreiner, *Romans*, BECNT (Grand Rapids: Baker Academic, 1998), 598–99; James D. G. Dunn, *Romans 9–16*, WBC 38b (Nashville, TN: Thomas Nelson, 1988), 658; Moo, *Epistle to the Romans*, 694–96.

[31] Schreiner, *Romans*, 599 (emphasis in original).

[32] Saucy, *The Case for Progressive Dispensationalism*, 261.

[33] Vlach, *Has the Church Replaced Israel?*, 172 (emphasis added).

conception; it is also national restoration. Nevertheless, when the "fullness" (πλήρωμα) of the Gentiles is spoken of in Romans 11:25, it only includes their present salvation—not their future restoration. In this way dispensationalists present two different understandings of "fullness" in Romans 11. In reference to Israel, it means a complete national restoration; but in reference to the Gentiles, it is only spiritual salvation that is incomplete in some way and still requires some kind of future, mediated, restoration blessings through Israel. These different meanings of "fullness" for Jew and Gentile are difficult to reconcile with the portrait Paul paints in Romans 11 of a symmetrical salvation experience between each group. Both Jew and Gentile were disobedient, and both have received mercy (Rom 11:30–32). God has brought salvation to the Gentiles *through* Israel and to Israel *through* the Gentiles. The nature of the mystery Paul reveals involves the interdependence of the salvation of the Gentiles and Jews. The Gentiles are not waiting for Israel to achieve a national restoration before they can receive the mediated blessings that grant them their own separate restoration.

If the dispensational solution for solving the dilemma of two different salvation-historical patterns is unsatisfactory, then how can they be reconciled? Positing a fourth step in the salvation-historical pattern is not necessarily wrong, but it should be placed before the sequence spelled out in Romans 11, not after it. Greg Beale and Benjamin Gladd have a helpful discussion concerning how the NT actually fulfills both patterns of salvation for Jews and Gentiles. They write, "It is likely that those Jews first hearing and accepting the gospel at Pentecost and shortly thereafter in Jerusalem (Acts 2–7) represent the beginning fulfillment of the order 'Jew first, then Greek.'"[34] The first believers in the church were all Israelites. The massive numbers of Jews embracing Jesus as Messiah and repenting of their sin were certainly a revival and part of the "restoration" of Israel (Acts 3:19–21; cf. 1:6).[35] "Three thou-

---

[34] G. K. Beale and Benjamin L. Gladd, *Hidden but Now Revealed: A Biblical Theology of Mystery* (Downers Grove, IL: InterVarsity, 2014), 88.

[35] The "restoration" process referenced in these verses is not exclusively future. It reaches a dramatic climax with the return of Jesus at the second coming, but it is already presently taking place beginning in these early chapters of Acts with the preaching of the gospel and the pouring out of the Spirit. See David G. Peterson, *The Acts of*

sand souls" were added on the day of Pentecost (Acts 2:41), and then not many days later another five thousand men, and presumably many of their wives and some of their children, heard the word and believed (Acts 4:4). Even at the end of Acts 3, right before Luke records this second large embrace of the gospel, he quotes Peter's words concerning the Abrahamic covenant. This covenant included both that all the families of the earth will be blessed (i.e., Gentile inclusion) and that God sent the Messiah to Israel first (Acts 3:25–26). So the salvation-historical priority is not undone; it just becomes clear to Paul later that the final eschatological restoration of Israel will not be complete "until the fullness of the Gentiles comes in" (Rom 11:25).[36]

Luke recounts a major turning point in the progression of the gospel in Acts 13. After focusing on Jewish salvation in the beginning of Acts, the gospel has come to the Gentiles in Acts 8 with the Ethiopian eunuch and in Acts 10 with Cornelius. Now at Pisidian Antioch, in response to the jealous Jews (Acts 13:45), Paul and Barnabas reaffirm the necessity of the gospel going to the Jews first (Acts 13:46). Then, because of the rejection by the Jews, they declare that they are turning to the Gentiles and even cite Isaiah 49:6 as support (Acts 13:46–47). Throughout the rest of the narrative in Acts, the majority of those saved are no longer Jews but Gentiles. This is the vantage point from which Paul writes Romans 11. He is addressing a situation in which the majority of the church is now composed of Gentiles. This reality, however, does not mean God has rejected his people. To the contrary, God will use the inclusion of the Gentiles to provoke the Jews to jealousy, who will then turn and embrace Christ. For the remainder of

---

the *Apostles*, PNTC (Grand Rapids: Eerdmans, 2009), 109–10, 182–83; and Eckhard J. Schnabel, *Acts*, ZECNT (Grand Rapids: Zondervan, 2012), 75–78, 214–17.

[36] The four steps spelled out would then look like this: (1) initial Jewish salvation (which turns out to be a remnant quantitatively speaking, Rom 11:5–7), then (2) the rest of Israel is hardened, which resulted in (3) the inclusion of the Gentiles, which in turn will provoke the Jews to jealous emulation resulting in (4) the final Jewish salvation (Rom 11:26). Therefore, there is an initial Jewish salvation at Christ's first coming and a final Jewish salvation at his second coming. This two-stage fulfillment of Israel's salvation is in contrast to the dispensational solution that argues for an initial Gentile salvation during the church age and a final Gentile restoration during the millennial kingdom.

the present age, the salvation-historical pattern is now "Gentiles first, then Jews." Therefore, as Beale and Gladd explain:

> According to the New Testament, the way redemption is actually accomplished fulfills both patterns: the majority of the first Christians were converts from Judaism, which sparked off initial Gentile salvation, as the pattern in Acts reveals. Yet as Acts unfolds, the Gentiles predominately compose the church with only a minority of Jews, which Paul interprets in Romans 11 as the pattern of "Gentile first, then Jew provoked to jealousy and salvation." It is only the actual fulfillment that shows how this mystery of the order salvation is unraveled.[37]

Dispensationalists are leery of explanations that suggest Paul is transforming or altering the OT picture "of the nations streaming to Jerusalem and being blessed through restored Israel (e.g., Isa 2:1–4)."[38] Nevertheless, the solution just presented maintains the clearer OT expectation of "Jews first, then Gentiles" but also recognizes that Paul reveals another pattern. He refers to this reversal of the OT expectations as a *mystery* (Rom 11:25) because "such an *explicit* chronological two-stage salvation [of Israel] cannot be found in the Old Testament."[39] However, this does not mean there are no clues in the OT of the notion that the salvation of the Gentiles would precede the majority of Israel. Beale and Gladd point to Deuteronomy 29:22–30:10 and 32:21 (cf. Rom 10:19) as texts that indicate a possible reversal in the sequence.[40] D. A. Carson suggests that a hint of the Gentile-Israel order may be found in Isaiah 45:14–17, 20–25 and Micah 4:1–8.[41] Even in Isaiah 2, a

---

[37] Beale and Gladd, *Hidden but Now Revealed*, 98. The authors understand the Jewish salvation flowing from the Gentile inclusion to be the elect remnant throughout the church age instead of a future mass conversion. Yet, as they admit, this understanding of "all Israel will be saved" (Rom 11:26) "does not significantly affect the present discussion" (88n3).

[38] Saucy, *The Case for Progressive Dispensationalism*, 259.

[39] Beale and Gladd, *Hidden but Now Revealed*, 89 (emphasis in original).

[40] Ibid., 89–93, 98–108.

[41] Carson, "Mystery and Fulfillment," 420. For these references Carson is drawing on Otfried Hofius, "Das Evangelium und Israel: Erwägungen zu Römer 9–11," *ZTK* 83

passage frequently cited as paradigmatic for the Israel-Gentile order, the picture might be more complex than is often acknowledged. The first four verses
certainly speak of the word of the Lord flowing out of an exalted Zion and the
influx of the nations in response, but the contribution of Isaiah 2:5 is often
left out of the discussion.[42] This verse reads, "O house of Jacob, come, let us
walk in the light of the LORD" (ESV). It is understood by some commentators
as an "appeal to join these other nations"[43] by following in their example. The
nations have already heeded their call to "come" and "walk" in the Lord's path
(Isa 2:3); now it is time for Israel to do the same. "Surely, [Isaiah] seems to be
saying, if the Gentiles will come seeking the truth we have . . . , if they will
come to the light we hold . . . , then we ought to walk in that light."[44] "The
prophet is attempting to use the example of the Gentiles to provoke God's
people to a holy jealousy."[45] This seems to correlate well with Paul's purposes
in Romans 11,[46] especially when Isaiah 2:6 is taken into account. Jacob/Israel
is exhorted to come because they have been rejected by the Lord because of
their sin. Paul, in Romans 11, tells an all too familiar story: Israel's sin led to
God's rejecting them (Isa 2:6); meanwhile the Gentiles were streaming to
the Lord (Isa 2:2–4), which in turn will provoke Israel to finally come and
join in the salvation enjoyed by the Gentiles (Isa 2:5). "The ironic twist in the
Book of Isaiah is that the nations finally turn and seek Zion (2:1–3), leaving
the house of Jacob to follow their lead (2:5)."[47] So "this order of salvation

---

(1986): 324.

[42] "When compared with Micah 4:1–3, the most distinctive feature of Isaiah's version of this prophecy is the 'application' in verse 5" (John Goldingay, *Isaiah*, UBCS 13
[Grand Rapids: Baker, 1995], 44).

[43] Christopher R. Seitz, *Isaiah 1–39*, Interpretation 20 (Louisville: John Knox,
1993), 38–39.

[44] John N. Oswalt, *The Book of Isaiah: Chapters 1–39*, NICOT (Grand Rapids:
Eerdmans, 1986), 119.

[45] Ibid., 118. He continues, "The emphatic position of 'House of Jacob' and its correlation with 'God of Jacob' in v. 3 supports this contention" (118–19).

[46] A point that is also explicitly made in C. F. Keil and F. Delitzsch, *Isaiah*, Commentary
on the Old Testament, vol. 7, trans. James Martin (Grand Rapids: Eerdmans, 1969), 117.

[47] Seitz, *Isaiah 1–39*, 72.

was, to some small degree, anticipated in the Old Testament, but it was not explained in detail and later Old Testament prophecies do not develop it."[48]

The reversal in the salvation sequence *is* developed by Paul, possibly even in his appeal to the OT. To buttress the "mystery" statement in Romans 11:25–26a, he quotes a combination of texts from Isaiah. Space does not provide the ability to elaborate, but this quotation in Romans 11:26b–27 (Isa 59:20–21a with Isa 27:9b),[49] with Paul's interpretive modifications, also provides OT grounding to the whole mystery statement.[50] The gospel now goes out of Zion to the Gentiles, which will in turn have the effect of removing ungodliness from Jacob.[51] In light of Paul's new revelation, the sequence of Gentiles preceding Israel's final salvation gains more clarity.

In summary, dispensationalists are right to attempt to reconcile Romans 11 with OT prophetic expectations; but their reading fails to account for the significance of Israel's initial salvation following Christ's first coming, and it underappreciates the climactic end of salvation-history ushered in by Christ's second coming. They are again presupposing the nature of the fulfillment for both Israel and the nations and then seeking to find it in this passage. Nothing in Romans 11:12 and 15 provides evidence for the anticipation of a separate age during the millennial kingdom where a restored national Israel will mediate some sort of greater salvation blessings to the nations. The implication that dispensationalists read into this text is unwarranted.

---

[48] Beale and Gladd, *Hidden but Now Revealed*, 93.

[49] Christopher R. Bruno ("The Deliverer from Zion: The Source(s) and Function of Paul's Citation in Romans 11:26–27," *TynBul* 59 [2008]: 119–34) has also made the case for an allusion to Isa 2:3 as part of the compound citation.

[50] See J. R. Daniel Kirk, "Why Does the Deliverer Come ἐκ Σιών (Romans 11.26)?," *JSNT* 33 (2010): 81–99 and Eusebio González, "Interdependencia entre judíos y gentiles en Rm 11,25–27," *Scripta Theologica* 43 (2011): 125–42. Cf. also N. T. Wright, *Paul and the Faithfulness of God* (Minneapolis: Fortress, 2013), 2:1248–52.

[51] For a more developed discussion of the function of the quotation in Rom 11:26b–27, as well as further grounding for the other exegetical decisions in this chapter, see Richard James Lucas Jr., "Was Paul Prooftexting? Paul's Use of the Old Testament as Illustrated Through Three Debated Texts" (PhD diss., The Southern Baptist Theological Seminary, 2014), 21–103.

Conclusion

Romans 11 does not provide support for dispensationalism's distinctive teachings concerning a restored national Israel mediating blessings to Gentile nations in the millennial kingdom. Even admitting that Romans 11 teaches that there is a future for ethnic Israel is not sufficient to claim this passage as support for their distinctive teachings. Dispensationalists read into Romans 11 their predetermined expectations concerning the nature of the fulfillment of these promises. Even prominent dispensationalist Darrell Bock admits, "How one answers this question about the implications of Romans 11 [for only the future *salvation* of ethnic Jews or for a national *restoration* of Israel] is dependent less on this text than how one reads the hope of Scripture as a whole."[52] The alternate proposal provided in this chapter for the nature of new covenant fulfillment and the interconnected salvific relationship between Jews and Gentiles better accounts for the details of Romans 11 and the larger canonical story. Dispensationalists may want to continue to seek support for their theological system from various texts, but I suggest they cease appealing to Romans 11 as a major proof text. The implications they attempt to read out of Romans 11 fail to convince.

At the heart of dispensationalism is the continuance of distinct national identities and roles for both Israel and the Gentiles.[53] That is why dispensationalists strictly reject any attempts to make the church supersede national Israel as the people of God. The church is not Israel, and Israel is not the church. On the other hand, more traditional forms of covenant theology have tended essentially to equate Israel and the church.[54] Neither view does justice to how Paul presents the relationship between Jew and Gentile in Romans 11. Douglas Moo nicely explains how Romans 11 actually presents a *via media* between these two more traditional options when he writes:

---

[52] Darrell L. Bock, "Summary Essay," in *Three Views on the Millennium and Beyond,* ed. D. L. Bock (Grand Rapids: Zondervan, 1999), 292.

[53] Vlach even claims that this distinction persists into the eternal state (*Has the Church Replaced Israel?,* 173–76).

[54] Louis Berkhof, *Systematic Theology* (Grand Rapids: Eerdmans, 1996), 570–72.

The relationship between Israel and the church in Paul's perspective is much more historically oriented and continuous than [the Israel = church model] might suggest. As his olive tree analogy in Romans 11 makes clear, Paul views Gentiles who are experiencing the messianic salvation as belonging not to a new body discontinuous with Israel but to Israel itself. True, this is not simply national Israel—for unbelieving Jews can be, and are, cut off from it. But it is the spiritual Israel within Israel that, according to Romans 9, has always been in existence and, according to [Rom] 11:16, grows from the seed of God's promises to the patriarchs. If we follow the logic of this analogy, then, the church is not so much a replacement for Israel or even a "new" Israel; it is the continuation of "Israel" in the era of fulfillment. As has always been the case, believing Jews, the remnant, are part of this spiritual Israel. And Paul's "to the Jew first" makes clear that the Jewish presence in the new Israel is both fitting and necessary. Now, however, in the fulfillment of the promise to Abraham and in line with the prophetic expectation of the universal extent of God's kingdom, Gentiles are becoming part of Israel. And in the eschatological consummation, as I understand Romans 11, many more Jews will be added to spiritual Israel.[55]

It should also be stated clearly that the means by which both Jews and Gentiles become part of the people of God, spiritual Israel, is by believing in the Messiah, Jesus Christ.[56] Ethnic Israel and Gentiles become part of spiritual Israel by believing in the true Israelite, Jesus Christ.[57]

---

[55] Douglas Moo, "Paul's Universalizing Hermeneutic in Romans," *SBTJ* 11 (2007): 77.

[56] A good case can be made that Christ is actually "the root" of the olive tree that holds together both Israel and the Gentiles in Rom 11:16–24. See Svetlana Khobnya, "'The Root' in Paul's Olive Tree Metaphor (Romans 11:16–24)," *TynBul* 64 (2013): 257–73.

[57] Cf. Thomas R. Schreiner, "The Church as the New Israel and the Future of Ethnic Israel in Paul," *Studia Biblica et Theologica* 13 (1983): 37.

Publication of Robert L. Saucy, "Does the Apostle Paul Reverse the Prophetic Tradition of the Salvation of Israel and the Nations?," in *Building on the Foundations of Evangelical Theology: Essays in Honor of John S. Feinberg*, ed. Gregg R. Allison and Stephen J. Wellum (Wheaton, IL: Crossway, 2015), 66–90, came too late to include as a resource.

CHAPTER 10

The Land Promise Biblically and Theologically Understood

OREN R. MARTIN

Introduction

Peter Gentry and Stephen Wellum's book *Kingdom Through Covenant* has received a variety of responses.[1] This chapter will address and respond to a few issues specifically related to dispensationalism: Israel and the land promise. I will proceed in two steps. First, I will briefly describe dispensational theology in regard to how the land promise is fulfilled. Second, in light of that discussion, I will offer an evaluation and critique of various hermeneutical issues related to the fulfillment of the land promise such as the progression of land promise through the biblical covenants, typology, and inaugurated eschatology.

In short, the dispensational argument that the OT land promise must be fulfilled by national Israel in the millennial age does not do justice to the biblical story line of God's redemptive plan from creation to new creation, from Adam to Christ. Instead, the land promised to Abraham begins the process of recapturing and advancing what was lost in Eden and will not be fulfilled until a "new Eden" is regained. At every point in Israel's history,

---

[1] Peter J. Gentry and Stephen J. Wellum, *Kingdom Through Covenant: A Biblical-Theological Understanding of the Covenants* (Wheaton, IL: Crossway, 2012). See the introduction of this volume for a list of reviews of *Kingdom Through Covenant*.

the promised land served as a place that anticipated, in Edenic terms, an even greater land to come. Although the territorial promise related initially to Israel's settlement in the land of Canaan, by divine design it also pointed to something greater. Let us develop these points in greater detail.[2]

Dispensationalism, Israel, and the Land

Dispensationalism has changed over the years, making it difficult to present a unified theology of land.[3] Nevertheless, it is possible to distill dispensational theology into an essential core. That is, all forms of dispensational theology derive a theology of land from an interconnected set of convictions.[4] First, the *sine qua non* of dispensationalism is the distinction between the nation of Israel and the church.[5] Second, dispensationalists believe God's

---

[2] For a more comprehensive treatment of this argument, see Oren R. Martin, *Bound for the Promised Land: The Land Promise in God's Redemptive Plan*, NSBT 34 (Downers Grove, IL: InterVarsity, 2015). Permission has been granted to use and build on portions of *Bound for the Promised Land* in this chapter.

[3] See, e.g., Herbert W. Bateman IV, ed., *Three Central Issues in Contemporary Dispensationalism: A Comparison of Traditional and Progressive Views* (Grand Rapids: Kregel, 1999); John S. Feinberg, "Systems of Discontinuity," in *Continuity and Discontinuity: Perspectives on the Relationship Between the Old and New Testaments*, ed. John S. Feinberg (Wheaton, IL: Crossway, 1988), 63–86; Craig A. Blaising, "Dispensationalism: The Search for Definition," in *Dispensationalism, Israel and the Church: The Search for Definition*, ed. Craig A. Blaising and Darrell L. Bock (Grand Rapids: Zondervan, 1992), 13–34; Craig A. Blaising and Darrell L. Bock, *Progressive Dispensationalism* (Grand Rapids: Baker, 1993), 9–56; Charles C. Ryrie, *Dispensationalism*, rev. ed. (Chicago: Moody, 2007); Robert L. Saucy, *The Case for Progressive Dispensationalism: The Interface Between Dispensational and Non-Dispensational Theology* (Grand Rapids: Zondervan, 1993).

[4] These points have been adapted from Feinberg, "Systems of Discontinuity," 63–86, and Michael Vlach, "What Is Dispensationalism?," in *Christ's Prophetic Plans: A Futuristic Premillennial Primer*, ed. John MacArthur and Richard Mayhue (Chicago: Moody, 2012), 24–35.

[5] Ryrie, *Dispensationalism*, 46; Blaising, "Dispensationalism: The Search for Definition," 23. For Feinberg, "What is distinctive of dispensational thinking is recognition of [the four distinct senses of seed: (1) biological, ethnic, national; (2) political; (3) spiritual; (4) typological] as operative in both Testaments coupled with a demand that no sense (spiritually especially) is more important than any other, and that no

unconditional promise of land in the Abrahamic covenant must be fulfilled
to national Israel in the future. This future fulfillment "includes at least the
millennial reign of Christ and for some dispensationalists, extends into the
eternal state as well."[6] Feinberg writes, "If an OT prophecy or promise is
made unconditionally to a given people and is still unfulfilled to them even
in the NT era, then the prophecy must still be fulfilled to them."[7] Third, and
building off the second point, is a hermeneutical concern: the NT does not
reinterpret or spiritualize the land promise to Israel.[8] Again, Feinberg writes,
"Lack of repetition in the NT does not render an OT teaching inoperative
during the NT era so long as nothing explicitly or implicitly cancels it."[9]
Feinberg's contention applies to types and antitypes and, when applied to
the issue of the land, leads to the fourth point. Feinberg writes,

> My contention is that understanding that both type and antitype
> must have their own meaning even while bearing a typological
> relation to the other, understanding the implications of NT
> reinterpretation of the OT, and realizing that progress of revelation
> only renders earlier truth inoperative if God says so, leads one

---

sense cancels out the meaning and implications of the other senses. The more one
emphasizes the distinctness and importance of the various senses, the more dispensational and discontinuity-oriented his system becomes, for the distinct senses neces-
sitate speaking of Israel ethnically, politically, and spiritually, as well as speaking of
the church" (Feinberg, "Systems of Discontinuity," 72–73). Bruce Ware defines this
distinction when he writes, "Israel and the church share theologically rich and important elements of commonality while at the same time maintaining distinct identities"
("The New Covenant and the People(s) of God," in *Dispensationalism, Israel, and the
Church*, 92).

[6] Blaising and Bock, *Progressive Dispensationalism*, 21; Feinberg, "Systems of
Discontinuity," 68; Walter Kaiser writes, "The mark of God's new measure of grace, not
only to Israel as a nation but also to all the nations and Gentiles at large, will be Israel's
return to the land and enjoyment of it in the millennium" ("The Promised Land: A
Biblical-Historical View," *BibSac* 138 [1981]: 311). See also Ware, "The New Covenant
and the People(s) of God," 93–96.

[7] Feinberg, "Systems of Discontinuity," 76. See also Blaising and Bock, *Progressive
Dispensationalism*, 132–34.

[8] Saucy, *The Case for Progressive Dispensationalism*, 30–31.

[9] Feinberg, "Systems of Discontinuity," 76.

to see that the meaning of both OT and NT passages must be maintained.[10]

As a result, dispensationalists reject the idea that the land serves solely as a type of the new creation inhabited by all God's people—both Jew and Gentile—through Christ's finished work. Rather, it is a "literal" promise that culminates with Christ reigning and Israel performing a mediatorial role in the land during the millennium.[11] How, then, does a progressive covenantal proposal differ from the dispensational view? To answer this question is to summarize the biblical-theological arguments set forth in *Kingdom Through Covenant* and *Bound for the Promised Land*.

Progressive Covenantalism, Israel, and the Land

The Promise to Abraham

To begin, an appeal to the unconditional nature of the Abrahamic covenant does not prove that the land promise must be exclusively fulfilled to national Israel in the future.[12] To be sure, Genesis 15 shows that God will unilaterally fulfill the promise and conditions of the covenant even if it means taking the curse upon himself. Nevertheless, this unconditional emphasis does not remove the necessity of Abraham's obedience. For example, Genesis 17:2 and 22:17–18 (cf. 26:4–5) demonstrate that God requires an obedient partner in the covenant relationship. God promises the covenant

---

[10] Ibid., 79.

[11] Michael J. Vlach, "Israel in Church History," in *The People, the Land, and the Future of Israel: Israel and the Jewish People in the Plan of God*, ed. Darrell L. Bock and Mitch Glasser (Grand Rapids: Kregel, 2015), 198–99. John Feinberg ("Israel in the Land as an Eschatological Necessity?," in *The People, the Land, and the Future of Israel*, 184) forcefully asserts, "I believe that Israel not only *will* possess the land, but biblically speaking, she *must* possess it . . . [because] various end-time prophecies cannot be fulfilled unless Israel is in the land with both political and religious control over her own destiny."

[12] Gentry and Wellum, *Kingdom Through Covenant*, 608–11, 634–35; Martin, *Bound for the Promised Land*, 63–71.

blessings to Abraham, but these blessings are reserved for the people who trust and obey him. In other words, the ultimate fulfillment of the covenant is grounded in God's promises, but the means of fulfillment will come through Abraham's (and his descendants') obedience. The tension between God's promise and the necessity of obedience in the covenant relationship becomes clearer as the story line progresses and is crucial for understanding the nature and progression of the covenants as they reach their *appointed fulfillment* in Christ. That is, when the larger canonical story line is considered, the conditions are met by God himself when he sends his obedient Son—the seed of Abraham (Gal 3:16)—to fulfill the demands of the covenant. Furthermore, an appeal to the Abrahamic covenant actually supports the view that the land promise is finally fulfilled in a greater way than in the geographical boundaries of Canaan. That is, the Abrahamic covenant itself has *both* national/international *and* regional/global components, which is confirmed later in Scripture, a point to which I now turn.[13]

The calling of and promise to Abraham recovers the universal purpose of Adam in terms of both the blessing of offspring and land. In other words, the universal scope of Eden temporarily narrows to the land of Canaan, thus serving as "a small-scale version (microcosm) of the flourishing that God intended for all humanity,"[14] and in time would expand with the proliferation of Abraham's offspring. When Genesis 22:17–18 and 26:3–4 are taken together, the immediate context of the Abrahamic covenant already points to a universal expansion of the territorial promise. In other words, the propagation of Abraham's offspring would result in inheriting the world (cf. Rom 4:13). This interpretation, however, is not reinterpreting or spiritualizing the OT promise, contrary to the charge of dispensationalists. Rather, it begins to establish the type or pattern by which the ultimate fulfillment of the promise would encompass the entire world, which the OT develops and the NT confirms.

---

[13] See Paul R. Williamson, "Promise and Fulfillment: The Territorial Inheritance," in *The Land of Promise: Biblical, Theological, and Contemporary Perspectives*, ed. Philip Johnston and Peter Walker (Downers Grove, IL: InterVarsity, 2000), 15–34.

[14] Richard Middleton, *A New Heaven and a New Earth: Reclaiming Biblical Eschatology* (Grand Rapids: Baker, 2014), 61.

Another important aspect of the Abrahamic covenant is whether it is intended to be national (Gen 12:2, "nation") or international (Gen 17:4–6, "nations").[15] For example, Genesis 15 is a covenant made between God and Abraham and his "seed," while Genesis 17 broadens the category of "seed." Furthermore, God changes Abram's name to Abraham since he is to be "the father of a multitude of nations" (Gen 17:5).[16] An intended ambiguity exists in the text, then, for Abraham's "seed" *both* encompasses a multitude of nations (Genesis 17) *and* relates to an individual descendant (Gen 22:17b) who will mediate blessing to all the nations.[17]

When these texts are put together, the ultimate inheritors of the patriarchal promises are not restricted to a national entity but extend to an international community. That is, God's programmatic agenda for humanity after Eden begins with the formation of a nation through Abraham and ends with an international people. This international component is picked up later in the prophets. It is difficult to see, then, how the territorial promise could be exhausted by any political borders, whether Israelite or otherwise, for the multiplication of descendants naturally expands the territorial borders until the earth is filled.

The Promise and the Nation

Exodus to Deuteronomy depicts Israel's future entrance into the promised land as a return to Edenic conditions, for they will multiply, subdue, and enjoy blessing in the land.[18] Moreover, when Israel—God's son—inherits

---

[15] Gentry and Wellum, *Kingdom Through Covenant*, 707–8; cf. Williamson, "Promise and Fulfillment," 18.

[16] Williamson, "Promise and Fulfillment," 19.

[17] T. Desmond Alexander, "Seed," in *NDBT*, 770. One can already see hermeneutical warrant for Paul to pick up on this idea when interpreted in light of Christ (Gal 3:16, 28–29). Williamson, "Promise and Fulfillment," 20; see also James M. Hamilton, "The Seed of the Woman and the Blessing of Abraham," *TynBul* 58 (2007): 258; T. Desmond Alexander, "Further Observations on the Term 'Seed' in Genesis," *TynBul* 48 (1997): 363–67; John H. Sailhamer, *The Meaning of the Pentateuch: Revelation, Composition and Interpretation* (Downers Grove, IL: InterVarsity, 2009), 439–42.

[18] For example, the land is described as being (very) good (Deut 1:25, 35; 3:25; 4:21, 22; 6:18; 8:7, 10; 9:6; 11:17. This language harkens back to God's "very good" creation in Gen 1:31. See also Josh 23:13, 15–16, and Num 14:7, which also describe

the land, rest will follow (Exod 33:14; Deut 12:10). Securing their inheritance of the promised land advances the pattern of Israel's entering into God's eternal rest, of which Canaan was the beginning. Later, Joshua demonstrates initial fulfillment of the Abrahamic promise (11:23; 14:15; 21:44–45) while anticipating a greater fulfillment that will bring Eden-like rest (13:1, 6–7; 15:63; 24:4–13). The end of Joshua, however, points to Israel's future failure and further need for subsequent repossession (24:14–28).

A significant advance of God's promise to plant his people in the land comes with the arrival of David and Solomon, for they, in escalating degrees, enjoy expansive and international reigns, and the nation enjoys rest from its enemies. The construction of the temple and subsequent rest represents a new Eden, for God once again dwells with his people in a more intensive sense (1 Kings 8). While the Solomonic reign typifies a return to Edenic conditions, the pattern of Solomon's disobedience leads to the second expulsion from the land, this time from Canaan.[19] Subsequently, the kingdom is divided and exiled. In the midst of judgment, however, the prophets resound with the eschatological hope of restoration that will bring the universal purposes of Eden, Abraham, and David back into focus.

The Prophets

The writing prophets bring into focus the Abrahamic promises and advance the pattern of God's promise by portraying the return from exile in various ways and stages, including both a physical and spiritual return, with national and international results. For example, Isaiah's prophecy describes Israel's return from exile in both imminent and distant ways. Moreover, it is cast in language resembling the exodus, projecting an ideal community established under messianic leadership, having experienced a greater

---

the land in a similar way to Gen 1:31), having luxurious pasturelands and flowers and containing abundant fruit (Deut 7:13; 28:4). The fruit of the womb and the fruit of the livestock will be blessed (Deut 7:13; 28:3–5, 11), and no male or female among the people or among the beasts will be barren (Deut 7:14; 28:4, 11; cf. Exod 23:26; Lev 26:9).

[19] John A. Davis, "Discerning Between Good and Evil: Solomon as a New Adam in 1 Kings," *WTJ* 73 (2011): 40.

exodus (e.g., Isa 11:1–16; 35:1–10; 51:9–11; 52:11–12). The first return from exile is a physical release and return to the land (42:18–43:21) that will be accomplished by God's servant Cyrus, who will permit enslaved Israel to return to their homeland (44:24–45:1; cf. Ezra 1:1–3). Although this return is another fulfillment of God's promised restoration, it in no way compares to the prophets' final vision—a large scale restoration beyond what was represented by the community in Jerusalem.

Isaiah. A deeper captivity kept Israel from being fully restored. That is, though God had delivered Israel from idolatrous nations, idolatry needed to be delivered from their hearts.[20] From Isaiah's perspective this deliverance will be accomplished by the Servant-King who will bring back Israel so that God's salvation may reach the nations (Isa 49:1–53:12).[21] Forgiveness will come through Yahweh's (individual) Servant who will deliver his (corporate) servant Israel (42:1–9; 49:1–6), redeem his people (9:2–7), rule over them (11:1–5), and atone for sin by suffering, dying, and taking upon himself the punishment they deserve (42:1–9; 49:5–6; 50:4–9; 52:13–53:12).[22] This Servant is of such a stature that he will save not only Israel but also the nations!

Furthermore, the Servant's substitutionary atonement will initiate a new covenant that offers life and enjoyment of the blessings of both the Abrahamic and Davidic covenants for Israel *and* the nations (54:1–55:13; cf. 19:19–25). This international scope in God's plan goes back to the Abrahamic covenant. Moreover, the leader and commander of the peoples, a new Davidic king, will bless and rule the nations (55:4–5). This connects to the Servant-king in Isaiah 53, whose atoning death and resurrection fulfill the Davidic covenant and establish the basis for the new or everlasting covenant.[23] Astonishingly, not only is the remnant called the Lord's servants

---

[20] Gentry and Wellum, *Kingdom Through Covenant*, 437–38.

[21] The sequence of redemption is important, for it marks the fulfillment of the Abrahamic promise that through Israel the nations would be blessed (Gen 12:1–3).

[22] John N. Oswalt, *The Book of Isaiah: Chapters 1–39*, NICOT (Grand Rapids: Eerdmans, 1986), 41. See also Gentry and Wellum, *Kingdom Through Covenant*, 438–41; Martin, *Bound for the Promised Land*, 103–5.

[23] Peter J. Gentry, "Rethinking the 'Sure Mercies of David' in Isaiah 55:3," *WTJ* 69 (2009): 301; cf. James M. Hamilton, *God's Glory in Salvation Through Judgment: A Biblical Theology* (Wheaton, IL: Crossway, 2010), 209.

(Isa 65:13–25); the foreigners are also deemed servants of the Lord (56:6). In fulfillment of the Abrahamic covenant, the Lord will give his *name* and *blessing* to his servants in the land (65:13–16; cf. Gen 12:3; 17:5; 22:18; 26:4). The result of the Servant's saving work, then, creates *servants*, and all—Israel as well as foreigners—will go to God's holy mountain in a pilgrimage of worship (Isa 2:2–4; 27:13; cf. Mic 4:1–5).

Isaiah proceeds to describe more clearly the result of this new order. Isaiah 65:17–66:24 provides a succinct summary of the eschatological themes that occur throughout the entire book and elaborates on the hope of restoration to the city of Jerusalem and the land that reaches an astounding climax (cf. 2:1–4; 4:2–6; 9:1–16; 11:1–10).[24] These eschatological themes have appeared throughout Isaiah, but what is new is their joining together in one concluding oracle. When the various strands are drawn together, Isaiah's vision of final restoration involves new heavens and a new earth (65:17; 66:22), a new Jerusalem (65:18–19; cf. 4:2–6), and a holy mountain, Zion (65:25; cf. 2:1–4; 4:2–6). Moreover, in fulfillment of the covenant promises to Abraham, God will give them a new *name*, and they will receive *blessing* in the *land* by the God of truth (Isa 65:15–16). By the end of Isaiah, then, this temple-mountain-city is coextensive with the new creation. The final vision resounds with astonishing realities cast in terms of God's kingdom coming to and filling the earth. Thus, God will save his people by the work of the Servant-king and make the place where they will live. The order is crucial since it is a reversal of the old creation. In the old creation God first created the place and then made and set his people there to live. In the new creation God first makes his people and then will make the new creation where they will live.[25]

Jeremiah. In Jeremiah, Yahweh promises to take back his people if they return, and "then nations shall bless themselves in him, and in him shall

---

[24] See J. Alec Motyer, *Isaiah*, TOTC (Downers Grove, IL: InterVarsity, 1999), 27.

[25] Gentry and Wellum, *Kingdom Through Covenant*, 467–68; cf. Craig G. Bartholomew, "The Theology of Place in Genesis 1–3," in *Reading the Law: Studies in Honour of Gordon J. Wenham*, ed. J. G. McConville and Karl Möller (New York: T&T Clark, 2007), 173–95.

they glory" (4:1–2 ESV).[26] The reference to the nations blessing themselves in him "indicates that the promises to Abraham would be realized (cf. Gen 12:3) if Israel would repent and glorify Yahweh."[27] Like Isaiah, the nations are in view in the restoration of Israel and Judah, and this cosmological and teleological goal is in fulfillment of the Abrahamic promises.[28] Jeremiah proclaims that Israel will return from exile in terms of a new exodus (16:14–15). In fact, this exodus will be so great that the former exodus will no longer be spoken of.

Then, in chapters 30–33, Jeremiah unfolds the great promises of salvation and offers hope beyond the exile that will come in the form of a new covenant and return to the land. Of particular importance is 31:38–40, which concerns the rebuilding and expansion of Jerusalem. In addition to the restoration of Davidic leadership (30:8–11), priesthood (31:14), and people (31:31–34), the restoration of the city brings to completion the glorious reversal of Jeremiah's pronouncements of judgment.[29] Though the city had been destroyed, the future age of redemption will see its restoration *and more*. Derek Kidner comments that "the promise [in 31:38–40] is 'earthed' not merely in this planet but in the familiar details of Israel's capital, naming rubbish dumps and all. . . . But the vision outruns that exercise, in scale and in significance."[30] Therefore, the new Jerusalem will be both different

---

[26] Gentry and Wellum, *Kingdom Through Covenant*, 486–88.

[27] Hamilton, *God's Glory in Salvation Through Judgment*, 215; see also Gentry and Wellum, *Kingdom Through Covenant*, 487.

[28] Also see Jer 12:14–17, which speaks of an exile, not just for Judah but also for God's evil neighbors "who touch the heritage that I have given my people Israel to inherit" (v. 14 ESV). Astonishingly, "according to verse 15, *each land* and *people* will have a return from exile. And when all the exiles are brought home, if the nations learn from Israel to swear by the God of Israel, then they will be 'built up' or established in the midst of the restored Israel. If they do not, each will be permanently eradicated as a nation" (emphasis in original). Gentry and Wellum, *Kingdom Through Covenant*, 488.

[29] Paul R. House, *Old Testament Theology* (Downers Grove, IL: InterVarsity, 1998), 319.

[30] Derek Kidner, *The Message of Jeremiah*, BST (Downers Grove, IL: InterVarsity, 1987), 111.

and expanded from the old, and the rebuilt city will become the center of God's presence among his people (3:14–18; cf. Isa 65:17; 66:12; Rev 21:3).

Jeremiah describes the restoration of both people and place in the future and pins these hopes on a Davidic leader, a righteous branch, who, interestingly, is a combination of both king and priest (33:14–18; cf. Isa 9:6–7; 11:1–10; 53:1–3). This king-priest will secure a new covenant for his people—a certainty as sure as Yahweh's covenant with day and night. God will make them dwell securely in the land and multiply the offspring of David as numerous as the immeasurable sands of the sea in fulfillment of the Abrahamic covenant (33:14–26). Moreover, 31:35–40 hints that a new covenant would necessarily operate within the contours of a new creation, as Isaiah and Ezekiel also make clear. An idealized return to the land, therefore, is intimated in Jeremiah.

Ezekiel. As the last of the Major Prophets, Ezekiel prophesies that the renewed people will be purified in heart and spirit, and they will be one flock under a new David (34–37). As a result, "the nations will know that I the LORD make Israel holy, when my sanctuary is among them forever" (37:28 NIV). Whereas Yahweh had been a sanctuary to the exiles "for a little while" (11:16), Yahweh's presence will be with them forever. God will make a new covenant (36:16–38), which will deal with their sin and finally fulfill his covenant so he can say, "They will be my people, and I will be their God" (37:23, 27 NIV). In Ezekiel 37, resurrection imagery illustrates the promise of Israel's return to a new life in her own land from the deathlike existence of the Babylonian exile. The restoration to the land is linked with the resurrection motif. The dead shall be brought to life so they too may participate in the restoration. But Ezekiel's vision of restoration does not stop with Israel, for other nations are included in Yahweh's everlasting covenant (16:59–63). Hence Ezekiel 16:61, like similar passages in Isaiah and Jeremiah, indicates that the restoration will have international significance.

Ezekiel continues with his program by envisioning a rebuilt temple with revitalized worship in chapters 40–48. First, a new humanity is (re)created (chap. 37) and then placed in a new temple-Eden. The climactic vision in chapters 40–48 describes the fulfillment of the promises of chapters 1–39. In a significant passage, Ezekiel 37:25–28 pulls together various strands of the new place for God's people and prepares the way for even more glorious promises in chapters 40–48 (cf. 37:25–28 and 43:7–9). Ezekiel ends with a vision of a purified land with boundaries situated around a new temple complex. More specifically, Ezekiel 47:1–12 contains a profusion of Edenic imagery and describes a paradisiacal temple that extends to encompass the entire land. It can be said, then, that the new temple is the new creation and restores the consummate state of paradise. Significantly, Ezekiel uses the same language as Jeremiah regarding a measuring line extending the boundaries outward (Jer 31:39; Ezek 47:3; cf. Zechariah 2).[31] Thus, the promise concerning the renewed Israel living in the land under a new David is fulfilled in the vision of a temple, recreating an Edenic context, the boundaries of which are coterminous with the land.

From a canonical perspective Revelation presents this worldwide temple as the new creation—the new Jerusalem—in light of the fulfillment of Christ, the true temple.[32] For the NT writers this prophecy became a

---

[31] Daniel I. Block, *The Book of Ezekiel 25–48*, NICOT (Grand Rapids: Eerdmans, 1998), 692n53; J. A. Thompson, *The Book of Jeremiah*, NICOT (Grand Rapids: Eerdmans, 1980), 583.

[32] There is some discontinuity between the visions of Ezekiel and John (Rev 21–22). Daniel Block, *Ezekiel 25–48*, 503, contends that Ezekiel's temple is not fulfilled in Rev 21 for these reasons: First, the two cities have different names ("Yahweh is there" [Ezek 48:35]; "the new Jerusalem" [Rev 21:2]). Second, Ezekiel's city is square and composed of common stones, whereas John's is cubic and composed of precious stones. Third, Ezekiel's temple is at the center of everything, whereas the temple's existence is denied in Rev 21:22. Fourth, Ezekiel portrays a parochially Israelite city, whereas Revelation 21 describes a cosmopolitan place of Jews and Gentiles. Fifth, sacrificial animals are at the heart of Ezekiel's temple, whereas the sacrificial Lamb is at the heart of John's temple. Finally, in Ezekiel's temple the clean and unclean are distinguished, whereas John makes no such distinction. Nevertheless, Beale provides a satisfying response to Block's criticisms. First, the concepts of both names are true of both cities. In fact, Rev 21:2 develops 3:12 and recalls Ezek 48:35, where the names are mentioned together. Second, Ezekiel's square and John's cube are similar in shape, and John even uses the word "four-square" in 21:16, combining Ezekiel's vision with an allusion to the cubic shape of the holy of holies from Solomon's temple (1 Kgs 6:20). Furthermore, Ezekiel does not comment on the kind of stones making up the foundation and walls. Third, John does not deny the temple's existence, only its *physical* existence. The true temple, that is, God and the Lamb, is now central (Rev 21:22), which comes close to the essence of Ezekiel's temple that culminated in the Lord's glorious

brilliant way of speaking of what God had now achieved in and through Jesus. Although Ezekiel's vision focused much upon the temple, it found its ultimate fulfillment in that city where there was no temple because its temple is the Lord God Almighty and the Lamb (Rev 21:22).[33] Ezekiel, in line with the other prophets, describes astounding hope for the future that includes transformed land and human nature—a new Eden that has been enlarged to include the entire land of Israel with one immense river of life and many trees of life.

Before moving to the NT, an important observation must be made concerning an OT theology of land. There are exegetical grounds rooted in creation, in the immediate context of the Abrahamic covenant and the OT

---

presence (Ezek 48:35). Fourth, Ezekiel does picture Gentiles in the new Jerusalem (47:22–23), although this probably would have been understood as Gentiles who convert to the faith of Israel. Actually, Revelation depicts Jews and Gentiles who have been made one people—kingdom-priests—by the firstborn of the dead, the ruler of the kings of earth (1:5–6). Fifth, a solution to Ezekiel's animal sacrifices and John's living sacrificial Lamb is a matter of perspective. Ezekiel's vision employs language and imagery in terms the Jews of that day would understand. This picture is not a spiritualization of the promises since the sacrifice of Christ was no doubt the physical fulfillment of the sacrificial system. What appears in Ezekiel to be animal sacrifices, which formerly could give only incomplete and temporary covering for sin, find escalated fulfillment in Christ's sacrifice, which provides eternal salvation. Therefore, to say that Christ typologically fulfills Ezekiel's sacrifices as the Lamb sacrificed for sin is not a figurative or spiritualizing use of the OT but the eschatological reality to which the sacrificial system pointed (Hebrews 8–10). Finally, in response to Block's critique concerning Ezekiel's ongoing need to distinguish between the clean and unclean, Beale's answer is that Ezekiel depicts an inaugurated but not yet consummated eschatological temple. Paul understands the inaugurated temple described in Ezek 37:26–28 to be the church, yet there is still the ongoing need to "touch no unclean thing" (2 Cor 6:17 ESV) and to cleanse oneself "from every defilement of body and spirit" (2 Cor 7:1 ESV; cf. 1 Cor 6:18–19). Yet, in the consummated city-temple, sin and death shall be no more, neither shall there be mourning, nor crying, nor pain anymore, for the former things have passed away (Rev 21:4). Therefore, Revelation 21–22 further interprets the yet future fulfillment of Ezekiel by collapsing temple, city, and land into one end-time picture and describes the fulfillment of God's covenant promises. G. K. Beale, *The Temple in the Church's Mission: A Biblical Theology of the Dwelling Place of God*, NSBT 17 (Downers Grove, IL: InterVarsity, 2004), 348–53.

[33] Peter W. L. Walker, *Jesus and the Holy City: New Testament Perspectives on Jerusalem* (Grand Rapids: Eerdmans, 1996), 313.

prophets, to argue that God's intention for the land was not merely limited to the specific geographical boundaries of Canaan. Within the OT itself the land functions as a type of something greater that would recapture God's original design for creation.[34] This point is crucial since the dispensational charge is that those who disagree with them have not sufficiently developed a theology of the land *on OT terms*.[35] Feinberg writes: "Nondispensationalists begin with NT teaching as having priority, and then go back to the OT. Dispensationalists often go back to the OT, but wherever they begin they demand that the OT be taken on its own terms rather than reinterpreted in the light of the NT."[36]

Further, Blaising and Bock ask: "Is it possible that covenantalist approaches to the question of the relationship of Old Testament and New Testament hope are already determined by a traditional structure framed within the linguistic dimensions of the New Testament before the biblical theology of the Old Testament has been properly understood in its historical setting?"[37]

While this question is disputable,[38] progressive covenantalism does in fact argue that the NT shows both *when* and *how* the OT is brought to

---

[34] Gentry and Wellum, *Kingdom Through Covenant*, 706.

[35] For example, Bruce Waltke develops an OT theology of land but then argues that the NT redefines *land* in three ways: spiritually, transcendentally, and eschatologically. "By 'redefine' we mean that whereas 'Land' in the Old Testament refers to Israel's life in Canaan, in the New Testament 'Land' is transmuted to refer to life in Christ" (Bruce K. Waltke, *An Old Testament Theology: An Exegetical, Canonical, and Thematic Approach* [Grand Rapids: Zondervan, 2007], 560). G. K. Beale criticizes this definition for sounding "a bit too close to allegorization or undue spiritualization, even though Waltke contends that Christ has the authority to redefine the OT divine authorial intent in this manner." In its place Beale better defines *land* in this way: "That the land was a type of the new creation in that its true design was for Israel (as a corporate Adam) to be faithful and expand the land's borders to encompass the whole earth" (G. K. Beale *A New Testament Biblical Theology: The Transformation of the Old Testament in the New* [Grand Rapids: Baker, 2011], 769).

[36] Feinberg, "Systems of Discontinuity," 75.

[37] Craig A. Blaising and Darrell L. Bock, "Dispensationalism, Israel and the Church: Assessment and Dialogue," in *Dispensationalism, Israel, and the Church*, 393.

[38] Notable exceptions in covenant theology include Anthony A. Hoekema, *The Bible and the Future* (Grand Rapids: Eerdmans, 1979), 274–87; Beale, *A New Testament Biblical Theology*, 750–72; Sam Storms, *Kingdom Come: The Amillennial Alternative*

fulfillment in Christ, though in a way that does not reinterpret, spiritualize, or contravene the earlier texts.[39]

New Testament Fulfillment

The NT reveals that what was promised in the OT is fulfilled in Christ, the son of David, the son of Abraham, the son of Adam, the son of God. Jesus, the obedient Israelite, inaugurates the kingdom through his death and resurrection and finally delivers his people from the exile of sin (Matt 2:15; Col 1:13–14). Matthew interprets the eschatological land promises through the lens of the many typological and universalized texts in the OT (Matt 5:5). A few observations are important for interpreting Matthew 5:5 and the use of Psalm 37. To begin, Psalm 37 is eschatologically oriented (vv. 18, 29). The familiar theme of inheriting the land is projected forward and promised as a future hope to those who wait for the Lord and keep his way (v. 34). This motif is threaded throughout the entire psalm (vv. 3, 9, 11, 18, 22, 29, 34). Also, Psalm 37 was recognized as messianic in Jesus' day (4QpPs 37). This inaugurated eschatology is seen in the repetition of the present blessing in Matthew 5:3 and 5:10 ("for theirs is the kingdom of heaven" ESV) and the future blessings that are framed between these bookends ("for they shall" in vv. 4–9 ESV). Hence, Matthew is picking up and advancing the eschatological trajectory of Psalm 37. It is unlikely, given the typological nature of the land promise in the OT, that Jesus is referring strictly to the geographical territory initially promised to Abraham and possessed—and lost—by Israel. He appears to be interpreting the eschatological land inheritance of the psalm through the lens of other universalized texts in the OT. Thus, the anticipation of entering into the land ultimately became a pointer toward entrance into the new creation (cf. Isa 66:22; Rev 21:1), the consummation of the messianic kingdom.

(Fearn, Ross-shire, Scotland: Mentor, 2013), 344–48; Philip Johnston and Peter Walker, eds., *The Land of Promise: Biblical, Theological, and Contemporary Perspectives* (Downers Grove, IL: InterVarsity, 2000).

[39] Gentry and Wellum, *Kingdom Through Covenant*, 116; see also Martin, *Bound for the Promised Land*, chaps. 7–9.

Furthermore, through Christ's work and by union with him, the true temple (John 1:14; 2:19–22), he makes a new covenant people—described as a new creation and a new temple (2 Cor 5:17; 6:16). This new people, the church, made up of believing Jews and Gentiles, await their final home. In this way it can be said that Abraham would "inherit" the world (Rom 4:13) without contravening or spiritualizing OT promises.[40] This new creation is cast in terms of a paradisiacal garden-temple-city (Revelation 21–22; cf. Isaiah 65–66; Ezekiel 40–48). The variegated realities of the OT promises— the expansive city, temple, and land—overlap with the new creation won by Christ.[41] Thus, Israel's land promise ultimately reaches its fulfillment when

---

[40] While no explicit OT text states that Abraham will inherit the world, the idea is there. Of particular importance is Gen 26:3–4, where the unique plural "lands," when read in conjunction with the oath to which it alludes in Gen 22:17–18, makes clear that Abraham's seed will possess/inherit the gate of his enemies (see Douglas J. Moo, *Romans*, NICNT [Grand Rapids: Eerdmans, 1996], 274). This provides exegetical footing for Paul's assertion that Abraham would inherit the world. Paul is demonstrating sound biblical exegesis by putting all three elements of the Abrahamic covenant together (Thomas R. Schreiner, *Romans*, BECNT [Grand Rapids: Baker, 1998], 227). Through faith in Christ—Abraham's (singular) seed (Gal 3:16)—Abraham's (corporate) offspring will inherit the world. The same could be said of Eph 6:2–3, "Honor your father and mother" (this is the first commandment with a promise), "that it may go well with you and that you may live long in the land" (ESV). In the OT the promise relates to a long life in the promised land that God gave to Israel. Does it follow that Paul sees no significance in the promise to live long in the land? Schreiner (*Paul: Apostle of God's Glory in Christ* [Downers Grove, IL: InterVarsity, 2001], 328–29) writes: "If we understand Paul's theology, we know that the inheritance promised to Abraham has become the world (Rom 4:13). Paul does not restrict the inheritance to the land of Palestine. He understands the inheritance to refer to the future glory awaiting believers (Rom 8:17). The promise of long life in the land, in Paul's view, relates to our heavenly inheritance. In other words, those who obey their parents will receive an eschatological reward—the inheritance promised to Abraham, Isaac, and Jacob. . . . How Paul handles the command to honor one's parents is paradigmatic. The injunction to honor parents is fulfilled rather straightforwardly in the new covenant, but the promise to live long in the land no longer relates in the same way. The land now becomes the future world that belongs to the people of God, the heavenly Jerusalem (Gal 4:26). The land promised in the OT anticipates and is fulfilled in the eschatological inheritance awaiting the people of God."

[41] One could also explore the rich use of inheritance language in the NT in light of its OT background. For example, see Martin, *Bound for the Promised Land*, chap. 8.

redeemed people from every nation fill and inhabit the whole earth.[42] What believing Israel obtains is far greater than the land of Canaan, for they—along with the nations—will inherit the whole earth in fulfillment of God's gracious and irrevocable promises.

Typology in Progressive Covenantalism

The issue of the fulfillment of the land promise in the NT presents a crucial issue for a particular view of typology within dispensationalism. Dispensationalists contend that if the land promised to Israel is unconditional, then the ultimate fulfillment must be to national Israel in the future regardless of how the OT develops the promise and the NT applies it.[43] As a result, Edward Glenny notes that progressive dispensationalists, who agree with revised dispensationalists but go beyond them in their understanding of typology, allow some of the OT promises for Israel to find typological fulfillment in the church. Although the antitype is in a real sense a fulfillment of the type, the fulfillment is only a partial one. This initial fulfillment does not annul the original OT meaning for Israel.[44] When applied to the issue of land, this view maintains that, although some spiritual aspects are applied to the church, the territorial aspects of God's promise to national Israel will be fulfilled in the future.[45] Therefore, the original promises to the nation of Israel must still be kept, even if they have partial application to the church.[46]

Is this understanding of the fulfillment of the land promise correct? Although this view should be commended for attempting to apply the inaugurated eschatological nature of the kingdom to the land promise, for a variety of

---

[42] Contrary to the notion that this fulfillment is merely ethereal or spiritual, George Ladd is correct when he writes, "Throughout the entire Bible, the ultimate destiny of God's people is an earthly destiny." George Eldon Ladd, *A Commentary on the Revelation of John* (Grand Rapids: Eerdmans, 1972), 275.

[43] See, e.g., Feinberg, "Systems of Discontinuity," 77–83.

[44] W. Edward Glenny, "Typology: A Summary of the Present Evangelical Discussion," *JETS* 40 (1997): 627–38.

[45] Ware, "The New Covenant and the People(s) of God," 94.

[46] This both-and approach is tied to the inaugurated eschatology embraced by progressive dispensationalists.

reasons it does not account for the already-not yet character of the kingdom or the nature of typological fulfillment in Scripture. First, the application of inaugurated eschatology is not accurate *at this point*. While there is an already-not yet nature to the kingdom in the NT, this eschatological perspective does not *merely* mean that part of the kingdom is present now with the church and part of it (i.e., the territorial aspect) will be present later for national Israel. Instead, the NT shows that *all* of God's saving promises have *already* been fulfilled in Christ and these promises are expanding where Christ is present—in the church now, which is one new man composed of both Jews and Gentiles (Eph 2:11–22) and finally in the consummated new creation.

Second, Scripture presents the NT antitype of the OT type as fulfilled and reaching its *telos* in and through Christ. This point distinguishes our proposal from so-called replacement theology.[47] It is not that the church merely replaces Israel; rather Israel finds her fulfillment first in Christ, the obedient Son and true Israel, who then bestows blessings to his people, believing Jews and Gentiles alike. Hence, the charge that Gentile inclusion means Jewish exclusion is not accurate,[48] for all who are included *in Christ* receive every spiritual blessing in Christ as they await their future inheritance, the new creation. In other words, believing Israel does not receive less but more: the whole earth!

Richard Davidson has demonstrated this understanding of typology by examining every NT use of "type" and its cognates.[49] The Bible's use of typology is consistently characterized by an eschatological escalation, or intensification, in the progression from type to antitype and from promise to fulfillment. Old Testament types do not merely correspond analogically to NT types but were designed by God to be "a shadow of the good things to come" (Heb 10:1 HCSB).[50] Mark Karlberg rightly notes,

---

[47] See, for example, Michael J. Vlach, *Has the Church Replaced Israel? A Theological Evaluation* (Nashville, TN: B&H Academic, 2010), 104–7.

[48] See e.g., Darrell L. Bock, "Israel in Luke-Acts," in *The People, the Land, and the Future of Israel*, 112.

[49] Richard M. Davidson, *Typology in Scripture: A Study of Hermeneutical ΤΥΠΟΣ Structures*, Andrews University Seminary Doctoral Dissertation Series, vol. 2 (Berrien Springs, MI: Andrews University, 1981).

[50] For discussion of typology, see Brent Parker's chapter in this volume.

To be sure, there is still to be at the consummation an antitypical fulfillment of the land promise, a cosmic antitype to typological Canaan-land, such as does not obtain in the present Church-age stage of the new covenant. But genuine typological interpretation rules out any additional literal fulfillment of the land promise in a future restoration of national Israel subsequent to or alongside the messianic fulfillment.[51]

At this point dispensationalists, though they agree that the land promised to Israel reaches its ultimate fulfillment in the new heaven and the new earth, still want to maintain that the literal (literalistic) fulfillment requires that Israel's land be given to believing national Israel separate from Gentile Christians in the millennial age. But this is incorrect for two reasons. First, all of God's promises are fulfilled in relation to Christ and given to believing Jews and Gentiles *equally* as the church (Eph 2:11–22).[52] Second, in considering other types such as prophets, Levitical priests, Davidic kings, circumcision, temple, and sacrifices, they do not await final fulfillment in the consummation but instead reach their fulfillment, terminus, and *telos* in Christ, thus bringing them to their divinely appointed end, regardless of the already-not yet aspect of Christ's work. In other words, when Christ comes, *he* as the antitype is the true prophet, priest, king, temple, sacrifice, and so on.

Similarly, in Scripture the land is typological. Starting in creation, God's cosmological goal is to establish his kingdom on earth. God establishes his saving rule on earth through the biblical covenants, which progressively unfold God's promises, which reach their *telos* in Christ, the last Adam, true Israel, and Davidic king. What is developed in the OT is confirmed by the NT. No doubt, at this time in history the fulfillment is primarily focused on Christ, who himself has inaugurated a new creational kingdom through his physical resurrection and has made new creations out of those united with him—both Jew and Gentile—as we anticipate the consummation of the new creation in its final form (Revelation 21–22).

---

[51] Mark W. Karlberg, "The Significance of Israel in Biblical Typology," *JETS* 31 (1988): 259–60.

[52] See Brent Parker's chapter in this volume for development of this point.

Fundamentally, this view differs from the dispensational view in at least two ways. First, the land is viewed as a type that reaches its antitypical fulfillment first in Christ who inaugurates a new age, second in believers as God's new covenant people (2 Cor 5:17), and finally in the consummated new creation (Revelation 21–22). Second, both believing Jews and Gentiles as the "one new man" (Eph 2:11–22) equally receive their promised inheritance in the glorious new creation, of which the indwelling Holy Spirit is the guarantee (Eph 1:13–14).

Summary Reflection

In all of this discussion, it is crucial to stress that our promise-making triune God keeps his promises. In his ministry Jesus announced that God was working to fulfill his ancient promises of redemption and restoration from sin and to reestablish his universal and international kingdom through *him*. In this age, between the inauguration and consummation of those promises, we live as sojourners and exiles who seek the city that is to come, whose designer and builder is God (Heb 11:10; 13:14; 1 Pet 2:11). We should in faith, therefore, live with an eschatological anticipation in our minds and hearts and in our words to others until *that* day, when "the dwelling place of God is with man. He will dwell with them, and they will be his people, and God himself will be with them as their God" (Rev 21:3 ESV).

EDITORS

Stephen J. Wellum, professor of Christian Theology, The Southern Baptist Theological Seminary, and editor of *The Southern Baptist Journal of Theology*

Brent E. Parker, PhD candidate in Systematic Theology, The Southern Baptist Theological Seminary, and assistant editor of *The Southern Baptist Journal of Theology*

CONTRIBUTORS

Ardel B. Caneday, professor of New Testament Studies and Greek, University of Northwestern

Christopher W. Cowan, editor for Bibles and Reference Books, B&H Publishing Group

Jason S. DeRouchie, associate professor of Old Testament and Biblical Theology, Bethlehem College and Seminary

Richard J. Lucas, Greek and Hebrew mentor at The NETS Center for Church Planting and Revitalization and associate pastor, Christ Memorial Church, Williston, VT

Oren R. Martin, assistant professor of Christian Theology, The Southern Baptist Theological Seminary and Boyce College

John D. Meade, assistant professor of Old Testament, Phoenix Seminary, and contributor of The Hexapla Institute

Jason C. Meyer, pastor for preaching and vision, Bethlehem Baptist Church, and associate professor of New Testament, Bethlehem College and Seminary

Thomas R. Schreiner, James Buchanan Harrison Professor of New Testament Interpretation and professor of Biblical Theology and associate dean of the School of Theology, The Southern Baptist Theological Seminary

NAME INDEX

SUBJECT INDEX

SCRIPTURE INDEX